1040

THIS BOOKLET DOES NOT CONTAIN INSTRUCTIONS FOR ANY FORM 1040 SCHEDULES

INSTRUCTIONS

2015

 makes doing your taxes faster and easier.

 is the fast, safe, and free way to prepare and *e-file* your taxes. See *www.irs.gov/freefile.*

Get a faster refund, reduce errors, and save paper. For more information on **IRS** *e-file* and Free File, see *Options for e-filing your returns* in these instructions or click on **IRS** *e-file* at IRS.gov.

2015 TAX CHANGES

See *What's New* in these instructions.

FUTURE DEVELOPMENTS

For the latest information about developments related to Form 1040 and its instructions, such as legislation enacted after they were published, go to *www.irs.gov/form1040*.

IRS

Department of the Treasury **Internal Revenue Service** IRS.gov

Jan 05, 2016   Cat. No. 24811V

Table of Contents

Department of the Treasury

Internal Revenue Service

The Taxpayer Advocate Service Is Here To Help You

What is the Taxpayer Advocate Service?
The Taxpayer Advocate Service (TAS) is an *independent* organization within the Internal Revenue Service (IRS) that helps taxpayers and protects taxpayer rights. Our job is to ensure that every taxpayer is treated fairly and that you know and understand your rights under the *Taxpayer Bill of Rights*.

What can the Taxpayer Advocate Service do for you?
We can help you resolve problems that you can't resolve with the IRS. And our service is free. If you qualify for our assistance, your advocate will be with you at every turn and do everything possible. TAS can help you if:

*   Your problem is causing financial difficulty for you, your family, or your business.
*   You face (or your business is facing) an immediate threat of adverse action.
*   You've tried repeatedly to contact the IRS but no one has responded, or the IRS hasn't responded by the date promised.

How can you reach us?
We have offices in *every state, the District of Columbia, and Puerto Rico*. Your local advocate's number is at *www.TaxpayerAdvocate.irs.gov*, at *www.irs.gov/advocate*, and in your local directory. You can also call us at 1-877-777-4778.

How can you learn about your taxpayer rights?
The Taxpayer Bill of Rights describes ten basic rights that all taxpayers have when dealing with the IRS. Our Tax Toolkit at *www.TaxpayerAdvocate.irs.gov* can help you understand *what these rights mean to you* and how they apply. These are *your* rights. Know them. Use them.

How else does the Taxpayer Advocate Service help taxpayers?
TAS works to resolve large-scale problems that affect many taxpayers. If you know of one of these broad issues, please report it to us at *www.irs.gov/sams*.

Low Income Taxpayer Clinics Help Taxpayers

Low Income Taxpayer Clinics (LITCs) are independent from the IRS. Some serve individuals whose income is below a certain level and who need to resolve a tax problem. These clinics provide professional representation before the IRS or in court on audits, appeals, tax collection disputes, and other issues for free or for a small fee. Some clinics provide information about taxpayer rights and responsibilities in many different languages for individuals who speak English as a second language. For more information, and to find a clinic near you, read the LITC page on *www.irs.gov/litc* or IRS *Publication 4134, Low Income Taxpayer Clinic List*. You can also get this publication at your local IRS office or by calling 1-800-829-3676.

Suggestions for Improving the IRS

Taxpayer Advocacy Panel

Have a suggestion for improving the IRS and do not know who to contact? The Taxpayer Advocacy Panel (TAP) is a diverse group of citizen volunteers who listen to taxpayers, identify taxpayers' issues, and make suggestions for improving IRS service and customer satisfaction. The panel is demographically and geographically diverse, with at least one member from each state, the District of Columbia, and Puerto Rico. Contact TAP at *www.improveirs.org* or 1-888-912-1227 (toll-free).

Options for *e-filing* your returns—safely, quickly, and easily.

Why do 85% of Americans file their taxes electronically?

- *Security*—The IRS uses the latest encryption technology to safeguard your information.
- *Flexible Payments*—File early; pay by the due date of your return (not counting extensions)—April 18, 2016, for most people.
- *Greater Accuracy*—Fewer errors mean faster processing.
- *Quick Receipt*—Get an acknowledgment that your return was received and accepted.
- *Go Green*—Reduce the amount of paper used.
- *It's Free*—through Free File.
- *Faster Refunds*—Join the eight in 10 taxpayers who get their refunds faster by using direct deposit and *e-file*.

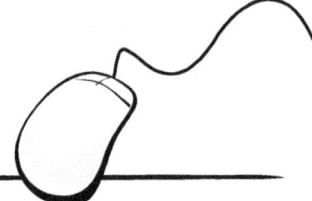

IRS *e-file:* It's Safe. It's Easy. It's Time.

Joining the more than 125 million Americans who already are using *e-file* is easy. Just ask your paid or volunteer tax preparer, use commercial software, or use Free File. IRS *e-file* is the safest, most secure way to transmit your tax return to the IRS. Since 1990, the IRS has processed more than 1 billion *e-filed* tax returns safely and securely. There's no paper return to be lost or stolen.

Most tax return preparers are now required to use IRS *e-file*. If you are asked if you want to *e-file*, just give it a try. IRS *e-file* is now the norm, not the exception. Most states also use electronic filing.

Free Tax Help Available Nationwide

Volunteers are available in communities nationwide providing free tax assistance to low to moderate income (generally under $54,000 in adjusted gross income) and elderly taxpayers (age 60 and older). At selected sites, taxpayers can input and electronically file their own tax return with the assistance of an IRS-certified volunteer.

See *How To Get Tax Help* near the end of these instructions for additional information or visit IRS.gov (Keyword: VITA) for a VITA/TCE site near you!

Do Your Taxes for Free

If your adjusted gross income was $62,000 or less in 2015, you can use free tax software to prepare and *e-file* your tax return. Earned more? Use Free File Fillable Forms.

Free File. This public-private partnership, between the IRS and tax software providers, makes approximately 15 brand name commercial software products and *e-file* available for free. Seventy percent of the nation's taxpayers are eligible.

Just visit *www.irs.gov/freefile* for details. Free File combines all the benefits of *e-file* and easy-to-use software at no cost. Guided questions will help ensure you get all the tax credits and deductions you are due. It's fast, safe, and free.

You can review each software provider's criteria for free usage or use an online tool to find which free software products match your situation. Some software providers offer state tax return preparation for free.

Free File Fillable Forms. The IRS offers electronic versions of IRS paper forms that also can be *e-filed* for free. Free File Fillable Forms is best for people experienced in preparing their own tax returns. There are no income limitations. Free File Fillable Forms does basic math calculations. It supports only federal tax forms.

IRS.gov is the gateway to all electronic services offered by the IRS, as well as the spot to download forms at *www.irs.gov/formspubs*.

Make your tax payments electronically—it's easy.

You can make electronic payments online, by phone, or from a mobile device. Paying electronically is safe and secure. The IRS uses the latest encryption technology and does not store the bank account number you use to submit your payment. When you use any of the IRS electronic payment options, it puts you in control of paying your tax bill and gives you peace of mind. You determine the payment date, and you will receive an immediate confirmation from the IRS. It's easy, secure, and much quicker than mailing in a check or money order. Go to *www.irs.gov/payments* to see all your electronic payment options.

What's New

Information reporting about health coverage. If you or someone in your family had health coverage in 2015, the provider of that coverage is required to send you a Form 1095-A, 1095-B, or 1095-C (with Part III completed), that lists individuals in your family who were enrolled in the coverage and shows their months of coverage. You may use this information to help complete line 61. However, you do not need to wait to receive these forms to file your return. You may have had health care coverage for some or all of 2015 even if you didn't receive a form with this information, and you may rely on other information about your coverage to complete line 61.

For more information on why your health provider might be asking for your social security number, go to *www.irs.gov/ACASSN*.

Information reporting about employer offer of coverage. If you or someone in your family was an employee in 2015, the employer may be required to send you a Form 1095-C. Part II of Form 1095-C shows whether your employer offered you health insurance coverage and, if so, information about the offer. This information may be relevant if you purchased health insurance coverage for 2015 through the Health Insurance Marketplace and wish to claim the premium tax credit on line 69. However, you do not need to wait to receive this form to file your return. You may rely on other information received from your employer. If you do not wish to claim the premium tax credit for 2015, you do not need the information in Part II. For more information on who is eligible for the premium tax credit, see the instructions for Form 8962.

Achieving a Better Life Experience (ABLE) account. This is a new type of savings account for individuals with disabilities and their families. For 2015, you can contribute up to $14,000. Distributions are tax-free if used to pay the beneficiary's qualified disability expenses. Do not deduct your contributions on your tax return. For details, see Pub. 907 and the instructions for lines 21 and 59.

Due date of return. File Form 1040 by April 18, 2016. The due date is April 18, instead of April 15, because of the Emancipation Day holiday in the District of Columbia—even if you do not live in the District of Columbia. If you live in Maine or Massachusetts, you have until April 19, 2016. That is because of the Patriots' Day holiday in those states.

Public safety officers. Certain amounts received because of the death of a public safety officer are nontaxable. See Pub. 525 for details.

Certain charitable contributions. A special rule applies to cash contributions made between January 1, 2015, and April 15, 2015, to benefit the families of slain New York detectives Wenjian Liu or Rafael Ramos. See Pub. 526 for details.

Direct deposits of refund to a *my*RA® account. You now can have your refund directly deposited to a new retirement savings program called *my*RA®. This is a starter retirement account offered by the Department of the Treasury. See the instructions for lines 76a through 76d. For more information and to open a *my*RA account online, visit *www.myRA.gov*.

Health coverage tax credit. The health coverage tax credit, which expired at the end of 2013, has been reinstated retroactive to January 1, 2014. To see if you are eligible for the credit, and to see how to claim the credit for 2014 and 2015, visit *www.irs.gov/HCTC*, or see Form 8885 and its instructions.

Earned income credit. If you didn't have a social security number (an SSN) by the due date of your 2015 return (including extensions), you can't claim the EIC on either your original or an amended 2015 return, even if you later get an SSN. Also, if a child didn't have an SSN by the due date of your return (including extensions), you can't count that child as a qualifying child in figuring the EIC on either your original or an amended 2015 return, even if that child later gets an SSN. See the instructions for lines 66a and 66b.

Child tax credit. If you didn't have an SSN (or ITIN) by the due date of your 2015 return (including extensions), you can't claim the child tax credit on either your original or an amended 2015 return, even if you later get an SSN (or ITIN). Also, no credit is allowed on either your original or an amended 2015 return with respect to a child who didn't have an SSN, ATIN, or ITIN by the due date of your return (including extensions), even if that child later gets one of those numbers. See the instructions for line 52.

American opportunity credit. If you didn't have an SSN (or ITIN) by the due date of your 2015 return (including extensions), you can't claim the American opportunity credit on either your original or an amended 2015 return, even if you later get an SSN (or ITIN). Also, you can't claim this credit on your original or an amended 2015 return for a student who didn't have an SSN, ATIN, or ITIN by the due date of your return (including extensions), even if the student later gets one of those numbers. See Pub. 970 and the instructions for Form 8863 for more information.

Additional child tax credit. You can't claim the additional child tax credit on line 67 if you file Form 2555, Foreign Earned Income, or Form 2555-EZ, Foreign Earned Income Exclusion. See Schedule 8812 and its instructions.

Health care individual responsibility payment increased. If you or someone in your household didn't have qualifying health care coverage or qualify for a coverage exemption for one or more months of 2015, the amount of your shared responsibility payment may be much more this year than it was last year. Like last year, you must either:

• Indicate on line 61 that you, your spouse (if filing jointly), and anyone you can or do claim as a dependent had qualifying health care coverage throughout 2015,

- Attach Form 8965 to claim an exemption from the requirement to have health care coverage, or

- Make a shared responsibility payment if, for any month in 2015, you, your spouse (if filing jointly), or anyone you can or do claim as a dependent didn't have coverage and do not qualify for a coverage exemption.

For more information, see the instructions for line 61 and Form 8965.

Requirement to reconcile advance payments of the premium tax credit. If you or a family member enrolled in health insurance through the Marketplace and advance payments of the premium tax credit were made to your insurance company to reduce your monthly premium payment, you must attach Form 8962 to your return to reconcile (compare) the advance payments with your premium tax credit for the year, which you figure on Form 8962. The Marketplace is required to send Form 1095-A by February 1, 2016, listing the advance payments and other information you need to figure your premium tax credit. Use Form 1095-A to complete Form 8962. Attach Form 8962 to your return. Do not attach Form 1095-A to your return.

Form W-2 verification code. The IRS is testing the use of a 16-character code to verify certain Forms W-2. If you are *e-filing* and your Form W-2 includes a code in a box labeled "Verification Code," enter the code when prompted by your software; disregard the prompt if your Form W-2 doesn't have the code. If you are filing a paper Form 1040, you do not have to use the code.

Filing Requirements

These rules apply to all U.S. citizens, regardless of where they live, and resident aliens.

 Have you tried IRS *e-file*? It's the fastest way to get your refund and it's free if you are eligible. Visit IRS.gov for details.

Do You Have To File?

Use Chart A, B, or C to see if you must file a return. U.S. citizens who lived in or had income from a U.S. possession should see Pub. 570. Residents of Puerto Rico can use *Tax Topic 901* to see if they must file.

 Even if you do not otherwise have to file a return, you should file one to get a refund of any federal income tax withheld. You should also file if you are eligible for any of the following credits.
- *Earned income credit.*
- *Additional child tax credit.*
- *American opportunity credit.*
- *Credit for federal tax on fuels.*
- *Premium tax credit.*
- *Health coverage tax credit.*

See Pub. 501 for details. Also see Pub. 501 if you do not have to file but received a Form 1099-B (or substitute statement).

Premium tax credit. If advance payments of the premium tax credit were made for you, your spouse with whom you are filing a joint return, or a dependent who enrolled in coverage through the Marketplace, you must file a 2015 return and attach Form 8962.

You (or whoever enrolled you) should have received Form 1095-A from the Marketplace with information about your coverage and any advance payments. You must attach Form 8962 even if someone else enrolled you, your spouse, or your dependent. If you are a dependent who is claimed on someone else's 2015 return, you do not have to attach Form 8962.

Exception for certain children under age 19 or full-time students. If certain conditions apply, you can elect to include on your return the income of a child who was under age 19 at the end of 2015 or was a full-time student under age 24 at the end of 2015. To do so, use Form 8814. If you make this election, your child doesn't have to file a return. For details, use *Tax Topic 553* or see Form 8814.

A child born on January 1, 1992, is considered to be age 24 at the end of 2015. Do not use Form 8814 for such a child.

Resident aliens. These rules also apply if you were a resident alien. Also, you may qualify for certain tax treaty benefits. See Pub. 519 for details.

Nonresident aliens and dual-status aliens. These rules also apply if you were a nonresident alien or a dual-status alien and both of the following apply.
- You were married to a U.S. citizen or resident alien at the end of 2015.
- You elected to be taxed as a resident alien.

See Pub. 519 for details.

 Specific rules apply to determine if you are a resident alien, nonresident alien, or dual-status alien. Most nonresident aliens and dual-status aliens have different filing requirements and may have to file Form 1040NR or Form 1040NR-EZ. Pub. 519 discusses these requirements and other information to help aliens comply with U.S. tax law.

When and Where Should You File?

File Form 1040 by **April 18, 2016.** (The due date is April 18, instead of April 15, because of the Emancipation Day holiday in the District of Columbia – even if you do not live in the District of Columbia. If you live in Maine or Massachusetts, you have until April 19, 2016, because of the Patriots' Day holiday in those states.) If you file after this date, you may have to pay interest and penalties. See *Interest and Penalties,* later.

If you were serving in, or in support of, the U.S. Armed Forces in a designated combat zone or contingency operation, you may be able to file later. See Pub. 3 for details.

If you *e-file* your return, there is no need to mail it. See the *e-file* page, earlier, or IRS.gov for more information. However, if you choose to mail it, filing instructions and addresses are at the end of these instructions.

What if You Can't File on Time?

You can get an automatic 6-month extension if, no later than the date your return is due, you file Form 4868. For details, see Form 4868. Instead of filing Form 4868, you can apply for an automatic extension by making an electronic payment by the due date of your return.

 An automatic 6-month extension to file doesn't extend the time to pay your tax. If you do not pay your tax by the original due date of your return, you will owe interest on the unpaid tax and may owe penalties. See Form 4868.

If you are a U.S. citizen or resident alien, you may qualify for an automatic extension of time to file without filing Form 4868. You qualify if, on the due date of your return, you meet one of the following conditions.
- You live outside the United States and Puerto Rico and your main place of business or post of duty is outside the United States and Puerto Rico.
- You are in military or naval service on duty outside the United States and Puerto Rico.

This extension gives you an extra 2 months to file and pay the tax, but interest will be charged from the original due date of the return on any unpaid tax. You must include a statement showing that you meet the requirements. If you are still unable to file your return by the end of the 2-month period, you can get an additional 4 months if, no later than June 15, 2016, you file Form 4868. This 4-month extension of time to file doesn't extend the time to pay your tax. See Form 4868.

Private Delivery Services

If you choose to mail your return, you can use certain private delivery services designated by the IRS to meet the "timely mailing treated as timely filing/paying" rule for tax returns and payments. These private delivery services include only the following.

- FedEx First Overnight, FedEx Priority Overnight, FedEx Standard Overnight, FedEx 2 Day, FedEx International Next Flight Out, FedEx International Priority, FedEx International First, and FedEx International Economy.
- UPS Next Day Air Early AM, UPS Next Day Air, UPS Next Day Air Saver, UPS 2nd Day Air, UPS 2nd Day Air A.M., UPS Worldwide Express Plus, and UPS Worldwide Express.

For more information, go to IRS.gov and enter "private delivery service" in the search box. The search results will direct you to the IRS mailing address to use if you are using a private delivery service. You will also find any updates to the list of designated private delivery services.

The private delivery service can tell you how to get written proof of the mailing date.

Chart A—For Most People

IF your filing status is . . .	AND at the end of 2015 you were* . . .	THEN file a return if your gross income** was at least . . .
Single (see the instructions for line 1)	under 65 65 or older	$10,300 11,850
Married filing jointly*** (see the instructions for line 2)	under 65 (both spouses) 65 or older (one spouse) 65 or older (both spouses)	$20,600 21,850 23,100
Married filing separately (see the instructions for line 3)	any age	$4,000
Head of household (see the instructions for line 4)	under 65 65 or older	$13,250 14,800
Qualifying widow(er) with dependent child (see the instructions for line 5)	under 65 65 or older	$16,600 17,850

*If you were born on January 1, 1951, you are considered to be age 65 at the end of 2015. (If your spouse died in 2015 or if you are preparing a return for someone who died in 2015, see Pub. 501.)

**Gross income means all income you received in the form of money, goods, property, and services that isn't exempt from tax, including any income from sources outside the United States or from the sale of your main home (even if you can exclude part or all of it). Do not include any social security benefits unless (a) you are married filing a separate return and you lived with your spouse at any time in 2015 or (b) one-half of your social security benefits plus your other gross income and any tax-exempt interest is more than $25,000 ($32,000 if married filing jointly). If (a) or (b) applies, see the instructions for lines 20a and 20b to figure the taxable part of social security benefits you must include in gross income. Gross income includes gains, but not losses, reported on Form 8949 or Schedule D. Gross income from a business means, for example, the amount on Schedule C, line 7, or Schedule F, line 9. But, in figuring gross income, do not reduce your income by any losses, including any loss on Schedule C, line 7, or Schedule F, line 9.

***If you didn't live with your spouse at the end of 2015 (or on the date your spouse died) and your gross income was at least $4,000, you must file a return regardless of your age.

Chart B—For Children and Other Dependents (See the instructions for line 6c to find out if someone can claim you as a dependent.)

> If your parent (or someone else) can claim you as a dependent, use this chart to see if you must file a return.
>
> In this chart, **unearned income** includes taxable interest, ordinary dividends, and capital gain distributions. It also includes unemployment compensation, taxable social security benefits, pensions, annuities, and distributions of unearned income from a trust. **Earned income** includes salaries, wages, tips, professional fees, and taxable scholarship and fellowship grants. **Gross income** is the total of your unearned and earned income.

Single dependents. Were you **either** age 65 or older **or** blind?

☐ **No.** You must file a return if **any** of the following apply.
- Your unearned income was over $1,050.
- Your earned income was over $6,300.
- Your gross income was more than the **larger** of—
  - $1,050, or
  - Your earned income (up to $5,950) plus $350.

☐ **Yes.** You must file a return if **any** of the following apply.
- Your unearned income was over $2,600 ($4,150 if 65 or older **and** blind).
- Your earned income was over $7,850 ($9,400 if 65 or older **and** blind).
- Your gross income was more than the **larger** of—
  - $2,600 ($4,150 if 65 or older **and** blind), or
  - Your earned income (up to $5,950) plus $1,900 ($3,450 if 65 or older **and** blind).

Married dependents. Were you **either** age 65 or older **or** blind?

☐ **No.** You must file a return if **any** of the following apply.
- Your unearned income was over $1,050.
- Your earned income was over $6,300.
- Your gross income was at least $5 and your spouse files a separate return and itemizes deductions.
- Your gross income was more than the **larger** of—
  - $1,050, or
  - Your earned income (up to $5,950) plus $350.

☐ **Yes.** You must file a return if **any** of the following apply.
- Your unearned income was over $2,300 ($3,550 if 65 or older **and** blind).
- Your earned income was over $7,550 ($8,800 if 65 or older **and** blind).
- Your gross income was at least $5 and your spouse files a separate return and itemizes deductions.
- Your gross income was more than the **larger** of—
  - $2,300 ($3,550 if 65 or older **and** blind), or
  - Your earned income (up to $5,950) plus $1,600 ($2,850 if 65 or older **and** blind).

Chart C—Other Situations When You Must File

You must file a return if any of the five conditions below apply for 2015.

1. You owe any special taxes, including any of the following.
   a. Alternative minimum tax.
   b. Additional tax on a qualified plan, including an individual retirement arrangement (IRA), or other tax-favored account. But if you are filing a return only because you owe this tax, you can file **Form 5329** by itself.
   c. Household employment taxes. But if you are filing a return only because you owe this tax, you can file **Schedule H** by itself.
   d. Social security and Medicare tax on tips you didn't report to your employer or on wages you received from an employer who didn't withhold these taxes.
   e. Recapture of first-time homebuyer credit. See the instructions for line 60b.
   f. Write-in taxes, including uncollected social security and Medicare or RRTA tax on tips you reported to your employer or on group-term life insurance and additional taxes on health savings accounts. See the instructions for line 62.
   g. Recapture taxes. See the instructions for lines 44, 60b, and line 62.

2. You (or your spouse, if filing jointly) received health savings account, Archer MSA, or Medicare Advantage MSA distributions.

3. You had net earnings from self-employment of at least $400.

4. You had wages of $108.28 or more from a church or qualified church-controlled organization that is exempt from employer social security and Medicare taxes.

5. Advance payments of the premium tax credit were made for you, your spouse, or a dependent who enrolled in coverage through the Marketplace. You or whoever enrolled you should have received Form(s) 1095-A showing the amount of the advance payments.

Where To Report Certain Items From 2015 Forms W-2, 1097, 1098, and 1099

File electronically. You may be eligible for free tax software that will take the guesswork out of preparing your return. Free File makes available free brand-name software and free *e-file*. Visit *www.irs.gov/freefile* for details.

If any federal income tax withheld is shown on these forms, include the tax withheld on Form 1040, line 64. If any state or local income tax withheld is shown on these forms and you deduct state and local income taxes on Schedule A, line 5, include the tax withheld in your deduction on that line.

Form	Item and Box in Which It Should Appear	Where To Report
W-2	Wages, tips, other compensation (box 1)	Form 1040, line 7
	Allocated tips (box 8)	See *Wages, Salaries, Tips, etc.*
	Dependent care benefits (box 10)	Form 2441, Part III
	Adoption benefits (box 12, code T)	Form 8839, line 20
	Employer contributions to an Archer MSA (box 12, code R)	Form 8853, line 1
	Employer contributions to a health savings account (box 12, code W)	Form 8889, line 9
	Uncollected social security and Medicare or RRTA tax (box 12, code A, B, M, or N)	See the instructions for Form 1040, line 62
W-2G	Gambling winnings (box 1)	Form 1040, line 21 (Schedule C or C-EZ for professional gamblers)
1097-BTC	Bond tax credit	See Form 8912 and its instructions
1098	Mortgage interest (box 1) Points (box 2)	Schedule A, line 10, but first see the instructions on Form 1098*
	Refund of overpaid interest (box 3)	Form 1040, line 21, but first see the instructions on Form 1098*
	Mortgage insurance premiums (box 4)	See the instructions for Schedule A, line 13*
1098-C	Contributions of motor vehicles, boats, and airplanes	Schedule A, line 17
1098-E	Student loan interest (box 1)	See the instructions for Form 1040, line 33*
1098-MA	Homeowner mortgage payments (box 3)	Schedule A, but first see the instructions on Form 1098-MA
1098-T	Qualified tuition and related expenses (box 1)	See the instructions for Form 1040, line 34, or Form 1040, line 50; but first see the instructions on Form 1098-T*
1099-A	Acquisition or abandonment of secured property	See Pub. 4681
1099-B	Sales price of stocks, bonds, etc. (box 1d), cost or other basis (box 1e), and adjustments (box 1g)	Form 8949 or Schedule D, whichever applies; see the Instructions for Form 8949
	Aggregate profit or (loss) on contracts (box 11)	Form 6781, line 1
	Bartering (box 13)	See Pub. 525
1099-C	Canceled debt (box 2)	See Pub. 4681
1099-DIV	Total ordinary dividends (box 1a)	Form 1040, line 9a
	Qualified dividends (box 1b)	See the instructions for Form 1040, line 9b
	Total capital gain distributions (box 2a)	Form 1040, line 13, or, if required, Schedule D, line 13
	Unrecaptured section 1250 gain (box 2b)	See the instructions for Schedule D, line 19
	Section 1202 gain (box 2c)	See *Exclusion of Gain on Qualified Small Business (QSB) Stock* in the instructions for Schedule D
	Collectibles (28%) gain (box 2d)	See the instructions for Schedule D, line 18
	Nondividend distributions (box 3)	See the instructions for Form 1040, line 9a
	Investment expenses (box 5)	Schedule A, line 23
	Foreign tax paid (box 6)	Form 1040, line 48, or Schedule A, line 8; but first see the instructions for line 48
	Exempt-interest dividends (box 10)	Form 1040, line 8b
	Specified private activity bond interest dividends (box 11)	Form 6251, line 12
1099-G	Unemployment compensation (box 1)	See the instructions for Form 1040, line 19
	State or local income tax refunds, credits, or offsets (box 2)	See the instructions for Form 1040, line 10, and if box 8 on Form 1099-G is checked, see the box 8 instructions
	RTAA payments (box 5)	Form 1040, line 21
	Taxable grants (box 6)	Form 1040, line 21*
	Agriculture payments (box 7)	See the Instructions for Schedule F or Pub. 225*
	Market gain (box 9)	See the Instructions for Schedule F

*If the item relates to an activity for which you are required to file Schedule C, C-EZ, E, or F or Form 4835, report the taxable or deductible amount allocable to the activity on that schedule or form instead.

Form	Item and Box in Which It Should Appear	Where To Report
1099-INT	Interest income (box 1)	See the instructions on Form 1099-INT
	Early withdrawal penalty (box 2)	Form 1040, line 30
	Interest on U.S. savings bonds and Treasury obligations (box 3)	See the instructions on Form 1099-INT and the instructions for Form 1040, line 8a
	Investment expenses (box 5)	Schedule A, line 23
	Foreign tax paid (box 6)	Form 1040, line 48, or Schedule A, line 8; but first see the instructions for line 48
	Tax-exempt interest (box 8)	Form 1040, line 8b
	Specified private activity bond interest (box 9)	Form 6251, line 12
	Market discount (box 10)	Form 1040, line 8a
	Bond premium (box 11) and bond premium on tax-exempt bond (box 13)	See the instructions on Form 1099-INT and Pub. 550
1099-K	Payment card and third party network transactions	Schedule C, C-EZ, E, or F
1099-LTC	Long-term care and accelerated death benefits	See Pub. 525 and the Instructions for Form 8853
1099-MISC	Rents (box 1)	See the Instructions for Schedule E*
	Royalties (box 2)	See the Instructions for Schedule E* (for timber, coal, and iron ore royalties, see Pub. 544)*
	Other income (box 3)	Form 1040, line 21*
	Nonemployee compensation (box 7)	Schedule C, C-EZ, or F; but if you were not self-employed, see the instructions on Form 1099-MISC
	Excess golden parachute payments (box 13)	See the instructions for Form 1040, line 62
	Other (boxes 5, 6, 8, 9, 10, 14, and 15b)	See the instructions on Form 1099-MISC
1099-OID	Original issue discount (box 1) Other periodic interest (box 2)	See the instructions on Form 1099-OID
	Early withdrawal penalty (box 3)	Form 1040, line 30
	Market discount (box 5)	Form 1040, line 8a
	Acquisition premium (box 6)	See the instructions on Form 1099-OID and Pub. 550
	Original issue discount on U.S. Treasury obligations (box 8)	See the instructions on Form 1099-OID
	Investment expenses (box 9)	Schedule A, line 23
1099-PATR	Patronage dividends and other distributions from a cooperative (boxes 1, 2, 3, and 5)	Schedule C, C-EZ, or F or Form 4835; but first see the instructions on Form 1099-PATR
	Domestic production activities deduction (box 6)	Form 8903, line 23
	Credits and other deductions (boxes 7, 8, and 10)	See the instructions on Form 1099-PATR
	Patron's AMT adjustment (box 9)	Form 6251, line 27
1099-Q	Qualified education program payments	See the instructions for Form 1040, line 21
1099-QA	Distributions from ABLE accounts	See the instructions for line 21, Form 5329, and Pub. 907
1099-R	Distributions from IRAs**	See the instructions for Form 1040, lines 15a and 15b
	Distributions from pensions, annuities, etc.	See the instructions for Form 1040, lines 16a and 16b
	Capital gain (box 3)	See the instructions on Form 1099-R
	Disability income with code 3 in box 7	See the instructions for Form 1040, line 7
1099-S	Gross proceeds from real estate transactions (box 2)	Form 4797, Form 6252, Form 8824, or Form 8949
	Buyer's part of real estate tax (box 5)	See the instructions for Schedule A, line 6*
1099-SA	Distributions from health savings accounts (HSAs)	Form 8889, line 14a
	Distributions from MSAs***	Form 8853
SSA-1099	Social security benefits	See the instructions for lines 20a and 20b
RRB-1099	Railroad retirement benefits	See the instructions for lines 20a and 20b

*If the item relates to an activity for which you are required to file Schedule C, C-EZ, E, or F or Form 4835, report the taxable or deductible amount allocable to the activity on that schedule or form instead.

**This includes distributions from Roth, SEP, and SIMPLE IRAs.

***This includes distributions from Archer and Medicare Advantage MSAs.

Line Instructions for Form 1040

You may be eligible for free tax software that will take the guesswork out of preparing your return. Free File makes available free brand-name software and free *e-file*. Visit *www.irs.gov/freefile* for details.

Section references are to the Internal Revenue Code.

Name and Address

Print or type the information in the spaces provided. If you are married filing a separate return, enter your spouse's name on line 3 instead of below your name.

 If you filed a joint return for 2014 and you are filing a joint return for 2015 with the same spouse, be sure to enter your names and SSNs in the same order as on your 2014 return.

Name Change

If you changed your name because of marriage, divorce, etc., be sure to report the change to the Social Security Administration (SSA) before filing your return. This prevents delays in processing your return and issuing refunds. It also safeguards your future social security benefits.

Address Change

If you plan to move after filing your return, use Form 8822 to notify the IRS of your new address.

P.O. Box

Enter your box number only if your post office doesn't deliver mail to your home.

Foreign Address

If you have a foreign address, enter the city name on the appropriate line. Do not enter any other information on that line, but also complete the spaces below that line. Do not abbreviate the country name. Follow the country's practice for entering the postal code and the name of the province, county, or state.

Death of a Taxpayer

See *Death of a Taxpayer* under *General Information,* later.

Social Security Number (SSN)

An incorrect or missing SSN can increase your tax, reduce your refund, or delay your refund. To apply for an SSN, fill in Form SS-5 and return it, along with the appropriate evidence documents, to the Social Security Administration (SSA). You can get Form SS-5 online at *www.socialsecurity.gov*, from your local SSA office, or by calling the SSA at 1-800-772-1213. It usually takes about 2 weeks to get an SSN once the SSA has all the evidence and information it needs.

Check that both the name and SSN on your Forms 1040, W-2, and 1099 agree with your social security card. If they do not, certain deductions and credits on your Form 1040 may be reduced or disallowed and you may not receive credit for your social security earnings. If your Form W-2 shows an incorrect SSN or name, notify your employer or the form-issuing agent as soon as possible to make sure your earnings are credited to your social security record. If the name or SSN on your social security card is incorrect, call the SSA.

IRS Individual Taxpayer Identification Numbers (ITINs) for Aliens

If you are a nonresident or resident alien and you do not have and are not eligible to get an SSN, you must apply for an ITIN. For more information, see Form W-7 and its instructions. It takes about 7 weeks to get an ITIN.

If you already have an ITIN, enter it wherever your SSN is requested on your tax return.

An ITIN is for tax use only. It doesn't entitle you to social security benefits or change your employment or immigration status under U.S. law.

If you receive an SSN after previously using an ITIN, stop using your ITIN. Use your SSN instead. Visit a local IRS office or write a letter to the IRS explaining that you now have an SSN and want all your tax records combined under your SSN. Details about what to include with the letter and where to mail it are at *www.irs.gov/Individuals/Additional-ITIN-Information*.

Nonresident Alien Spouse

If your spouse is a nonresident alien, he or she must have either an SSN or an ITIN if:
- You file a joint return,
- You file a separate return and claim an exemption for your spouse, or
- Your spouse is filing a separate return.

Presidential Election Campaign Fund

This fund helps pay for Presidential election campaigns. The fund reduces candidates' dependence on large contributions from individuals and groups and places candidates on an equal financial footing in the general election. The fund also helps pay for pediatric medical research. If you want $3 to go to this fund, check the box. If you are filing a joint return, your spouse can also have $3 go to the fund. If you check a box, your tax or refund won't change.

Filing Status

Check only the filing status that applies to you. The ones that will usually give you the lowest tax are listed last.
- Married filing separately.
- Single.
- Head of household.

Need more information or forms? Visit IRS.gov.

- Married filing jointly.
- Qualifying widow(er) with dependent child.

For information about marital status, see Pub. 501.

 More than one filing status can apply to you. You can choose the one that will give you the lowest tax.

Line 1

Single

You can check the box on line 1 if any of the following was true on December 31, 2015.

- You were never married.
- You were legally separated according to your state law under a decree of divorce or separate maintenance. But if, at the end of 2015, your divorce wasn't final (an interlocutory decree), you are considered married and can't check the box on line 1.
- You were widowed before January 1, 2015, and didn't remarry before the end of 2015. But if you have a dependent child, you may be able to use the qualifying widow(er) filing status. See the instructions for line 5.

Line 2

Married Filing Jointly

You can check the box on line 2 if any of the following apply.

- You were married at the end of 2015, even if you didn't live with your spouse at the end of 2015.
- Your spouse died in 2015 and you didn't remarry in 2015.
- You were married at the end of 2015, and your spouse died in 2016 before filing a 2015 return.

A married couple filing jointly report their combined income and deduct their combined allowable expenses on one return. They can file a joint return even if only one had income or if they didn't live together all year. However, both persons must sign the return. Once you file a joint return, you can't choose to file separate returns for that year after the due date of the return.

Joint and several tax liability. If you file a joint return, both you and your spouse are generally responsible for the

tax and interest or penalties due on the return. This means that if one spouse doesn't pay the tax due, the other may have to. Or, if one spouse doesn't report the correct tax, both spouses may be responsible for any additional taxes assessed by the IRS. You may want to file separately if:

- You believe your spouse isn't reporting all of his or her income, or
- You do not want to be responsible for any taxes due if your spouse doesn't have enough tax withheld or doesn't pay enough estimated tax.

See the instructions for line 3. Also see *Innocent Spouse Relief* under *General Information,* later.

Nonresident aliens and dual-status aliens. Generally, a married couple can't file a joint return if either spouse is a nonresident alien at any time during the year. However, if you were a nonresident alien or a dual-status alien and were married to a U.S. citizen or resident alien at the end of 2015, you can elect to be treated as a resident alien and file a joint return. See Pub. 519 for details.

Line 3

Married Filing Separately

If you are married and file a separate return, you generally report only your own income, exemptions, deductions, and credits. Generally, you are responsible only for the tax on your own income. Different rules apply to people in community property states; see Pub. 555.

However, you will usually pay more tax than if you use another filing status for which you qualify. Also, if you file a separate return, you can't take the student loan interest deduction, the tuition and fees deduction, the education credits, or the earned income credit. You also can't take the standard deduction if your spouse itemizes deductions.

Be sure to enter your spouse's SSN or ITIN on Form 1040. If your spouse doesn't have and isn't required to have an SSN or ITIN, enter "NRA."

 You may be able to file as head of household if you had a child living with you and you lived apart from your spouse during the last 6 months of 2015. See Married persons who live apart.

Line 4

Head of Household

This filing status is for unmarried individuals who provide a home for certain other persons. You are considered unmarried for this purpose if any of the following applies.

- You were legally separated according to your state law under a decree of divorce or separate maintenance at the end of 2015. But if, at the end of 2015, your divorce wasn't final (an interlocutory decree), you are considered married.
- You are married but lived apart from your spouse for the last 6 months of 2015 and you meet the other rules under *Married persons who live apart.*
- You are married to a nonresident alien at any time during the year and you do not choose to treat him or her as a resident alien.

Check the box on line 4 only if you are unmarried (or considered unmarried) and either *Test 1* or *Test 2* applies.

Test 1. You paid over half the cost of keeping up a home that was the main home for all of 2015 of your parent whom you can claim as a dependent on line 6c, except under a multiple support agreement (see the line 6c instructions). Your parent didn't have to live with you.

Test 2. You paid over half the cost of keeping up a home in which you lived and in which one of the following also lived for more than half of the year (if half or less, see *Exception to time lived with you*).

1. Any person whom you can claim as a dependent on line 6c. But do not include:

a. Your child whom you claim as your dependent because of the rule for *Children of divorced or separated parents* in the line 6c instructions,

b. Any person who is your dependent only because he or she lived with you for all of 2015, or

c. Any person you claimed as a dependent under a multiple support agreement. See the line 6c instructions.

2. Your unmarried qualifying child who isn't your dependent.

3. Your married qualifying child who isn't your dependent only because you can be claimed as a dependent on line 6c of someone else's 2015 return.

4. Your qualifying child who, even though you are the custodial parent, isn't your dependent because of the rule for *Children of divorced or separated parents* in the line 6c instructions.

If the child isn't claimed as your dependent on line 6c, enter the child's name on line 4. If you do not enter the name, it will take us longer to process your return.

Qualifying child. To find out if someone is your qualifying child, see Step 1 of the line 6c instructions.

Dependent. To find out if someone is your dependent, see the instructions for line 6c.

Exception to time lived with you. Temporary absences by you or the other person for special circumstances, such as school, vacation, business, medical care, military service, or detention in a juvenile facility, count as time lived in the home. Also see *Kidnapped child* in the line 6c instructions, if applicable.

If the person for whom you kept up a home was born or died in 2015, you still may be able to file as head of household. If the person is your qualifying child, the child must have lived with you for more than half the part of the year he or she was alive. If the person is anyone else, see Pub. 501.

Keeping up a home. To find out what is included in the cost of keeping up a home, see Pub. 501.

If you used payments you received under Temporary Assistance for Needy Families (TANF) or other public assistance programs to pay part of the cost of keeping up your home, you can't count them as money you paid. However, you must include them in the total cost of keeping up your home to figure if you paid over half the cost.

Married persons who live apart. Even if you were not divorced or legally sepa-

rated at the end of 2015, you are considered unmarried if all of the following apply.

• You lived apart from your spouse for the last 6 months of 2015. Temporary absences for special circumstances, such as for business, medical care, school, or military service, count as time lived in the home.

• You file a separate return from your spouse.

• You paid over half the cost of keeping up your home for 2015.

• Your home was the main home of your child, stepchild, or foster child for more than half of 2015 (if half or less, see *Exception to time lived with you*, earlier).

• You can claim this child as your dependent or could claim the child except that the child's other parent can claim him or her under the rule for *Children of divorced or separated parents* in the line 6c instructions.

Adopted child. An adopted child is always treated as your own child. An adopted child includes a child lawfully placed with you for legal adoption.

Foster child. A foster child is any child placed with you by an authorized placement agency or by judgment, decree, or other order of any court of competent jurisdiction.

Line 5

Qualifying Widow(er) With Dependent Child

You can check the box on line 5 and use joint return tax rates for 2015 if all of the following apply.

1. Your spouse died in 2013 or 2014 and you didn't remarry before the end of 2015.

2. You have a child or stepchild you can claim as a dependent on line 6c. This doesn't include a foster child.

3. This child lived in your home for all of 2015. If the child didn't live with you for the required time, see *Exception to time lived with you*, later.

4. You paid over half the cost of keeping up your home.

5. You could have filed a joint return with your spouse the year he or she died, even if you didn't actually do so.

If your spouse died in 2015, you can't file as qualifying widow(er) with dependent child. Instead, see the instructions for line 2.

Adopted child. An adopted child is always treated as your own child. An adopted child includes a child lawfully placed with you for legal adoption.

Dependent. To find out if someone is your dependent, see the instructions for line 6c.

Exception to time lived with you. Temporary absences by you or the child for special circumstances, such as school, vacation, business, medical care, military service, or detention in a juvenile facility, count as time lived in the home. Also see *Kidnapped child* in the line 6c instructions, if applicable.

A child is considered to have lived with you for all of 2015 if the child was born or died in 2015 and your home was the child's home for the entire time he or she was alive.

Keeping up a home. To find out what is included in the cost of keeping up a home, see Pub. 501.

If you used payments you received under Temporary Assistance for Needy Families (TANF) or other public assistance programs to pay part of the cost of keeping up your home, you can't count them as money you paid. However, you must include them in the total cost of keeping up your home to figure if you paid over half the cost.

Exemptions

You usually can deduct $4,000 on line 42 for each exemption you can take.

Line 6b

Spouse

Check the box on line 6b if either of the following applies.

1. Your filing status is married filing jointly and your spouse can't be claimed as a dependent on another person's return.

2. You were married at the end of 2015, your filing status is married filing separately or head of household, and both of the following apply.

Need more information or forms? Visit IRS.gov.

a. Your spouse had no income and isn't filing a return.

b. Your spouse can't be claimed as a dependent on another person's return.

If your filing status is head of household and you check the box on line 6b, enter the name of your spouse on the dotted line next to line 6b. Also, enter your spouse's social security number in the space provided at the top of your return. If you became divorced or legally separated during 2015, you can't take an exemption for your former spouse.

Death of your spouse. If your spouse died in 2015 and you didn't remarry by the end of 2015, check the box on line 6b if you could have taken an exemption for your spouse on the date of death. For other filing instructions, see *Death of a Taxpayer* under *General Information,* later.

Line 6c—Dependents

Dependents and Qualifying Child for Child Tax Credit

Follow the steps below to find out if a person qualifies as your dependent, qualifies you to take the child tax credit, or both. If you have more than four dependents, check the box to the left of line 6c and include a statement showing the information required in columns (1) through (4).

Step 1   Do You Have a Qualifying Child?

A qualifying child is a child who is your...

Son, daughter, stepchild, foster child, brother, sister, stepbrother, stepsister, half brother, half sister, or a descendant of any of them (for example, your grandchild, niece, or nephew)

AND

was ...

Under age 19 at the end of 2015 and younger than you (or your spouse, if filing jointly)

or

Under age 24 at the end of 2015, a student (defined later), and younger than you (or your spouse, if filing jointly)

or

Any age and permanently and totally disabled (defined later)

AND

Who didn't provide over half of his or her own support for 2015 (see Pub. 501)

AND

Who isn't filing a joint return for 2015
or is filing a joint return for 2015 only to claim a refund of withheld income tax or estimated tax paid (see Pub. 501 for details and examples)

AND

Who lived with you for more than half of 2015. If the child didn't live with you for the required time, see *Exception to time lived with you,* later.

 *If the child meets the conditions to be a qualifying child of any other person (other than your spouse if filing jointly) for 2015, see* Qualifying child of more than one person, *later.*

1. Do you have a child who meets the conditions to be your qualifying child?

   ☐ **Yes.** Go to Step 2.   ☐ **No.** Go to Step 4.

Step 2   Is Your Qualifying Child Your Dependent?

1. Was the child a U.S. citizen, U.S. national, U.S. resident alien, or a resident of Canada or Mexico? (See Pub. 519 for the definition of a U.S. national or U.S. resident alien. If the child was adopted, see *Exception to citizen test,* later.)

   ☐ **Yes.** Continue   ☐ **No.** (STOP)

                                        You can't claim this child as a dependent.

2. Was the child married?

   ☐ **Yes.** See *Married person,* later.   ☐ **No.** Continue

3. Could you, or your spouse if filing jointly, be claimed as a dependent on someone else's 2015 tax return? See Steps 1, 2, and 4.

   ☐ **Yes.** You can't claim any dependents. Go to Form 1040, line 7.   ☐ **No.** You can claim this child as a dependent. Complete Form 1040, line 6c, columns (1) through (3) for this child. Then, go to Step 3.

Step 3   Does Your Qualifying Child Qualify You for the Child Tax Credit?

1. Was the child under age 17 at the end of 2015?

   ☐ **Yes.** Continue   ☐ **No.** (STOP)

                                        This child isn't a qualifying child for the child tax credit.

2. Was the child a U.S. citizen, U.S. national, or U.S. resident alien? (See Pub. 519 for the definition of a U.S. national or U.S. resident alien. If the child was adopted, see *Exception to citizen test,* later.)

   ☐ **Yes.** This child is a qualifying child for the child tax credit. Check the box on Form 1040, line 6c, column (4).   ☐ **No.** (STOP)

                                        This child isn't a qualifying child for the child tax credit.

Step 4 Is Your Qualifying Relative Your Dependent?

A qualifying relative is a person who is your...

Son, daughter, stepchild, foster child, or a descendant of any of them (for example, your grandchild)

or

Brother, sister, half brother, half sister, or a son or daughter of any of them (for example, your niece or nephew)

or

Father, mother, or an ancestor or sibling of either of them (for example, your grandmother, grandfather, aunt, or uncle)

or

Stepbrother, stepsister, stepfather, stepmother, son-in-law, daughter-in-law, father-in-law, mother-in-law, brother-in-law, or sister-in-law

or

Any other person (other than your spouse) who lived with you all year as a member of your household if your relationship didn't violate local law. If the person didn't live with you for the required time, see *Exception to time lived with you,* later

Who wasn't a qualifying child (see Step 1) of any taxpayer for 2015. For this purpose, a person isn't a taxpayer if he or she isn't required to file a U.S. income tax return **and** either doesn't file such a return or files only to get a refund of withheld income tax or estimated tax paid. See Pub. 501 for details and examples

Who had gross income of less than $4,000 in 2015. If the person was permanently and totally disabled, see *Exception to gross income test,* later

For whom you provided over half of his or her support in 2015. But see *Children of divorced or separated parents, Multiple support agreements,* and *Kidnapped child,* later.

1. Does any person meet the conditions to be your qualifying relative?

☐ **Yes.** Continue ↘   ☐ **No.** (STOP)
　　　　　　　　　　　　　　Go to Form 1040, line 7.

2. Was your qualifying relative a U.S. citizen, U.S. national, U.S. resident alien, or a resident of Canada or Mexico? (See Pub. 519 for the definition of a U.S. national or U.S. resident alien. If your qualifying relative was adopted, see *Exception to citizen test,* later.)

☐ **Yes.** Continue ↘   ☐ **No.** (STOP)
　　　　　　　　　　　　　　You can't claim this
　　　　　　　　　　　　　　person as a dependent.

3. Was your qualifying relative married?

☐ **Yes.** See *Married person,* later.   ☐ **No.** Continue ↘

4. Could you, or your spouse if filing jointly, be claimed as a dependent on someone else's 2015 tax return? See Steps 1, 2, and 4.

☐ **Yes.** (STOP)
You can't claim any dependents. Go to Form 1040, line 7.

☐ **No.** You can claim this person as a dependent. Complete Form 1040, line 6c, columns (1) through (3). Do not check the box on Form 1040, line 6c, column (4).

Definitions and Special Rules

Adopted child. An adopted child is always treated as your own child. An adopted child includes a child lawfully placed with you for legal adoption.

Adoption taxpayer identification numbers (ATINs). If you have a dependent who was placed with you for legal adoption and you do not know his or her SSN, you must get an ATIN for the dependent from the IRS. See Form W-7A for details. If the dependent isn't a U.S. citizen or resident alien, apply for an ITIN instead, using Form W-7.

If you didn't have an SSN (or ITIN) by the due date of your 2015 return (including extensions), you can't claim the child tax credit on either your original or an amended 2015 return, even if you later get an SSN (or ITIN). Also, no child tax credit is allowed on your original or an amended 2015 return with respect to a child who didn't have an SSN, ATIN, or ITIN by the due date of your return (including extensions), even if that child later gets one of those numbers. See the instructions for line 52.

Children of divorced or separated parents. A child will be treated as the qualifying child or qualifying relative of his or her noncustodial parent (defined later) if all of the following conditions apply.

1. The parents are divorced, legally separated, separated under a written separation agreement, or lived apart at all times

during the last 6 months of 2015 (whether or not they are or were married).

2. The child received over half of his or her support for 2015 from the parents (and the rules on *Multiple support agreements*, later, do not apply). Support of a child received from a parent's spouse is treated as provided by the parent.

3. The child is in custody of one or both of the parents for more than half of 2015.

4. Either of the following applies.

a. The custodial parent signs Form 8332 or a substantially similar statement that he or she won't claim the child as a dependent for 2015, and the noncustodial parent includes a copy of the form or statement with his or her return. If the divorce decree or separation agreement went into effect after 1984 and before 2009, the noncustodial parent may be able to include certain pages from the decree or agreement instead of Form 8332. See *Post-1984 and pre-2009 decree or agreement* and *Post-2008 decree or agreement*.

b. A pre-1985 decree of divorce or separate maintenance or written separation agreement between the parents provides that the noncustodial parent can claim the child as a dependent, and the noncustodial parent provides at least $600 for support of the child during 2015.

If conditions (1) through (4) apply, only the noncustodial parent can claim the child for purposes of the dependency exemption (line 6c) and the child tax credits (lines 52 and 67). However, this doesn't allow the noncustodial parent to claim head of household filing status, the credit for child and dependent care expenses, the exclusion for dependent care benefits, the earned income credit, or the health coverage tax credit. See Pub. 501 for details.

Example. Even if conditions (1) through (4) are met and the custodial parent signs Form 8332 or a substantially similar statement that he or she will not claim the child as a dependent for 2015, this doesn't allow the noncustodial parent to claim the child as a qualifying child for the earned income credit. The custodial parent or another taxpayer, if eligible, can claim the child for the earned income credit.

Custodial and noncustodial parents. The custodial parent is the parent with whom the child lived for the greater number of nights in 2015. The noncustodial parent is the other parent. If the child was with each parent for an equal number of nights, the custodial parent is the parent with the higher adjusted gross income. See Pub. 501 for an exception for a parent who works at night, rules for a child who is emancipated under state law, and other details.

Post-1984 and pre-2009 decree or agreement. The decree or agreement must state all three of the following.

1. The noncustodial parent can claim the child as a dependent without regard to any condition, such as payment of support.

2. The other parent won't claim the child as a dependent.

3. The years for which the claim is released.

The noncustodial parent must include all of the following pages from the decree or agreement.

- Cover page (include the other parent's SSN on that page).
- The pages that include all the information identified in (1) through (3) above.
- Signature page with the other parent's signature and date of agreement.

 You must include the required information even if you filed it with your return in an earlier year.

Post-2008 decree or agreement. If the divorce decree or separation agreement went into effect after 2008, the noncustodial parent can't include pages from the decree or agreement instead of Form 8332. The custodial parent must sign either Form 8332 or a substantially similar statement the only purpose of which is to release the custodial parent's claim to an exemption for a child, and the noncustodial parent must include a copy with his or her return. The form or statement must release the custodial parent's claim to the child without any conditions. For example, the release must not depend on the noncustodial parent paying support.

Release of exemption revoked. A custodial parent who has revoked his or her previous release of a claim to exemption for a child must include a copy of the revocation with his or her return. For details, see Form 8332.

Exception to citizen test. If you are a U.S. citizen or U.S. national and your adopted child lived with you all year as a member of your household, that child meets the requirement to be a U.S. citizen in Step 2, question 1; Step 3, question 2; and Step 4, question 2.

Exception to gross income test. If your relative (including a person who lived with you all year as a member of your household) is permanently and totally disabled (defined later), certain income for services performed at a sheltered workshop may be excluded for this test. For details, see Pub. 501.

Exception to time lived with you. Temporary absences by you or the other person for special circumstances, such as school, vacation, business, medical care, military service, or detention in a juvenile facility, count as time the person lived with you. Also see *Children of divorced or separated parents*, earlier, or *Kidnapped child*, later.

If the person meets all other requirements to be your qualifying child but was born or died in 2015, the person is considered to have lived with you for more than half of 2015 if your home was this person's home for more than half the time he or she was alive in 2015.

Any other person is considered to have lived with you for all of 2015 if the person was born or died in 2015 and your home was this person's home for the entire time he or she was alive in 2015.

Foster child. A foster child is any child placed with you by an authorized placement agency or by judgment, decree, or other order of any court of competent jurisdiction.

Kidnapped child. If your child is presumed by law enforcement authorities to have been kidnapped by someone who isn't a family member, you may be able to take the child into account in determining your eligibility for head of household or

Need more information or forms? Visit IRS.gov.

qualifying widow(er) filing status, the dependency exemption, the child tax credit, and the earned income credit (EIC). For details, see Pub. 501 (Pub. 596 for the EIC).

Married person. If the person is married and files a joint return, you can't claim that person as your dependent. However, if the person is married but doesn't file a joint return or files a joint return only to claim a refund of withheld income tax or estimated tax paid, you may be able to claim him or her as a dependent. (See Pub. 501 for details and examples.) In that case, go to Step 2, question 3 (for a qualifying child) or Step 4, question 4 (for a qualifying relative).

Multiple support agreements. If no one person contributed over half of the support of your relative (or a person who lived with you all year as a member of your household) but you and another person(s) provided more than half of your relative's support, special rules may apply that would treat you as having provided over half of the support. For details, see Pub. 501.

Permanently and totally disabled. A person is permanently and totally disabled if, at any time in 2015, the person can't engage in any substantial gainful activity because of a physical or mental condition and a doctor has determined that this condition has lasted or can be expected to last continuously for at least a year or can be expected to lead to death.

Qualifying child of more than one person. Even if a child meets the conditions to be the qualifying child of more than one person, only one person can claim the child as a qualifying child for all of the following tax benefits, unless the special rule for *Children of divorced or separated parents,* described earlier, applies.

1. Dependency exemption (line 6c).
2. Child tax credits (lines 52 and 67).
3. Head of household filing status (line 4).
4. Credit for child and dependent care expenses (line 49).
5. Exclusion for dependent care benefits (Form 2441, Part III).
6. Earned income credit (lines 66a and 66b).

No other person can take any of the six tax benefits just listed unless he or she has a different qualifying child. If you and any other person can claim the child as a qualifying child, the following rules apply.

• If only one of the persons is the child's parent, the child is treated as the qualifying child of the parent.

• If the parents file a joint return together and can claim the child as a qualifying child, the child is treated as the qualifying child of the parents.

• If the parents do not file a joint return together but both parents claim the child as a qualifying child, the IRS will treat the child as the qualifying child of the parent with whom the child lived for the longer period of time in 2015. If the child lived with each parent for the same amount of time, the IRS will treat the child as the qualifying child of the parent who had the higher adjusted gross income (AGI) for 2015.

• If no parent can claim the child as a qualifying child, the child is treated as the qualifying child of the person who had the highest AGI for 2015.

• If a parent can claim the child as a qualifying child but no parent does so claim the child, the child is treated as the qualifying child of the person who had the highest AGI for 2015, but only if that person's AGI is higher than the highest AGI of any parent of the child who can claim the child.

Example. Your daughter meets the conditions to be a qualifying child for both you and your mother. Your daughter doesn't meet the conditions to be a qualifying child of any other person, including her other parent. Under the rules just described, you can claim your daughter as a qualifying child for all of the six tax benefits just listed for which you otherwise qualify. Your mother can't claim any of those six tax benefits unless she has a different qualifying child. However, if your mother's AGI is higher than yours and you do not claim your daughter as a qualifying child, your daughter is the qualifying child of your mother.

For more details and examples, see Pub. 501.

If you will be claiming the child as a qualifying child, go to Step 2. Otherwise, stop; you can't claim any benefits based on this child.

Social security number. You must enter each dependent's social security number (SSN). Be sure the name and SSN entered agree with the dependent's social security card. Otherwise, at the time we process your return, we may disallow the exemption claimed for the dependent and reduce or disallow any other tax benefits (such as the child tax credit) based on that dependent. If the name or SSN on the dependent's social security card isn't correct or you need to get an SSN for your dependent, contact the Social Security Administration. See *Social Security Number (SSN),* earlier. If your dependent won't have a number by the date your return is due, see *What if You can't File on Time?* earlier.

If your dependent child was born and died in 2015 and you do not have an SSN for the child, enter "Died" in column (2) and include a copy of the child's birth certificate, death certificate, or hospital records. The document must show the child was born alive.

If you didn't have an SSN (or ITIN) by the due date of your 2015 return (including extensions), you can't claim the child tax credit on either your original or an amended 2015 return, even if you later get an SSN (or ITIN). Also, no child tax credit is allowed on your original or an amended 2015 return with respect to a child who didn't have an SSN, ATIN, or ITIN by the due date of your return (including extensions), even if that child later gets one of those numbers. See the instructions for line 52.

Student. A student is a child who during any part of 5 calendar months of 2015 was enrolled as a full-time student at a school, or took a full-time, on-farm training course given by a school or a state, county, or local government agency. A school includes a technical, trade, or mechanical school. It doesn't include an on-the-job training course, correspondence school, or school offering courses only through the Internet.

Income

Generally, you must report all income except income that is exempt from tax by law. For details, see the following instructions, especially the instructions for lines 7 through 21. Also see Pub. 525.

Foreign-Source Income

You must report unearned income, such as interest, dividends, and pensions, from sources outside the United States unless exempt by law or a tax treaty. You must also report earned income, such as wages and tips, from sources outside the United States.

If you worked abroad, you may be able to exclude part or all of your foreign earned income. For details, see Pub. 54 and Form 2555 or 2555-EZ.

Foreign retirement plans. If you were a beneficiary of a foreign retirement plan, you may have to report the undistributed income earned in your plan. However, if you were the beneficiary of a Canadian registered retirement plan, see Revenue Procedure 2014-55, 2014-44 I.R.B. 753, available at *www.irs.gov//irb/2014-44_IRB/ar10.html*, to find out if you can elect to defer tax on the undistributed income.

Report distributions from foreign pension plans on lines 16a and 16b.

Foreign accounts and trusts. You must complete Part III of Schedule B if you:
• Had a foreign account, or
• Received a distribution from, or were a grantor of, or a transferor to, a foreign trust.

Foreign financial assets. If you had foreign financial assets in 2015, you may have to file Form 8938. See Form 8938 and its instructions.

Chapter 11 Bankruptcy Cases

If you are a debtor in a chapter 11 bankruptcy case, income taxable to the bankruptcy estate and reported on the estate's income tax return includes:
• Earnings from services you performed after the beginning of the case (both wages and self-employment income), and
• Income from property described in section 541 of title 11 of the U.S. Code that you either owned when the case began or that you acquired after the case began and before the case was closed, dismissed, or converted to a case under a different chapter.

Because this income is taxable to the estate, do not include this income on your own individual income tax return. The only exception is for purposes of figuring your self-employment tax. For that purpose, you must take into account all your self-employment income for the year from services performed both before and after the beginning of the case. Also, you (or the trustee, if one is appointed) must allocate between you and the bankruptcy estate the wages, salary, or other compensation and withheld income tax reported to you on Form W-2. A similar allocation is required for income and withheld income tax reported to you on Forms 1099. You must also include a statement that indicates you filed a chapter 11 case and that explains how income and withheld income tax reported to you on Forms W-2 and 1099 are allocated between you and the estate. For more details, including acceptable allocation methods, see Notice 2006-83, 2006-40 I.R.B. 596, available at *www.irs.gov/irb/2006-40_IRB/ar12.html*.

Community Property States

Community property states are Arizona, California, Idaho, Louisiana, Nevada, New Mexico, Texas, Washington, and Wisconsin. If you and your spouse lived in a community property state, you must usually follow state law to determine what is community income and what is separate income. For details, see Form 8958 and Pub. 555.

Nevada, Washington, and California domestic partners. A registered domestic partner in Nevada, Washington, or California generally must report half the combined community income of the individual and his or her domestic partner. See Form 8958 and Pub. 555.

Rounding Off to Whole Dollars

You can round off cents to whole dollars on your return and schedules. If you do round to whole dollars, you must round all amounts. To round, drop amounts under 50 cents and increase amounts from 50 to 99 cents to the next dollar. For example, $1.39 becomes $1 and $2.50 becomes $3.

If you have to add two or more amounts to figure the amount to enter on a line, include cents when adding the amounts and round off only the total.

Line 7

Wages, Salaries, Tips, etc.

Enter the total of your wages, salaries, tips, etc. If a joint return, also include your spouse's income. For most people, the amount to enter on this line should be shown in box 1 of their Form(s) W-2. But the following types of income must also be included in the total on line 7.
• All wages received as a household employee for which you didn't receive a Form W-2 because an employer paid you less than $1,900 in 2015. Also, enter "HSH" and the total amount not reported on Form(s) W-2 on the dotted line next to line 7.
• Tip income you didn't report to your employer. This should include any allocated tips shown in box 8 on your Form(s) W-2 unless you can prove that your unreported tips are less than the amount in box 8. Allocated tips aren't included as income in box 1. See Pub. 531 for more details. Also include the value of any noncash tips you received, such as tickets, passes, or other items of value. Although you do not report these noncash tips to your employer, you must report them on line 7.

 You may owe social security and Medicare or railroad retirement (RRTA) tax on unreported tips. See the instructions for line 58.

• Dependent care benefits, which should be shown in box 10 of your Form(s) W-2. But first complete Form 2441 to see if you can exclude part or all of the benefits.
• Employer-provided adoption benefits, which should be shown in box 12 of your Form(s) W-2 with code T. But see the Instructions for Form 8839 to find out if you can exclude part or all of the benefits. You may also be able to exclude amounts if you adopted a child

with special needs and the adoption became final in 2015.

- Scholarship and fellowship grants not reported on Form W-2. Also, enter "SCH" and the amount on the dotted line next to line 7. However, if you were a degree candidate, include on line 7 only the amounts you used for expenses other than tuition and course-related expenses. For example, amounts used for room, board, and travel must be reported on line 7.
- Excess salary deferrals. The amount deferred should be shown in box 12 of your Form W-2, and the "Retirement plan" box in box 13 should be checked. If the total amount you (or your spouse if filing jointly) deferred for 2015 under all plans was more than $18,000 (excluding catch-up contributions as explained later), include the excess on line 7. This limit is (a) $12,500 if you have only SIMPLE plans, or (b) $21,000 for section 403(b) plans if you qualify for the 15-year rule in Pub. 571. Although designated Roth contributions are subject to this limit, do not include the excess attributable to such contributions on line 7. They are already included as income in box 1 of your Form W-2.

A higher limit may apply to participants in section 457(b) deferred compensation plans for the 3 years before retirement age. Contact your plan administrator for more information.

If you were age 50 or older at the end of 2015, your employer may have allowed an additional deferral (catch-up contributions) of up to $6,000 ($3,000 for section 401(k)(11) and SIMPLE plans). This additional deferral amount isn't subject to the overall limit on elective deferrals.

 *You can't deduct the amount deferred. It isn't included as income in box 1 of your Form W-2.*

- Disability pensions shown on Form 1099-R if you have not reached the minimum retirement age set by your employer. But see *Insurance Premiums for Retired Public Safety Officers* in the instructions for lines 16a and 16b. Disability pensions received after you reach minimum retirement age and other payments shown on Form 1099-R (other than payments from an IRA*) are reported on lines 16a and 16b. Payments from an IRA are reported on lines 15a and 15b.

- Corrective distributions from a retirement plan shown on Form 1099-R of excess salary deferrals and excess contributions (plus earnings). But do not include distributions from an IRA* on line 7. Instead, report distributions from an IRA on lines 15a and 15b.
- Wages from Form 8919, line 6.

This includes a Roth, SEP, or SIMPLE IRA.

Were You a Statutory Employee?

If you were, the "Statutory employee" box in box 13 of your Form W-2 should be checked. Statutory employees include full-time life insurance salespeople and certain agent or commission drivers, traveling salespeople, and homeworkers. If you have related business expenses to deduct, report the amount shown in box 1 of your Form W-2 on Schedule C or C-EZ along with your expenses.

Missing or Incorrect Form W-2?

Your employer is required to provide or send Form W-2 to you no later than February 1, 2016. If you do not receive it by early February, use *Tax Topic 154* to find out what to do. Even if you do not get a Form W-2, you must still report your earnings on line 7. If you lose your Form W-2 or it is incorrect, ask your employer for a new one.

Line 8a

Taxable Interest

Each payer should send you a Form 1099-INT or Form 1099-OID. Enter your total taxable interest income on line 8a. But you must fill in and attach Schedule B if the total is over $1,500 or any of the other conditions listed at the beginning of the Schedule B instructions apply to you.

For more details about reporting taxable interest, including market discount on bonds, see Pub. 550.

Interest credited in 2015 on deposits that you couldn't withdraw because of the bankruptcy or insolvency of the financial institution may not have to be included in your 2015 income. For details, see Pub. 550.

 If you get a 2015 Form 1099-INT for U.S. savings bond interest that includes amounts you reported before 2015, see Pub. 550.

Line 8b

Tax-Exempt Interest

If you received any tax-exempt interest, such as from municipal bonds, each payer should send you a Form 1099-INT. Your tax-exempt interest should be shown in box 8 of Form 1099-INT. Enter the total on line 8b. Also include on line 8b any exempt-interest dividends from a mutual fund or other regulated investment company. This amount should be shown in box 10 of Form 1099-DIV.

Do not include interest earned on your IRA, health savings account, Archer or Medicare Advantage MSA, or Coverdell education savings account.

Line 9a

Ordinary Dividends

Each payer should send you a Form 1099-DIV. Enter your total ordinary dividends on line 9a. This amount should be shown in box 1a of Form(s) 1099-DIV.

You must fill in and attach Schedule B if the total is over $1,500 or you received, as a nominee, ordinary dividends that actually belong to someone else.

Nondividend Distributions

Some distributions are a return of your cost (or other basis). They won't be taxed until you recover your cost (or other basis). You must reduce your cost (or other basis) by these distributions. After you get back all of your cost (or other basis), you must report these distributions as capital gains on Form 8949. For details, see Pub. 550.

Dividends on insurance policies are a partial return of the premiums you paid. Do not report them as dividends. Include them in income on line 21 only if they exceed the total of all net premiums you paid for the contract.

Line 9b

Qualified Dividends

Enter your total qualified dividends on line 9b. Qualified dividends are also included in the ordinary dividend total required to be shown on line 9a. Qualified dividends are eligible for a lower tax rate than other ordinary income. Generally, these dividends are shown in box 1b of Form(s) 1099-DIV. See Pub. 550 for the definition of qualified dividends if you received dividends not reported on Form 1099-DIV.

Exception. Some dividends may be reported as qualified dividends in box 1b of Form 1099-DIV but aren't qualified dividends. These include:

• Dividends you received as a nominee. See the Schedule B instructions.

• Dividends you received on any share of stock that you held for less than 61 days during the 121-day period that began 60 days before the ex-dividend date. The ex-dividend date is the first date following the declaration of a dividend on which the purchaser of a stock isn't entitled to receive the next dividend payment. When counting the number of days you held the stock, include the day you disposed of the stock but not the day you acquired it. See the examples that follow. Also, when counting the number of days you held the stock, you can't count certain days during which your risk of loss was diminished. See Pub. 550 for more details.

• Dividends attributable to periods totaling more than 366 days that you received on any share of preferred stock held for less than 91 days during the 181-day period that began 90 days before the ex-dividend date. When counting the number of days you held the stock, you can't count certain days during which your risk of loss was diminished. See Pub. 550 for more details. Preferred dividends attributable to periods totaling less than 367 days are subject to the 61-day holding period rule just described.

• Dividends on any share of stock to the extent that you are under an obligation (including a short sale) to make related payments with respect to positions in substantially similar or related property.

• Payments in lieu of dividends, but only if you know or have reason to know that the payments aren't qualified dividends.

Example 1. You bought 5,000 shares of XYZ Corp. common stock on July 8, 2015. XYZ Corp. paid a cash dividend of 10 cents per share. The ex-dividend date was July 16, 2015. Your Form 1099-DIV from XYZ Corp. shows $500 in box 1a (ordinary dividends) and in box 1b (qualified dividends). However, you sold the 5,000 shares on August 11, 2015. You held your shares of XYZ Corp. for only 34 days of the 121-day period (from July 9, 2015, through August 11, 2015). The 121-day period began on May 17, 2015 (60 days before the ex-dividend date), and ended on September 14, 2015. You have no qualified dividends from XYZ Corp. because you held the XYZ stock for less than 61 days.

Example 2. The facts are the same as in Example 1 except that you bought the stock on July 15, 2015 (the day before the ex-dividend date), and you sold the stock on September 16, 2015. You held the stock for 63 days (from July 16, 2015, through September 16, 2015). The $500 of qualified dividends shown in box 1b of Form 1099-DIV are all qualified dividends because you held the stock for 61 days of the 121-day period (from July 16, 2015, through September 14, 2015).

Example 3. You bought 10,000 shares of ABC Mutual Fund common stock on July 8, 2015. ABC Mutual Fund paid a cash dividend of 10 cents a share. The ex-dividend date was July 16, 2015. The ABC Mutual Fund advises you that the part of the dividend eligible to be treated as qualified dividends equals 2 cents a share. Your Form 1099-DIV from ABC Mutual Fund shows total ordinary dividends of $1,000 and qualified dividends of $200. However, you sold the 10,000 shares on August 11, 2015. You have no qualified dividends from ABC Mutual Fund because you held the ABC Mutual Fund stock for less than 61 days.

 Use the Qualified Dividends and Capital Gain Tax Worksheet or the Schedule D Tax Worksheet, whichever applies, to figure your tax. See the instructions for line 44 for details.

Line 10

Taxable Refunds, Credits, or Offsets of State and Local Income Taxes

 None of your refund is taxable if, in the year you paid the tax, you either (a) didn't itemize deductions, or (b) elected to deduct state and local general sales taxes instead of state and local income taxes.

If you received a refund, credit, or offset of state or local income taxes in 2015, you may be required to report this amount. If you didn't receive a Form 1099-G, check with the government agency that made the payments to you. Your 2015 Form 1099-G may have been made available to you only in an electronic format, and you will need to get instructions from the agency to retrieve this document. Report any taxable refund you received even if you didn't receive Form 1099-G.

If you chose to apply part or all of the refund to your 2015 estimated state or local income tax, the amount applied is treated as received in 2015. If the refund was for a tax you paid in 2014 and you deducted state and local income taxes on line 5 of your 2014 Schedule A, use the State and Local Income Tax Refund Worksheet in these instructions to see if any of your refund is taxable.

Exception. See *Itemized Deduction Recoveries* in Pub. 525 instead of using the State and Local Income Tax Refund Worksheet in these instructions if any of the following applies.

1. You received a refund in 2015 that is for a tax year other than 2014.

2. You received a refund other than an income tax refund, such as a general sales tax or real property tax refund, in

Need more information or forms? Visit IRS.gov.

State and Local Income Tax Refund Worksheet—Line 10
Keep for Your Records

Before you begin: ✓ Be sure you have read the **Exception** in the instructions for this line to see if you can use this worksheet instead of Pub. 525 to figure if any of your refund is taxable.

1. Enter the income tax refund from **Form(s) 1099-G** (or similar statement). But **do not** enter more than the amount of your state and local income taxes shown on your 2014 Schedule A, line 5 .... **1.** _____

2. Enter your total itemized deductions from your 2014 Schedule A, line 29 .... **2.** _____

   Note. If the filing status on your 2014 Form 1040 was married filing separately and your spouse itemized deductions in 2014, skip lines 3 through 5, enter the amount from line 2 on line 6, and go to line 7.

3. Enter the amount shown below for the filing status claimed on your **2014** Form 1040.
   - Single or married filing separately—$6,200
   - Married filing jointly or qualifying widow(er)—$12,400
   - Head of household—$9,100   } **3.** _____

4. Did you fill in line 39a on your 2014 Form 1040?

   ☐ **No.** Enter -0-.

   ☐ **Yes.** Multiply the number in the box on line 39a of your 2014 Form 1040 by $1,200 ($1,550 if your 2014 filing status was single or head of household). } **4.** _____

5. Add lines 3 and 4 .... **5.** _____

6. Is the amount on line 5 less than the amount on line 2?

   ☐ **No.** 🛑 None of your refund is taxable.

   ☐ **Yes.** Subtract line 5 from line 2 .... **6.** _____

7. **Taxable part of your refund.** Enter the **smaller** of line 1 or line 6 here and on Form 1040, line 10 .... **7.** _____

2015 of an amount deducted or credit claimed in an earlier year.

3. The amount on your 2014 Form 1040, line 42, was more than the amount on your 2014 Form 1040, line 41.

4. You had taxable income on your 2014 Form 1040, line 43, but no tax on your Form 1040, line 44, because of the 0% tax rate on net capital gain and qualified dividends in certain situations.

5. Your 2014 state and local income tax refund is more than your 2014 state and local income tax deduction minus the amount you could have deducted as your 2014 state and local general sales taxes.

6. You made your last payment of 2014 estimated state or local income tax in 2015.

7. You owed alternative minimum tax in 2014.

8. You couldn't use the full amount of credits you were entitled to in 2014 because the total credits were more than the amount shown on your 2014 Form 1040, line 47.

9. You could be claimed as a dependent by someone else in 2014.

10. You received a refund because of a jointly filed state or local income tax return, but you aren't filing a joint 2015 Form 1040 with the same person.

11. You had to use the Itemized Deductions Worksheet in the 2014 Instructions for Schedule A and both of the following apply.

   a. You couldn't deduct all of the amount on the 2014 Itemized Deductions Worksheet, line 1.

   b. The amount on line 8 of that 2014 worksheet would be more than the amount on line 4 of that worksheet if the amount on line 4 were reduced by 80% of the refund you received in 2015.

Line 11

Alimony Received

Enter amounts received as alimony or separate maintenance. You must let the person who made the payments know your social security number. If you do not, you may have to pay a penalty. For more details, see Pub. 504.

Line 12

Business Income or (Loss)

If you operated a business or practiced your profession as a sole proprietor, report your income and expenses on Schedule C or C-EZ.

Line 13

Capital Gain or (Loss)

If you sold a capital asset, such as a stock or bond, you must complete and attach Form 8949 and Schedule D.

Exception 1. You do not have to file Form 8949 or Schedule D if both of the following apply.

1. You have no capital losses, and your only capital gains are capital gain distributions from Form(s) 1099-DIV, box 2a (or substitute statements).

2. None of the Form(s) 1099-DIV (or substitute statements) have an amount in box 2b (unrecaptured section 1250 gain), box 2c (section 1202 gain), or box 2d (collectibles (28%) gain).

Exception 2. You must file Schedule D, but generally do not have to file Form 8949, if *Exception 1* doesn't apply and your only capital gains and losses are:

- Capital gain distributions,
- A capital loss carryover from 2014,
- A gain from Form 2439 or 6252 or Part I of Form 4797,
- A gain or loss from Form 4684, 6781, or 8824,
- A gain or loss from a partnership, S corporation, estate, or trust, or
- Gains and losses from transactions for which you received a Form 1099-B (or substitute statement) that shows basis was reported to the IRS and for which you do not need to make any adjustments in column (g) of Form 8949 or enter any codes in column (f) of Form 8949.

If *Exception 1* applies, enter your total capital gain distributions (from box 2a of Form(s) 1099-DIV) on line 13 and check the box on that line. If you received capital gain distributions as a nominee (that is, they were paid to you but actually belong to someone else), report on line 13 only the amount that belongs to you. Include a statement showing the full amount you received and the amount you received as a nominee. See the Schedule B instructions for filing requirements for Forms 1099-DIV and 1096.

 If you do not have to file Schedule D, use the Qualified Dividends and Capital Gain Tax Worksheet in the line 44 instructions to figure your tax.

Line 14

Other Gains or (Losses)

If you sold or exchanged assets used in a trade or business, see the Instructions for Form 4797.

Lines 15a and 15b

IRA Distributions

You should receive a Form 1099-R showing the total amount of any distribution from your IRA before income tax or other deductions were withheld. This amount should be shown in box 1 of Form 1099-R. Unless otherwise noted in the line 15a and 15b instructions, an IRA includes a traditional IRA, Roth IRA (including a *my*RA), simplified employee pension (SEP) IRA, and a savings incentive match plan for employees (SIMPLE) IRA. Except as provided next, leave line 15a blank and enter the total distribution (from Form 1099-R, box 1) on line 15b.

Exception 1. Enter the total distribution on line 15a if you rolled over part or all of the distribution from one:

- IRA to another IRA of the same type (for example, from one traditional IRA to another traditional IRA),
- SEP or SIMPLE IRA to a traditional IRA, or
- IRA to a qualified plan other than an IRA.

Also, enter "Rollover" next to line 15b. If the total distribution was rolled over in a qualified rollover, enter -0- on line 15b. If the total distribution wasn't rolled over in a qualified rollover, enter the part not rolled over on line 15b unless *Exception 2* applies to the part not rolled over. Generally, a qualified rollover must be made within 60 days after the day you received the distribution. For more details on rollovers, see Pub. 590-A and Pub. 590-B.

If you rolled over the distribution into a qualified plan other than an IRA or you made the rollover in 2016, include a statement explaining what you did.

Exception 2. If any of the following apply, enter the total distribution on line 15a and see Form 8606 and its instructions to figure the amount to enter on line 15b.

1. You received a distribution from an IRA (other than a Roth IRA) and you made nondeductible contributions to any of your traditional or SEP IRAs for 2015 or an earlier year. If you made nondeductible contributions to these IRAs for 2015, also see Pub. 590-A and Pub. 590-B.

2. You received a distribution from a Roth IRA. But if either (a) or (b) below applies, enter -0- on line 15b; you do not have to see Form 8606 or its instructions.

a. Distribution code T is shown in box 7 of Form 1099-R and you made a contribution (including a conversion) to a Roth IRA for 2010 or an earlier year.

b. Distribution code Q is shown in box 7 of Form 1099-R.

3. You converted part or all of a traditional, SEP, or SIMPLE IRA to a Roth IRA in 2015.

4. You had a 2014 or 2015 IRA contribution returned to you, with the related earnings or less any loss, by the due date (including extensions) of your tax return for that year.

5. You made excess contributions to your IRA for an earlier year and had them returned to you in 2015.

6. You recharacterized part or all of a contribution to a Roth IRA as a traditional IRA contribution, or vice versa.

Exception 3. If the distribution is a qualified charitable distribution (QCD), enter the total distribution on line 15a. If the total amount distributed is a QCD, enter -0- on line 15b. If only part of the distribution is a QCD, enter the part that is not a QCD on line 15b unless *Exception 2* applies to that part. Enter "QCD" next to line 15b.

A QCD is a distribution made directly by the trustee of your IRA (other than an ongoing SEP or SIMPLE IRA) to an organization eligible to receive tax-deductible contributions (with certain exceptions). You must have been at least age 70½ when the distribution was made.

Need more information or forms? Visit IRS.gov.

Generally, your total QCDs for the year can't be more than $100,000. (On a joint return, your spouse can also have a QCD of up to $100,000.) The amount of the QCD is limited to the amount that would otherwise be included in your income. If your IRA includes nondeductible contributions, the distribution is first considered to be paid out of otherwise taxable income. See Pub. 590-A for details.

 You can't claim a charitable contribution deduction for any QCD not included in your income.

Exception 4. If the distribution is a health savings account (HSA) funding distribution (HFD), enter the total distribution on line 15a. If the total amount distributed is an HFD and you elect to exclude it from income, enter -0- on line 15b. If only part of the distribution is an HFD and you elect to exclude that part from income, enter the part that isn't an HFD on line 15b unless *Exception 2* applies to that part. Enter "HFD" next to line 15b.

An HFD is a distribution made directly by the trustee of your IRA (other than an ongoing SEP or SIMPLE IRA) to your HSA. If eligible, you generally can elect to exclude an HFD from your income once in your lifetime. You can't exclude more than the limit on HSA contributions or more than the amount that would otherwise be included in your income. If your IRA includes nondeductible contributions, the HFD is first considered to be paid out of otherwise taxable income. See Pub. 969 for details.

 The amount of an HFD reduces the amount you can contribute to your HSA for the year. If you fail to maintain eligibility for an HSA for the 12 months following the month of the HFD, you may have to report the HFD as income and pay an additional tax. See Form 8889, Part III.

More than one exception applies. If more than one exception applies, include a statement showing the amount of each exception, instead of making an entry next to line 15b. For example: "Line 15b – $1,000 Rollover and $500 HFD." But you do not need to attach a statement if

only *Exception 2* and one other exception apply.

More than one distribution. If you (or your spouse if filing jointly) received more than one distribution, figure the taxable amount of each distribution and enter the total of the taxable amounts on line 15b. Enter the total amount of those distributions on line 15a.

 You may have to pay an additional tax if (a) you received an early distribution from your IRA and the total wasn't rolled over, or (b) you were born before July 1, 1944, and received less than the minimum required distribution from your traditional, SEP, and SIMPLE IRAs. See the instructions for line 59 for details.

More information. For more information about IRAs, see Pub. 590-A and Pub. 590-B.

Lines 16a and 16b
Pensions and Annuities

You should receive a Form 1099-R showing the total amount of your pension and annuity payments before income tax or other deductions were withheld. This amount should be shown in box 1 of Form 1099-R. Pension and annuity payments include distributions from 401(k), 403(b), and governmental 457(b) plans. Rollovers and lump-sum distributions are explained later. Do not include the following payments on lines 16a and 16b. Instead, report them on line 7.

• Disability pensions received before you reach the minimum retirement age set by your employer.

• Corrective distributions (including any earnings) of excess salary deferrals or excess contributions to retirement plans. The plan must advise you of the year(s) the distributions are includible in income.

 Attach Form(s) 1099-R to Form 1040 if any federal income tax was withheld.

Fully Taxable Pensions and Annuities

Your payments are fully taxable if (a) you didn't contribute to the cost (see *Cost,* later) of your pension or annuity,

or (b) you got your entire cost back tax free before 2015. But see *Insurance Premiums for Retired Public Safety Officers,* later. If your pension or annuity is fully taxable, enter the total pension or annuity payments (from Form(s) 1099-R, box 1) on line 16b; do not make an entry on line 16a.

Fully taxable pensions and annuities also include military retirement pay shown on Form 1099-R. For details on military disability pensions, see Pub. 525. If you received a Form RRB-1099-R, see Pub. 575 to find out how to report your benefits.

Partially Taxable Pensions and Annuities

Enter the total pension or annuity payments (from Form 1099-R, box 1) on line 16a. If your Form 1099-R doesn't show the taxable amount, you must use the General Rule explained in Pub. 939 to figure the taxable part to enter on line 16b. But if your annuity starting date (defined later) was after July 1, 1986, see *Simplified Method,* later, to find out if you must use that method to figure the taxable part.

You can ask the IRS to figure the taxable part for you for a $1,000 fee. For details, see Pub. 939.

If your Form 1099-R shows a taxable amount, you can report that amount on line 16b. But you may be able to report a lower taxable amount by using the General Rule or the Simplified Method or if the exclusion for retired public safety officers, discussed next, applies.

Insurance Premiums for Retired Public Safety Officers

If you are an eligible retired public safety officer (law enforcement officer, firefighter, chaplain, or member of a rescue squad or ambulance crew), you can elect to exclude from income distributions made from your eligible retirement plan that are used to pay the premiums for coverage by an accident or health plan or a long-term care insurance contract. You can do this only if you retired because of disability or because you reached normal retirement age. The premiums can be for coverage for you, your spouse, or dependents. The distribution must be from a plan maintained by the employer from which you retired as a public safety officer. Also, the distribution must be made directly from the plan to the provider of the accident or health plan or long-term care insurance contract. You can exclude from income the smaller of the amount of the premiums or $3,000. You can make this election only for amounts that would otherwise be included in your income.

An eligible retirement plan is a governmental plan that is a qualified trust or a section 403(a), 403(b), or 457(b) plan.

If you make this election, reduce the otherwise taxable amount of your pension or annuity by the amount excluded. The amount shown in box 2a of Form 1099-R doesn't reflect the exclusion. Report your total distributions on line 16a and the taxable amount on line 16b. Enter "PSO" next to line 16b.

If you are retired on disability and reporting your disability pension on line 7, include only the taxable amount on that line and enter "PSO" and the amount excluded on the dotted line next to line 7.

Simplified Method

You must use the Simplified Method if either of the following applies.

1. Your annuity starting date was after July 1, 1986, and you used this method last year to figure the taxable part.

2. Your annuity starting date was after November 18, 1996, and both of the following apply.

a. The payments are from a qualified employee plan, a qualified employee annuity, or a tax-sheltered annuity.

b. On your annuity starting date, either you were under age 75 or the number of years of guaranteed payments was fewer than 5. See Pub. 575 for the definition of guaranteed payments.

If you must use the Simplified Method, complete the Simplified Method Worksheet in these instructions to figure the taxable part of your pension or annuity. For more details on the Simplified Method, see Pub. 575 (or Pub. 721 for U.S. Civil Service retirement benefits).

 If you received U.S. Civil Service retirement benefits and you chose the alternative annuity option, see Pub. 721 to figure the taxable part of your annuity. Do not use the Simplified Method Worksheet in these instructions.

Annuity Starting Date

Your annuity starting date is the later of the first day of the first period for which you received a payment or the date the plan's obligations became fixed.

Age (or Combined Ages) at Annuity Starting Date

If you are the retiree, use your age on the annuity starting date. If you are the survivor of a retiree, use the retiree's age on his or her annuity starting date. But if your annuity starting date was after 1997 and the payments are for your life and that of your beneficiary, use your combined ages on the annuity starting date.

If you are the beneficiary of an employee who died, see Pub. 575. If there is more than one beneficiary, see Pub. 575 or Pub. 721 to figure each beneficiary's taxable amount.

Cost

Your cost is generally your net investment in the plan as of the annuity starting date. It doesn't include pre-tax contributions. Your net investment should be shown in box 9b of Form 1099-R for the first year you received payments from the plan.

Rollovers

Generally, a qualified rollover is a tax-free distribution of cash or other assets from one retirement plan that is contributed to another plan within 60 days of receiving the distribution. However, a qualified rollover to a Roth IRA or a designated Roth account is generally not a tax-free distribution. Use lines 16a and 16b to report a qualified rollover, including a direct rollover, from one qualified employer's plan to another or to an IRA or SEP.

Enter on line 16a the distribution from Form 1099-R, box 1. From this amount, subtract any contributions (usually shown in box 5) that were taxable to you when made. From that result, subtract the amount of the qualified rollover. Enter the remaining amount on line 16b. If the remaining amount is zero and you have no other distribution to report on line 16b, enter zero on line 16b. Also, enter "Rollover" next to line 16b.

See Pub. 575 for more details on rollovers, including special rules that apply to rollovers from designated Roth accounts, partial rollovers of property, and distributions under qualified domestic relations orders.

Lump-Sum Distributions

If you received a lump-sum distribution from a profit-sharing or retirement plan, your Form 1099-R should have the "Total distribution" box in box 2b checked. You may owe an additional tax if you received an early distribution from a qualified retirement plan and the total amount wasn't rolled over in a qualified rollover. For details, see the instructions for line 59.

Enter the total distribution on line 16a and the taxable part on line 16b. For details, see Pub 575.

 *If you or the plan participant was born before January 2, 1936, you could pay less tax on the distribution. See Form 4972.*

Line 19

Unemployment Compensation

You should receive a Form 1099-G showing in box 1 the total unemployment compensation paid to you in 2015. Report this amount on line 19. However, if you made contributions to a governmental unemployment compensation program or to a governmental paid family leave program and you aren't itemizing deductions, reduce the amount you report on line 19 by those contributions. If you are itemizing deductions, see the instructions on Form 1099-G.

If you received an overpayment of unemployment compensation in 2015 and you repaid any of it in 2015, subtract the amount you repaid from the total amount you received. Enter the result on line 19. Also, enter "Repaid" and the amount you repaid on the dotted line

Simplified Method Worksheet—Lines 16a and 16b *Keep for Your Records*

Before you begin:	✓ If you are the beneficiary of a deceased employee or former employee who died **before** August 21, 1996, include any death benefit exclusion that you are entitled to (up to $5,000) in the amount entered on line 2 below.

More than one pension or annuity. If you had more than one partially taxable pension or annuity, figure the taxable part of each separately. Enter the total of the taxable parts on Form 1040, line 16b. Enter the total pension or annuity payments received in 2015 on Form 1040, line 16a.

1. Enter the total pension or annuity payments from Form 1099-R, box 1. Also, enter this amount on Form 1040, line 16a . . . . **1.** _____

2. Enter your cost in the plan at the annuity starting date . . . . **2.** _____

   Note. If you completed this worksheet last year, skip line 3 and enter the amount from line 4 of last year's worksheet on line 4 below (even if the amount of your pension or annuity has changed). Otherwise, go to line 3.

3. Enter the appropriate number from **Table 1** below. **But** if your annuity starting date was **after** 1997 **and** the payments are for your life and that of your beneficiary, enter the appropriate number from **Table 2** below . . . . **3.** _____

4. Divide line 2 by the number on line 3 . . . . **4.** _____

5. Multiply line 4 by the number of months for which this year's payments were made. If your annuity starting date was **before** 1987, skip lines 6 and 7 and enter this amount on line 8. Otherwise, go to line 6 . . . . **5.** _____

6. Enter the amount, if any, recovered tax free in years after 1986. If you completed this worksheet last year, enter the amount from line 10 of last year's worksheet . . . . . . **6.** _____

7. Subtract line 6 from line 2 . . . . **7.** _____

8. Enter the **smaller** of line 5 or line 7 . . . . **8.** _____

9. **Taxable amount.** Subtract line 8 from line 1. Enter the result, but not less than zero. Also, enter this amount on Form 1040, line 16b. If your Form 1099-R shows a larger amount, use the amount on this line instead of the amount from Form 1099-R. If you are a retired public safety officer, see *Insurance Premiums for Retired Public Safety Officers* before entering an amount on line 16b . . . . **9.** _____

10. Was your annuity starting date before 1987?

    ☐ **Yes.** (STOP) Do not complete the rest of this worksheet.

    ☐ **No.** Add lines 6 and 8. This is the **amount you have recovered tax free** through 2015. You will need this number if you need to fill out this worksheet next year . . . . **10.** _____

11. **Balance of cost to be recovered.** Subtract line 10 from line 2. If zero, you won't have to complete this worksheet next year. The payments you receive next year will generally be fully taxable . . . . **11.** _____

Table 1 for Line 3 Above

IF the age at annuity starting date was . . .	**AND your annuity starting date was—**	
	before November 19, 1996, enter on line 3 . . .	**after** November 18, 1996, enter on line 3 . . .
55 or under	300	360
56–60	260	310
61–65	240	260
66–70	170	210
71 or older	120	160

Table 2 for Line 3 Above

IF the combined ages at annuity starting date were . . .	THEN enter on line 3 . . .
110 or under	410
111–120	360
121–130	310
131–140	260
141 or older	210

next to line 19. If, in 2015, you repaid unemployment compensation that you included in gross income in an earlier year, you can deduct the amount repaid on Schedule A, line 23. But if you repaid more than $3,000, see *Repayments* in Pub. 525 for details on how to report the repayment.

Lines 20a and 20b

Social Security Benefits

You should receive a Form SSA-1099 showing in box 3 the total social security benefits paid to you. Box 4 will show the amount of any benefits you repaid in 2015. If you received railroad retirement benefits treated as social security, you should receive a Form RRB-1099.

Use the Social Security Benefits Worksheet in these instructions to see if any of your benefits are taxable.

Exception. Do not use the Social Security Benefits Worksheet in these instructions if any of the following applies.
* You made contributions to a traditional IRA for 2015 and you or your spouse were covered by a retirement plan at work or through self-employment. Instead, use the worksheets in Pub. 590-A to see if any of your social security benefits are taxable and to figure your IRA deduction.
* You repaid any benefits in 2015 and your total repayments (box 4) were more than your total benefits for 2015 (box 3). None of your benefits are taxable for 2015. Also, you may be able to take an itemized deduction or a credit for part of the excess repayments if they were for benefits you included in gross income in an earlier year. For more details, see Pub. 915.
* You file Form 2555, 2555-EZ, 4563, or 8815, or you exclude employer-provided adoption benefits or income from sources within Puerto Rico. Instead, use the worksheet in Pub. 915.

 Benefits for earlier year received in 2015? *If any of your benefits are taxable for 2015 and they include a lump-sum benefit payment that was for an earlier year, you may be able to reduce the taxable amount. See* Lump-Sum Election *in Pub. 915 for details.*

Social security information. Social security beneficiaries can now get a variety of information from the SSA website with a *my Social Security* account, including getting a replacement Form SSA-1099 if needed. For more information and to set up an account, go to *www.socialsecurity.gov/myaccount*.

Form RRB-1099. If you need a replacement Form RRB-1099, call the Railroad Retirement Board at 1-877-772-5772 or go to *www.rrb.gov*.

Line 21

Other Income

 Do not report on this line any income from self-employment or fees received as a notary public. Instead, you must use Schedule C, C-EZ, or F, even if you do not have any business expenses. Also, do not report on line 21 any nonemployee compensation shown on Form 1099-MISC (unless it isn't self-employment income, such as income from a hobby or a sporadic activity). Instead, see the instructions on Form 1099-MISC to find out where to report that income.

Taxable income. Use line 21 to report any taxable income not reported elsewhere on your return or other schedules. List the type and amount of income. If necessary, include a statement showing the required information. For more details, see *Miscellaneous Income* in Pub. 525.

Examples of income to report on line 21 include the following.
* Most prizes and awards.
* Jury duty pay. Also see the instructions for line 36.
* Alaska Permanent Fund dividends.
* Reimbursements or other amounts received for items deducted in an earlier year, such as medical expenses, real estate taxes, general sales taxes, or home mortgage interest. See *Recoveries* in Pub. 525 for details on how to figure the amount to report.
* Income from the rental of personal property if you engaged in the rental for profit but were not in the business of renting such property. Also see the instructions for line 36.
* Income from an activity not engaged in for profit. See Pub. 535.

* Amounts deemed to be income from a health savings account (HSA) because you didn't remain an eligible individual during the testing period. See Form 8889, Part III.
* Gambling winnings, including lotteries, raffles, a lump-sum payment from the sale of a right to receive future lottery payments, etc. For details on gambling losses, see the instructions for Schedule A, line 28.

 Attach Form(s) W-2G to Form 1040 if any federal income tax was withheld.

* Reemployment trade adjustment assistance (RTAA) payments. These payments should be shown in box 5 of Form 1099-G.
* Loss on certain corrective distributions of excess deferrals. See *Retirement Plan Contributions* in Pub. 525.
* Dividends on insurance policies if they exceed the total of all net premiums you paid for the contract.
* Recapture of a charitable contribution deduction relating to the contribution of a fractional interest in tangible personal property. See *Fractional Interest in Tangible Personal Property* in Pub. 526. Interest and an additional 10% tax apply to the amount of the recapture. See the instructions for line 62.
* Recapture of a charitable contribution deduction if the charitable organization disposes of the donated property within 3 years of the contribution. See *Recapture if no exempt use* in Pub. 526.
* Canceled debts. These amounts may be shown in box 2 of Form 1099-C. However, part or all of your income from the cancellation of debt may be nontaxable. See Pub. 4681 or go to IRS.gov and enter "canceled debt" or "foreclosure" in the search box.
* Taxable part of disaster relief payments. See Pub. 525 to figure the taxable part, if any. If any of your disaster relief payment is taxable, attach a statement showing the total payment received and how you figured the taxable part.
* Taxable distributions from a Coverdell education savings account (ESA) or a qualified tuition program (QTP). Distributions from these accounts may be taxable if (a) they are more than the qualified higher education expenses of the designated beneficiary in 2015, and

Need more information or forms? Visit IRS.gov.

Social Security Benefits Worksheet—Lines 20a and 20b
Keep for Your Records

Before you begin:	✓ Complete Form 1040, lines 21 and 23 through 32, if they apply to you.
	✓ Figure any write-in adjustments to be entered on the dotted line next to line 36 (see the instructions for line 36).
	✓ If you are married filing separately and you lived apart from your spouse for all of 2015, enter "D" to the right of the word "benefits" on line 20a. If you do not, you may get a math error notice from the IRS.
	✓ Be sure you have read the **Exception** in the line 20a and 20b instructions to see if you can use this worksheet instead of a publication to find out if any of your benefits are taxable.

1. Enter the total amount from **box 5** of **all** your **Forms SSA-1099** and **Forms RRB-1099.** Also, enter this amount on Form 1040, line 20a .... **1.** _____

2. Multiply line 1 by 50% (0.50) .... **2.** _____

3. Combine the amounts from Form 1040, lines 7, 8a, 9a, 10 through 14, 15b, 16b, 17 through 19, and 21 .... **3.** _____

4. Enter the amount, if any, from Form 1040, line 8b .... **4.** _____

5. Combine lines 2, 3, and 4 .... **5.** _____

6. Enter the total of the amounts from Form 1040, lines 23 through 32, plus any write-in adjustments you entered on the dotted line next to line 36 .... **6.** _____

7. Is the amount on line 6 less than the amount on line 5?

   ☐ **No.** (STOP) None of your social security benefits are taxable. Enter -0- on Form 1040, line 20b.

   ☐ **Yes.** Subtract line 6 from line 5 .... **7.** _____

8. If you are:
   - Married filing jointly, enter $32,000
   - Single, head of household, qualifying widow(er), or married filing separately and you **lived apart** from your spouse for all of 2015, enter $25,000

   - Married filing separately and you lived with your spouse at any time in 2015, skip lines 8 through 15; multiply line 7 by 85% (0.85) and enter the result on line 16. Then go to line 17
   .... **8.** _____

9. Is the amount on line 8 less than the amount on line 7?

   ☐ **No.** (STOP) None of your social security benefits are taxable. Enter -0- on Form 1040, line 20b. If you are married filing separately and you **lived apart** from your spouse for all of 2015, be sure you entered "D" to the right of the word "benefits" on line 20a.

   ☐ **Yes.** Subtract line 8 from line 7 .... **9.** _____

10. Enter: $12,000 if married filing jointly; $9,000 if single, head of household, qualifying widow(er), or married filing separately and you **lived apart** from your spouse for all of 2015 .... **10.** _____

11. Subtract line 10 from line 9. If zero or less, enter -0- .... **11.** _____

12. Enter the **smaller** of line 9 or line 10 .... **12.** _____

13. Enter one-half of line 12 .... **13.** _____

14. Enter the **smaller** of line 2 or line 13 .... **14.** _____

15. Multiply line 11 by 85% (0.85). If line 11 is zero, enter -0- .... **15.** _____

16. Add lines 14 and 15 .... **16.** _____

17. Multiply line 1 by 85% (0.85) .... **17.** _____

18. **Taxable social security benefits.** Enter the **smaller** of line 16 or line 17. Also enter this amount on Form 1040, line 20b .... **18.** _____

(TIP) *If any of your benefits are taxable for 2015 **and** they include a lump-sum benefit payment that was for an earlier year, you may be able to reduce the taxable amount. See Lump-Sum Election in Pub. 915 for details.*

(b) they were not included in a qualified rollover. See Pub. 970. Nontaxable distributions from these accounts, including rollovers, do not have to be reported on Form 1040.

 You may have to pay an additional tax if you received a taxable distribution from a Coverdell ESA or a QTP. See the Instructions for Form 5329.

• Taxable distributions from a health savings account (HSA) or an Archer MSA. Distributions from these accounts may be taxable if (a) they are more than the unreimbursed qualified medical expenses of the account beneficiary or account holder in 2015, and (b) they were not included in a qualified rollover. See Pub. 969.

 You may have to pay an additional tax if you received a taxable distribution from an HSA or an Archer MSA. See the Instructions for Form 8889 for HSAs or the Instructions for Form 8853 for Archer MSAs.

• Taxable distributions from an ABLE account. Distributions from this type of account may be taxable if (a) they are more than the designated beneficiary's qualified disability expenses, and (b) they were not included in a qualified rollover. Enter "ABLE" and the taxable amount on the dotted line next to line 21. See Pub. 907 for more information.

 You may have to pay an additional tax if you received a taxable distribution from an ABLE account. See the Instructions for Form 5329.

Nontaxable income. Do not report any nontaxable income on line 21. Examples of nontaxable income include the following.
• Child support.
• Payments you received to help you pay your mortgage loan under the HFA Hardest Hit Fund or the Emergency Homeowners' Loan Program or similar state program.
• Any Pay-for-Performance Success Payments that reduce the principal balance of your home mortgage under the Home Affordable Modification Program.

• Life insurance proceeds received because of someone's death (other than from certain employer-owned life insurance contracts).
• Gifts and bequests. However, if you received a gift or bequest from a foreign person of more than $15,601, you may have to report information about it on Form 3520, Part IV. See the Instructions for Form 3520.

Net operating loss (NOL) deduction. Include on line 21 any NOL deduction from an earlier year. Subtract it from any income on line 21 and enter the result. If the result is less than zero, enter it in parentheses. On the dotted line next to line 21, enter "NOL" and show the amount of the deduction in parentheses. See Pub. 536 for details.

Medicaid waiver payments to care provider. Certain Medicaid waiver payments you received for caring for someone living in your home with you may be nontaxable. If these payments were incorrectly reported to you in box 1 of Form(s) W-2, and you can't get a corrected Form W-2, include the amount on line 7. On line 21, subtract the nontaxable amount of the payments from any income on line 21 and enter the result. If the result is less than zero, enter it in parentheses. Enter "Notice 2014-7" and the nontaxable amount on the dotted line next to line 21. For more information about these payments, see Pub. 525.

Adjusted Gross Income

Line 23

Educator Expenses

If you were an eligible educator in 2015, you can deduct on line 23 up to $250 of qualified expenses you paid in 2015. If you and your spouse are filing jointly and both of you were eligible educators, the maximum deduction is $500. However, neither spouse can deduct more than $250 of his or her qualified expenses on line 23. You may be able to deduct expenses that are more than the $250 (or $500) limit on Schedule A, line 21. An eligible educator is a kinder-

garten through grade 12 teacher, instructor, counselor, principal, or aide who worked in a school for at least 900 hours during a school year.

Qualified expenses include ordinary and necessary expenses paid in connection with books, supplies, equipment (including computer equipment, software, and services), and other materials used in the classroom. An ordinary expense is one that is common and accepted in your educational field. A necessary expense is one that is helpful and appropriate for your profession as an educator. An expense does not have to be required to be considered necessary.

Qualified expenses do not include expenses for home schooling or for nonathletic supplies for courses in health or physical education.

You must reduce your qualified expenses by the following amounts.
• Excludable U.S. series EE and I savings bond interest from Form 8815.
• Nontaxable qualified tuition program earnings or distributions.
• Any nontaxable distribution of Coverdell education savings account earnings.
• Any reimbursements you received for these expenses that were not reported to you in box 1 of your Form W-2.

For more details, use *Tax Topic 458* or see Pub. 529.

Line 24

Certain Business Expenses of Reservists, Performing Artists, and Fee-Basis Government Officials

Include the following deductions on line 24.
• Certain business expenses of National Guard and reserve members who traveled more than 100 miles from home to perform services as a National Guard or reserve member.
• Performing-arts-related expenses as a qualified performing artist.
• Business expenses of fee-basis state or local government officials.

For more details, see Form 2106 or 2106-EZ.

Need more information or forms? Visit IRS.gov.

Self-Employed Health Insurance Deduction Worksheet—Line 29 *Keep for Your Records*

Before you begin:	✓ If, during 2015, you were an eligible trade adjustment assistance (TAA) recipient, alternative TAA (ATAA) recipient, reemployment TAA (RTAA) recipient, or Pension Benefit Guaranty Corporation pension payee, do not include on line 1 of this worksheet any amounts you included on Form 8885, line 4.
	✓ Be sure you have read the **Exceptions** in the instructions for this line to see if you can use this worksheet instead of Pub. 535 to figure your deduction.

1. Enter the total amount paid in 2015 for health insurance coverage established under your business (or the S corporation in which you were a more-than-2% shareholder) for 2015 for you, your spouse, and your dependents. Your insurance can also cover your child who was under age 27 at the end of 2015, even if the child wasn't your dependent. But do not include amounts for any month you were eligible to participate in an employer-sponsored health plan or amounts paid from retirement plan distributions that were nontaxable because you are a retired public safety officer .... **1.** _____

2. Enter your net profit* and any other earned income** from the business under which the insurance plan is established, minus any deductions on Form 1040, lines 27 and 28. Do not include Conservation Reserve Program payments exempt from self-employment tax .... **2.** _____

3. **Self-employed health insurance deduction.** Enter the **smaller** of line 1 or line 2 here and on Form 1040, line 29. **Do not** include this amount in figuring any medical expense deduction on Schedule A .... **3.** _____

If you used either optional method to figure your net earnings from self-employment, do not enter your net profit. Instead, enter the amount from Schedule SE, Section B, line 4b.

Earned income *includes net earnings and gains from the sale, transfer, or licensing of property you created. However, it doesn't include capital gain income. If you were a more-than-2% shareholder in the S corporation under which the insurance plan is established, earned income is your Medicare wages (box 5 of Form W-2) from that corporation.*

Line 25

Health Savings Account (HSA) Deduction

You may be able to take this deduction if contributions (other than employer contributions, rollovers, and qualified HSA funding distributions from an IRA) were made to your HSA for 2015. See Form 8889.

Line 26

Moving Expenses

If you moved in connection with your job or business or started a new job, you may be able to take this deduction. But your new workplace must be at least 50 miles farther from your old home than your old home was from your old workplace. If you had no former workplace, your new workplace must be at least 50 miles from your old home. Use *Tax Topic 455* or see Form 3903.

Line 27

Deductible Part of Self-Employment Tax

If you were self-employed and owe self-employment tax, fill in Schedule SE to figure the amount of your deduction. If you completed Section A of Schedule SE, the deductible part of your self-employment tax is on line 6. If you completed Section B of Schedule SE, it is on line 13.

Line 28

Self-Employed SEP, SIMPLE, and Qualified Plans

If you were self-employed or a partner, you may be able to take this deduction. See Pub. 560 or, if you were a minister, Pub. 517.

Line 29

Self-Employed Health Insurance Deduction

You may be able to deduct the amount you paid for health insurance for yourself, your spouse, and your dependents. The insurance can also cover your child who was under age 27 at the end of 2015, even if the child wasn't your dependent. A child includes your son, daughter, stepchild, adopted child, or foster child (defined in the line 6c instructions).

One of the following statements must be true.

• You were self-employed and had a net profit for the year reported on Schedule C, C-EZ, or F.

• You were a partner with net earnings from self-employment.

• You used one of the optional methods to figure your net earnings from self-employment on Schedule SE.

• You received wages in 2015 from an S corporation in which you were a more-than-2% shareholder. Health insurance premiums paid or reimbursed by the S corporation are shown as wages on Form W-2.

The insurance plan must be established under your business. Your personal services must have been a material income-producing factor in the business. If you are filing Schedule C, C-EZ, or F, the policy can be either in your name or in the name of the business.

If you are a partner, the policy can be either in your name or in the name of the partnership. You can either pay the premiums yourself or your partnership can pay them and report them as guaranteed payments. If the policy is in your name and you pay the premiums yourself, the partnership must reimburse you and report the premiums as guaranteed payments.

If you are a more-than-2% shareholder in an S corporation, the policy can be either in your name or in the name of the S corporation. You can either pay the premiums yourself or the S corporation can pay them and report them as wages. If the policy is in your name and you pay the premiums yourself, the S corporation must reimburse you. You can deduct the premiums only if the S corporation reports the premiums paid or reimbursed as wages in box 1 of your Form W-2 in 2015 and you also report the premium payments or reimbursements as wages on Form 1040, line 7.

But if you were also eligible to participate in any subsidized health plan maintained by your or your spouse's employer for any month or part of a month in 2015, amounts paid for health insurance coverage for that month can't be used to figure the deduction. Also, if you were eligible for any month or part of a month to participate in any subsidized health plan maintained by the employer of either your dependent or your child who was under age 27 at the end of 2015, do not use amounts paid for coverage for that month to figure the deduction.

Example. If you were eligible to participate in a subsidized health plan maintained by your spouse's employer from September 30 through December 31, you can't use amounts paid for health insurance coverage for September through December to figure your deduction.

Medicare premiums you voluntarily pay to obtain insurance in your name that is similar to qualifying private health insurance can be used to figure the deduction. Amounts paid for health insurance coverage from retirement plan distributions that were nontaxable because you are a retired public safety officer can't be used to figure the deduction.

For more details, see Pub. 535.

If you qualify to take the deduction, use the Self-Employed Health Insurance Deduction Worksheet to figure the amount you can deduct.

Exceptions. Use Pub. 535 instead of the Self-Employed Health Insurance Deduction Worksheet in these instructions to figure your deduction if any of the following applies.
• You had more than one source of income subject to self-employment tax.
• You file Form 2555 or 2555-EZ.
• You are using amounts paid for qualified long-term care insurance to figure the deduction.

Use Pub. 974 instead of the worksheet in these instructions if the insurance plan established, or considered to be established, under your business was obtained through the Marketplace and you are claiming the premium tax credit.

Line 30

Penalty on Early Withdrawal of Savings

The Form 1099-INT or Form 1099-OID you received will show the amount of any penalty you were charged.

Lines 31a and 31b

Alimony Paid

If you made payments to or for your spouse or former spouse under a divorce or separation instrument, you may be able to take this deduction. Use *Tax Topic 452* or see Pub. 504.

Line 32

IRA Deduction

 If you made any nondeductible contributions to a traditional individual retirement arrangement (IRA) for 2015, you must report them on Form 8606.

If you made contributions to a traditional IRA for 2015, you may be able to take an IRA deduction. But you, or your spouse if filing a joint return, must have had earned income to do so. For IRA purposes, earned income includes alimony and separate maintenance payments reported on line 11. If you were a member of the U.S. Armed Forces, earned income includes any nontaxable combat pay you received. If you were self-employed, earned income is generally your net earnings from self-employment if your personal services were a material income-producing factor. For more details, see Pub. 590-A. A statement should be sent to you by May 31, 2016, that shows all contributions to your traditional IRA for 2015.

Use the IRA Deduction Worksheet to figure the amount, if any, of your IRA deduction. But read the following 11-item list before you fill in the worksheet.

1. If you were age 70½ or older at the end of 2015, you can't deduct any contributions made to your traditional IRA for 2015 or treat them as nondeductible contributions.

2. You can't deduct contributions to a Roth IRA. But you may be able to take the retirement savings contributions credit (saver's credit). See the instructions for line 51.

3. If you are filing a joint return and you or your spouse made contributions to both a traditional IRA and a Roth IRA for 2015, do not use the IRA Deduction Worksheet in these instructions. Instead, see Pub. 590-A to figure the amount, if any, of your IRA deduction.

4. You can't deduct elective deferrals to a 401(k) plan, 403(b) plan, section 457 plan, SIMPLE plan, or the federal Thrift Savings Plan. These amounts aren't included as income in box 1 of your Form W-2. But you may be able to

Need more information or forms? Visit IRS.gov.

take the retirement savings contributions credit. See the instructions for line 51.

5. If you made contributions to your IRA in 2015 that you deducted for 2014, do not include them in the worksheet.

6. If you received income from a nonqualified deferred compensation plan or nongovernmental section 457 plan that is included in box 1 of your Form W-2, or in box 7 of Form 1099-MISC, do not include that income on line 8 of the worksheet. The income should be shown in (a) box 11 of your Form W-2, (b) box 12 of your Form W-2 with code Z, or (c) box 15b of Form 1099-MISC. If it isn't, contact your employer or the payer for the amount of the income.

7. You must file a joint return to deduct contributions to your spouse's IRA. Enter the total IRA deduction for you and your spouse on line 32.

8. Do not include qualified rollover contributions in figuring your deduction. Instead, see the instructions for lines 15a and 15b.

9. Do not include trustees' fees that were billed separately and paid by you for your IRA. These fees can be deducted only as an itemized deduction on Schedule A.

10. Do not include any repayments of qualified reservist distributions. You can't deduct them. For information on how to report these repayments, see *Qualified reservist repayments* in Pub. 590-A.

11. If the total of your IRA deduction on line 32 plus any nondeductible contribution to your traditional IRAs shown on Form 8606 is less than your total traditional IRA contributions for 2015, see Pub. 590-A for special rules.

 By April 1 of the year after the year in which you turn age 70½, you must start taking minimum required distributions from your traditional IRA. If you do not, you may have to pay a 50% additional tax on the amount that should have been distributed. For details, including how to figure the minimum required distribution, see Pub. 590-B.

Were You Covered by a Retirement Plan?

If you were covered by a retirement plan (qualified pension, profit-sharing (including 401(k)), annuity, SEP, SIMPLE, etc.) at work or through self-employment, your IRA deduction may be re-duced or eliminated. But you can still make contributions to an IRA even if you can't deduct them. In any case, the income earned on your IRA contributions isn't taxed until it is paid to you.

The "Retirement plan" box in box 13 of your Form W-2 should be checked if you were covered by a plan at work even if you were not vested in the plan. You are also covered by a plan if you were self-employed and had a SEP, SIMPLE, or qualified retirement plan.

If you were covered by a retirement plan and you file Form 2555, 2555-EZ, or 8815, or you exclude employer-provided adoption benefits, see Pub. 590-A to figure the amount, if any, of your IRA deduction.

Married persons filing separately. If you were not covered by a retirement plan but your spouse was, you are considered covered by a plan unless you lived apart from your spouse for all of 2015.

 *You may be able to take the retirement savings contributions credit. See the line 51 instructions.*

IRA Deduction Worksheet—Line 32

Keep for Your Records

 *If you were age 70½ or older at the end of 2015, you can't deduct any contributions made to your traditional IRA or treat them as nondeductible contributions. **Do not** complete this worksheet for anyone age 70½ or older at the end of 2015. If you are married filing jointly and only one spouse was under age 70½ at the end of 2015, complete this worksheet only for that spouse.*

Before you begin:
- ✓ Be sure you have read the 11-item list in the instructions for this line. You may not be able to use this worksheet.
- ✓ Figure any write-in adjustments to be entered on the dotted line next to line 36 (see the instructions for line 36).
- ✓ If you are married filing separately and you lived apart from your spouse for all of 2015, enter "D" on the dotted line next to Form 1040, line 32. If you do not, you may get a math error notice from the IRS.

		Your IRA	Spouse's IRA

1a. Were you covered by a retirement plan (see *Were You Covered by a Retirement Plan?*)? .... **1a.** ☐ Yes ☐ No

b. If married filing jointly, was your spouse covered by a retirement plan? .... **1b.** ☐ Yes ☐ No

Next. If you checked "No" on line 1a (and "No" on line 1b if married filing jointly), skip lines 2 through 6, enter the applicable amount below on line 7a (and line 7b if applicable), and go to line 8.
- • $5,500, if under age 50 at the end of 2015.
- • $6,500, if age 50 or older but under age 70½ at the end of 2015.

Otherwise, go to line 2.

2. Enter the amount shown below that applies to you.
- • Single, head of household, or married filing separately and you **lived apart** from your spouse for all of 2015, enter $71,000.
- • Qualifying widow(er), enter $118,000.
- • Married filing jointly, enter $118,000 in both columns. But if you checked "No" on either line 1a or 1b, enter $193,000 for the person who wasn't covered by a plan.
- • Married filing separately and you lived with your spouse at any time in 2015, enter $10,000.

2a. _____ **2b.** _____

3. Enter the amount from Form 1040, line 22 .... **3.** _____

4. Enter the total of the amounts from Form 1040, lines 23 through 31a, plus any write-in adjustments you entered on the dotted line next to line 36 .... **4.** _____

5. Subtract line 4 from line 3. If married filing jointly, enter the result in both columns .... **5a.** _____ **5b.** _____

6. Is the amount on line 5 less than the amount on line 2?

☐ **No.** (STOP) None of your IRA contributions are deductible. For details on nondeductible IRA contributions, see Form 8606.

☐ **Yes.** Subtract line 5 from line 2 in each column. Follow the instruction below that applies to you.
- • If single, head of household, or married filing separately, and the result is $10,000 or more, enter the applicable amount below on line 7 for that column and go to line 8.
  - i. $5,500, if under age 50 at the end of 2015.
  - ii. $6,500, if age 50 or older but under age 70½ at the end of 2015.

  If the result is less than $10,000, go to line 7.

- • If married filing jointly or qualifying widow(er), and the result is $20,000 or more ($10,000 or more in the column for the IRA of a person who wasn't covered by a retirement plan), enter the applicable amount below on line 7 for that column and go to line 8.
  - i. $5,500, if under age 50 at the end of 2015.
  - ii. $6,500 if age 50 or older but under age 70½ at the end of 2015.

  Otherwise, go to line 7.

6a. _____ **6b.** _____

Need more information or forms? Visit IRS.gov.

IRA Deduction Worksheet—*Continued*

		Your IRA		Spouse's IRA

7. Multiply lines 6a and 6b by the percentage below that applies to you. If the result isn't a multiple of $10, increase it to the next multiple of $10 (for example, increase $490.30 to $500). If the result is $200 or more, enter the result. But if it is less than $200, enter $200.

   - Single, head of household, or married filing separately, multiply by 55% (0.55) (or by 65% (0.65) in the column for the IRA of a person who is age 50 or older at the end of 2015).

   - Married filing jointly or qualifying widow(er), multiply by 27.5% (0.275) (or by 32.5% (0.325) in the column for the IRA of a person who is age 50 or older at the end of 2015). But if you checked "No" on either line 1a or 1b, then in the column for the IRA of the person who wasn't covered by a retirement plan, multiply by 55% (0.55) (or by 65% (0.65) if age 50 or older at the end of 2015).   **7a.** _____   **7b.** _____

8. Enter the total of your (and your spouse's if filing jointly):

   - Wages, salaries, tips, etc. Generally, this is the amount reported in box 1 of Form W-2. Exceptions are explained earlier in these instructions for line 32.

   - Alimony and separate maintenance payments reported on Form 1040, line 11.

   - Nontaxable combat pay. This amount should be reported in box 12 of Form W-2 with code Q.   **8.** _____

9. Enter the earned income you (and your spouse if filing jointly) received as a self-employed individual or a partner. Generally, this is your (and your spouse's if filing jointly) net earnings from self-employment if your personal services were a material income-producing factor, minus any deductions on Form 1040, lines 27 and 28. If zero or less, enter -0-. For more details, see Pub. 590-A . . . .   **9.** _____

10. Add lines 8 and 9 . . . .   **10.** _____

   ⚠️ **CAUTION** *If married filing jointly and line 10 is less than $11,000 ($12,000 if one spouse is age 50 or older at the end of 2015; $13,000 if both spouses are age 50 or older at the end of 2015), **stop here** and use the worksheet in Pub. 590-A to figure your IRA deduction.*

11. Enter traditional IRA contributions made, or that will be made by the due date of your 2015 return not counting extensions (April 18, 2016, for most people), for 2015 to your IRA on line 11a and to your spouse's IRA on line 11b . . . . . .   **11a.** _____   **11b.** _____

12. On line 12a, enter the **smallest** of line 7a, 10, or 11a. On line 12b, enter the **smallest** of line 7b, 10, or 11b. This is the most you can deduct. Add the amounts on lines 12a and 12b and enter the total on Form 1040, line 32. Or, if you want, you can deduct a smaller amount and treat the rest as a nondeductible contribution (see Form 8606) . . . .   **12a.** _____   **12b.** _____

Line 33

Student Loan Interest Deduction

You can take this deduction only if all of the following apply.

- You paid interest in 2015 on a qualified student loan (defined later).

- Your filing status is any status except married filing separately.

- Your modified adjusted gross income (AGI) is less than: $80,000 if single, head of household, or qualifying widow(er); $160,000 if married filing jointly. Use lines 2 through 4 of the worksheet in these instructions to figure your modified AGI.

- You, or your spouse if filing jointly, aren't claimed as a dependent on someone else's (such as your parent's) 2015 tax return.

Use the worksheet in these instructions to figure your student loan interest deduction.

Exception. Use Pub. 970 instead of the worksheet in these instructions to figure your student loan interest deduction if you file Form 2555, 2555-EZ, or 4563, or you exclude income from sources within Puerto Rico.

Qualified student loan. A qualified student loan is any loan you took out to pay the qualified higher education expenses for any of the following individuals who was an eligible student.

1. Yourself or your spouse.

2. Any person who was your dependent when the loan was taken out.

3. Any person you could have claimed as a dependent for the year the loan was taken out except that:

a. The person filed a joint return,

b. The person had gross income that was equal to or more than the exemption amount for that year ($4,000 for 2015), or

c. You, or your spouse if filing jointly, could be claimed as a dependent on someone else's return.

However, a loan isn't a qualified student loan if (a) any of the proceeds were used for other purposes, or (b) the loan was from either a related person or a person who borrowed the proceeds under a qualified employer plan or a contract purchased under such a plan. For details, see Pub. 970.

Qualified higher education expenses. Qualified higher education expenses generally include tuition, fees, room and board, and related expenses such as books and supplies. The expenses must be for education in a degree, certificate, or similar program at an eligible educational institution. An eligible educational institution includes most colleges, universities, and certain vocational schools. For details, see Pub. 970.

Student Loan Interest Deduction Worksheet—Line 33

Keep for Your Records

Before you begin:
✓ Figure any write-in adjustments to be entered on the dotted line next to line 36 (see the instructions for line 36).
✓ Be sure you have read the **Exception** in the instructions for this line to see if you can use this worksheet instead of Pub. 970 to figure your deduction.

1. Enter the total interest you paid in 2015 on qualified student loans (see the instructions for line 33). **Do not** enter more than $2,500 .... **1.** _____

2. Enter the amount from Form 1040, line 22 .... **2.** _____

3. Enter the total of the amounts from Form 1040, lines 23 through 32, plus any write-in adjustments you entered on the dotted line next to line 36 .... **3.** _____

4. Subtract line 3 from line 2 .... **4.** _____

5. Enter the amount shown below for your filing status.
   • Single, head of household, or qualifying widow(er)—$65,000
   • Married filing jointly—$130,000 } .... **5.** _____

6. Is the amount on line 4 more than the amount on line 5?
   ☐ **No.** Skip lines 6 and 7, enter -0- on line 8, and go to line 9.
   ☐ **Yes.** Subtract line 5 from line 4 .... **6.** _____

7. Divide line 6 by $15,000 ($30,000 if married filing jointly). Enter the result as a decimal (rounded to at least three places). If the result is 1.000 or more, enter 1.000 .... **7.** ___._____

8. Multiply line 1 by line 7 .... **8.** _____

9. **Student loan interest deduction.** Subtract line 8 from line 1. Enter the result here and on Form 1040, line 33. **Do not** include this amount in figuring any other deduction on your return (such as on Schedule A, C, E, etc.) .... **9.** _____

Line 34

Tuition and Fees

If you paid qualified tuition and fees for yourself, your spouse, or your dependent(s), you may be able to take this deduction. See Form 8917.

 You may be able to take a credit for your educational expenses instead of a deduction. See the instructions for lines 50 and 68 for details.

Line 35

Domestic Production Activities Deduction

You may be able to deduct up to 9% of your qualified production activities income from the following activities.

1. Construction of real property performed in the United States.

2. Engineering or architectural services performed in the United States for

Need more information or forms? Visit IRS.gov.

construction of real property in the United States.

3. Any lease, rental, license, sale, exchange, or other disposition of:

a. Tangible personal property, computer software, and sound recordings that you manufactured, produced, grew, or extracted in whole or in significant part in the United States,

b. Any qualified film you produced, or

c. Electricity, natural gas, or potable water you produced in the United States.

Your deduction may be reduced if you had oil-related qualified production activities income.

The deduction doesn't apply to income derived from:
* The sale of food and beverages you prepared at a retail establishment;
* Property you leased, licensed, or rented for use by any related person;
* The transmission or distribution of electricity, natural gas, or potable water; or
* The lease, rental, license, sale, exchange, or other disposition of land.

For details, see Form 8903 and its instructions.

Line 36

Include in the total on line 36 any of the following write-in adjustments. To find out if you can take the deduction, see the form or publication indicated. On the dotted line next to line 36, enter the amount of your deduction and identify it as indicated.
* Archer MSA deduction (see Form 8853). Identify as "MSA."
* Jury duty pay if you gave the pay to your employer because your employer paid your salary while you served on the jury. Identify as "Jury Pay."
* Deductible expenses related to income reported on line 21 from the rental of personal property engaged in for profit. Identify as "PPR."
* Reforestation amortization and expenses (see Pub. 535). Identify as "RFST."
* Repayment of supplemental unemployment benefits under the Trade Act of 1974 (see Pub. 525). Identify as "Sub-Pay TRA."

* Contributions to section 501(c)(18) (D) pension plans (see Pub. 525). Identify as "501(c)(18)(D)."
* Contributions by certain chaplains to section 403(b) plans (see Pub. 517). Identify as "403(b)."
* Attorney fees and court costs for actions involving certain unlawful discrimination claims, but only to the extent of gross income from such actions (see Pub. 525). Identify as "UDC."
* Attorney fees and court costs you paid in connection with an award from the IRS for information you provided that helped the IRS detect tax law violations, up to the amount of the award includible in your gross income. Identify as "WBF."

Line 37

If line 37 is less than zero, you may have a net operating loss that you can carry to another tax year. See the Instructions for Form 1045 for details.

Tax and Credits

Line 39a

If you were born before January 2, 1951, or were blind at the end of 2015, check the appropriate box(es) on line 39a. If you were married and checked the box on Form 1040, line 6b, and your spouse was born before January 2, 1951, or was blind at the end of 2015, also check the appropriate box(es) for your spouse. Be sure to enter the total number of boxes checked. Do not check any box(es) for your spouse if your filing status is head of household.

Death of spouse in 2015. If your spouse was born before January 2, 1951, but died in 2015 before reaching age 65, do not check the box that says "Spouse was born before January 2, 1951."

A person is considered to reach age 65 on the day before his or her 65th birthday.

Example. Your spouse was born on February 14, 1950, and died on February 13, 2015. Your spouse is considered age 65 at the time of death. Check the appropriate box for your spouse on line 39a. However, if your spouse died on Febru-

ary 12, 2015, your spouse isn't considered age 65. Do not check the box.

Death of taxpayer in 2015. If you are preparing a return for someone who died in 2015, see Pub. 501 before completing line 39a.

Blindness

If you were not totally blind as of December 31, 2015, you must get a statement certified by your eye doctor (ophthalmologist or optometrist) that:
* You can't see better than 20/200 in your better eye with glasses or contact lenses, or
* Your field of vision is 20 degrees or less.

If your eye condition isn't likely to improve beyond the conditions listed above, you can get a statement certified by your eye doctor (ophthalmologist or optometrist) to this effect instead.

You must keep the statement for your records.

Line 39b

If your filing status is married filing separately (box 3 is checked), and your spouse itemizes deductions on his or her return, check the box on line 39b. Also check that box if you were a dual-status alien. But if you were a dual-status alien and you file a joint return with your spouse who was a U.S. citizen or resident alien at the end of 2015 and you and your spouse agree to be taxed on your combined worldwide income, do not check the box.

Line 40

Itemized Deductions or Standard Deduction

In most cases, your federal income tax will be less if you take the larger of your itemized deductions or standard deduction.

Itemized Deductions

To figure your itemized deductions, fill in Schedule A.

Standard Deduction

Most people can find their standard deduction by looking at the amounts listed under "All others" to the left of line 40.

Exception 1 – dependent. If you, or your spouse if filing jointly, can be claimed as a dependent on someone else's 2015 return, use the Standard Deduction Worksheet for Dependents to figure your standard deduction.

Exception 2 – box on line 39a checked. If you checked any box on line 39a, figure your standard deduction using the Standard Deduction Chart for People Who Were Born Before January 2, 1951, or Were Blind.

Exception 3 – box on line 39b checked. If you checked the box on line 39b, your standard deduction is zero, even if you were born before January 2, 1951, or were blind.

Line 42

Exemptions

If the amount on line 38 is over $154,950, use the Deduction for Exemptions Worksheet to figure your deduction for exemptions.

Standard Deduction Worksheet for Dependents—Line 40

Keep for Your Records

Use this worksheet **only** if someone can claim you, or your spouse if filing jointly, as a dependent.

1. Is your **earned income*** more than $700?	
☐ **Yes.** Add $350 to your earned income. Enter the total	
☐ **No.** Enter $1,050	.... 1. _____
2. Enter the amount shown below for your filing status.	
• Single or married filing separately—$6,300	
• Married filing jointly—$12,600	
• Head of household—$9,250	.... 2. _____
3. **Standard deduction.**	
a. Enter the **smaller** of line 1 or line 2. If born after January 1, 1951, and not blind, **stop here** and enter this amount on Form 1040, line 40. Otherwise, go to line 3b .... 3a. _____	
b. If born before January 2, 1951, or blind, multiply the number on Form 1040, line 39a, by $1,250 ($1,550 if single or head of household) .... 3b. _____	
c. Add lines 3a and 3b. Enter the total here and on Form 1040, line 40 .... 3c. _____	

***Earned income** includes wages, salaries, tips, professional fees, and other compensation received for personal services you performed. It also includes any taxable scholarship or fellowship grant. Generally, your earned income is the total of the amount(s) you reported on Form 1040, lines 7, 12, and 18, minus the amount, if any, on line 27.*

Need more information or forms? Visit IRS.gov.

Standard Deduction Chart for People Who Were Born Before January 2, 1951, or Were Blind

Do not use this chart if someone can claim you, or your spouse if filing jointly, as a dependent. Instead, use the worksheet above.

Enter the number from the box on
Form 1040, line 39a .... ▶ [ ]

⚠ **CAUTION** Do not use the number of exemptions from line 6d.

IF your filing status is ...	AND the number in the box above is ...	THEN your standard deduction is ...
Single	1	$7,850
	2	9,400
Married filing jointly or Qualifying widow(er)	1	$13,850
	2	15,100
	3	16,350
	4	17,600
Married filing separately	1	$7,550
	2	8,800
	3	10,050
	4	11,300
Head of household	1	$10,800
	2	12,350

Deduction for Exemptions Worksheet—Line 42

Keep for Your Records

1. Is the amount on Form 1040, line 38, more than the amount shown on line 4 below for your filing status?

   ☐ **No.** (STOP) Multiply $4,000 by the total number of exemptions claimed on Form 1040, line 6d, and enter the result on line 42.

   ☐ **Yes. Continue.**

2. Multiply $4,000 by the total number of exemptions claimed on Form 1040, line 6d . . . . **2.** _____

3. Enter the amount from Form 1040, line 38 . . . . **3.** _____

4. Enter the amount shown below for your filing status.
   * Single —$258,250
   * Married filing jointly or qualifying widow(er)—$309,900
   * Married filing separately—$154,950
   * Head of household—$284,050

   } . . . . **4.** _____

5. Subtract line 4 from line 3. If the result is more than $122,500

   ($61,250 if married filing separately) , (STOP) Enter -0- on

   line 42 . . . . **5.** _____

6. Divide line 5 by $2,500 ($1,250 if married filing separately). If the result isn't a whole number, increase it to the next higher whole number (for example, increase .00004 to 1) . . . . **6.** _____

7. Multiply line 6 by 2% (0.02) and enter the result as a decimal (rounded to at least three places) . . . . **7.** _____

8. Multiply line 2 by line 7 . . . . **8.** _____

9. **Deduction for exemptions.** Subtract line 8 from line 2. Enter the result here and on Form 1040, line 42 . . . . **9.** _____

Line 44

Tax

Include in the total on line 44 all of the following taxes that apply.

• Tax on your taxable income. Figure the tax using one of the methods described here.

• Tax from Form(s) 8814 (relating to the election to report child's interest or dividends). Check the appropriate box.

• Tax from Form 4972 (relating to lump-sum distributions). Check the appropriate box.

• Tax due to making a section 962 election (the election made by a domestic shareholder of a controlled foreign corporation to be taxed at corporate rates). See section 962 for details. Check box c and enter the amount and "962" in the space next to that box. Attach a statement showing how you figured the tax.

• Recapture of an education credit. You may owe this tax if you claimed an education credit in an earlier year, and either tax-free educational assistance or a refund of qualified expenses was received in 2015 for the student. See Form 8863 for more details. Check box c and enter the amount and "ECR" in the space next to that box.

• Any tax from Form 8621, line 16e, relating to a section 1291 fund. Check box c and enter the amount of the tax and "1291TAX" in the space next to that box.

Do you want the IRS to figure the tax on your taxable income for you?

☐ **Yes.** See chapter 30 of Pub. 17 for details, including who is eligible and what to do. If you have paid too much, we will send you a refund. If you didn't pay enough, we will send you a bill.

☐ **No.** Use one of the following methods to figure your tax.

Tax Table or Tax Computation Worksheet. If your taxable income is less than $100,000, you must use the Tax Table, later in these instructions, to figure your tax. Be sure you use the correct column. If your taxable income is $100,000 or more, use the Tax Computation Worksheet right after the Tax Table.

However, do not use the Tax Table or Tax Computation Worksheet to figure your tax if any of the following applies.

Form 8615. Form 8615 generally must be used to figure the tax for any child who had more than $2,100 of unearned income, such as taxable interest, ordinary dividends, or capital gains (including capital gain distributions), and who either:

Need more information or forms? Visit IRS.gov.

1. Was under age 18 at the end of 2015,

2. Was age 18 at the end of 2015 and didn't have earned income that was more than half of the child's support, or

3. Was a full-time student at least age 19 but under age 24 at the end of 2015 and didn't have earned income that was more than half of the child's support.

But if the child files a joint return for 2015 or if neither of the child's parents was alive at the end of 2015, do not use Form 8615 to figure the child's tax.

A child born on January 1, 1998, is considered to be age 18 at the end of 2015; a child born on January 1, 1997, is considered to be age 19 at the end of 2015; a child born on January 1, 1992, is considered to be age 24 at the end of 2015.

Schedule D Tax Worksheet. If you have to file Schedule D, and line 18 or 19 of Schedule D is more than zero, use the Schedule D Tax Worksheet in the Instructions for Schedule D to figure the amount to enter on Form 1040, line 44. But if you are filing Form 2555 or 2555-EZ, you must use the Foreign Earned Income Tax Worksheet instead.

Qualified Dividends and Capital Gain Tax Worksheet. Use the Qualified Dividends and Capital Gain Tax Worksheet, later, to figure your tax if you do not have to use the Schedule D Tax Worksheet and if any of the following applies.
- You reported qualified dividends on Form 1040, line 9b.
- You do not have to file Schedule D and you reported capital gain distributions on Form 1040, line 13.

- You are filing Schedule D and Schedule D, lines 15 and 16, are both more than zero.

But if you are filing Form 2555 or 2555-EZ, you must use the Foreign Earned Income Tax Worksheet instead.

Schedule J. If you had income from farming or fishing (including certain amounts received in connection with the Exxon Valdez litigation), your tax may be less if you choose to figure it using income averaging on Schedule J.

Foreign Earned Income Tax Worksheet. If you claimed the foreign earned income exclusion, housing exclusion, or housing deduction on Form 2555 or 2555-EZ, you must figure your tax using the Foreign Earned Income Tax Worksheet.

Foreign Earned Income Tax Worksheet—Line 44

Keep for Your Records

> ⚠ **CAUTION** If Form 1040, line 43, is zero, do not complete this worksheet.

1. Enter the amount from Form 1040, line 43 .... **1.** _____

2a. Enter the amount from your (and your spouse's, if filing jointly) Form 2555, lines 45 and 50, or Form 2555-EZ, line 18 .... **2a.** _____

   b. Enter the total amount of any itemized deductions or exclusions you couldn't claim because they are related to excluded income .... **b.** _____

   c. Subtract line 2b from line 2a. If zero or less, enter -0- .... **c.** _____

3. Add lines 1 and 2c .... **3.** _____

4. **Figure the tax on the amount on line 3**. Use the Tax Table, Tax Computation Worksheet, Qualified Dividends and Capital Gain Tax Worksheet*, Schedule D Tax Worksheet*, or Form 8615, whichever applies. See the instructions for line 44 to see which tax computation method applies. (Do not use a second Foreign Earned Income Tax Worksheet to figure the tax on this line) .... **4.** _____

5. **Figure the tax on the amount on line 2c**. If the amount on line 2c is less than $100,000, use the Tax Table to figure this tax. If the amount on line 2c is $100,000 or more, use the Tax Computation Worksheet .... **5.** _____

6. Subtract line 5 from line 4. Enter the result. If zero or less, enter -0-. Also include this amount on Form 1040, line 44 .... **6.** _____

*Enter the amount from line 3 above on line 1 of the Qualified Dividends and Capital Gain Tax Worksheet or Schedule D Tax Worksheet if you use either of those worksheets to figure the tax on line 4 above. Complete the rest of that worksheet through line 6 (line 10 if you use the Schedule D Tax Worksheet). Next, you must determine if you have a capital gain excess. To find out if you have a capital gain excess, subtract Form 1040, line 43, from line 6 of your Qualified Dividends and Capital Gain Tax Worksheet (line 10 of your Schedule D Tax Worksheet). If the result is more than zero, that amount is your capital gain excess.

If you do not have a capital gain excess, complete the rest of either of those worksheets according to the worksheet's instructions. Then complete lines 5 and 6 above.

If you have a capital gain excess, complete a second Qualified Dividends and Capital Gain Tax Worksheet or Schedule D Tax Worksheet (whichever applies) as instructed above but in its entirety and with the following additional modifications. Then complete lines 5 and 6 above. These modifications are to be made only for purposes of filling out the Foreign Earned Income Tax Worksheet above.

1. Reduce (but not below zero) the amount you would otherwise enter on line 3 of your Qualified Dividends and Capital Gain Tax Worksheet or line 9 of your Schedule D Tax Worksheet by your capital gain excess.

2. Reduce (but not below zero) the amount you would otherwise enter on line 2 of your Qualified Dividends and Capital Gain Tax Worksheet or line 6 of your Schedule D Tax Worksheet by any of your capital gain excess not used in (1) above.

3. Reduce (but not below zero) the amount on your Schedule D (Form 1040), line 18, by your capital gain excess.

4. Include your capital gain excess as a loss on line 16 of your Unrecaptured Section 1250 Gain Worksheet in the Instructions for Schedule D (Form 1040).

Need more information or forms? Visit IRS.gov.

Qualified Dividends and Capital Gain Tax Worksheet—Line 44   *Keep for Your Records*

Before you begin:	✓ See the earlier instructions for line 44 to see if you can use this worksheet to figure your tax.
	✓ Before completing this worksheet, complete Form 1040 through line 43.
	✓ If you do not have to file Schedule D and you received capital gain distributions, be sure you checked the box on line 13 of Form 1040.

1. Enter the amount from Form 1040, line 43. However, if you are filing Form 2555 or 2555-EZ (relating to foreign earned income), enter the amount from line 3 of the Foreign Earned Income Tax Worksheet .... **1.** _____

2. Enter the amount from Form 1040, line 9b* .... **2.** _____

3. Are you filing Schedule D?*
☐ **Yes.** Enter the **smaller** of line 15 or 16 of Schedule D. If either line 15 or line 16 is blank or a loss, enter -0-
☐ **No.** Enter the amount from Form 1040, line 13   **3.** _____

4. Add lines 2 and 3 .... **4.** _____

5. If filing Form 4952 (used to figure investment interest expense deduction), enter any amount from line 4g of that form. Otherwise, enter -0- .... **5.** _____

6. Subtract line 5 from line 4. If zero or less, enter -0- .... **6.** _____

7. Subtract line 6 from line 1. If zero or less, enter -0- .... **7.** _____

8. Enter:
$37,450 if single or married filing separately,
$74,900 if married filing jointly or qualifying widow(er),
$50,200 if head of household.   .... **8.** _____

9. Enter the smaller of line 1 or line 8 .... **9.** _____

10. Enter the smaller of line 7 or line 9 .... **10.** _____

11. Subtract line 10 from line 9. This amount is taxed at 0% .... **11.** _____

12. Enter the smaller of line 1 or line 6 .... **12.** _____

13. Enter the amount from line 11 .... **13.** _____

14. Subtract line 13 from line 12 .... **14.** _____

15. Enter:
$413,200 if single,
$232,425 if married filing separately,
$464,850 if married filing jointly or qualifying widow(er),
$439,000 if head of household.   .... **15.** _____

16. Enter the smaller of line 1 or line 15 .... **16.** _____

17. Add lines 7 and 11 .... **17.** _____

18. Subtract line 17 from line 16. If zero or less, enter -0- .... **18.** _____

19. Enter the smaller of line 14 or line 18 .... **19.** _____

20. Multiply line 19 by 15% (0.15) .... **20.** _____

21. Add lines 11 and 19 .... **21.** _____

22. Subtract line 21 from line 12 .... **22.** _____

23. Multiply line 22 by 20% (0.20) .... **23.** _____

24. Figure the tax on the amount on line 7. If the amount on line 7 is less than $100,000, use the Tax Table to figure the tax. If the amount on line 7 is $100,000 or more, use the Tax Computation Worksheet .... **24.** _____

25. Add lines 20, 23, and 24 .... **25.** _____

26. Figure the tax on the amount on line 1. If the amount on line 1 is less than $100,000, use the Tax Table to figure the tax. If the amount on line 1 is $100,000 or more, use the Tax Computation Worksheet .... **26.** _____

27. **Tax on all taxable income.** Enter the **smaller** of line 25 or line 26. Also include this amount on Form 1040, line 44. If you are filing Form 2555 or 2555-EZ, do not enter this amount on Form 1040, line 44. Instead, enter it on line 4 of the Foreign Earned Income Tax Worksheet .... **27.** _____

If you are filing Form 2555 or 2555-EZ, see the footnote in the Foreign Earned Income Tax Worksheet before completing this line.

Line 45

Alternative Minimum Tax (AMT)

If you aren't sure whether you owe the AMT, complete the Worksheet To See if You Should Fill in Form 6251.

Exception. Fill in Form 6251 instead of using the worksheet if you claimed or received any of the following items.

- Accelerated depreciation.
- Tax-exempt interest from private activity bonds.
- Intangible drilling, circulation, research, experimental, or mining costs.
- Amortization of pollution-control facilities or depletion.
- Income or (loss) from tax-shelter farm activities, passive activities, partnerships, S corporations, or activities for which you aren't at risk.
- Income from long-term contracts not figured using the percentage-of-completion method.
- Interest paid on a home mortgage not used to buy, build, or substantially improve your home.
- Investment interest expense reported on Form 4952.
- Net operating loss deduction.
- Alternative minimum tax adjustments from an estate, trust, electing large partnership, or cooperative.
- Section 1202 exclusion.
- Stock by exercising an incentive stock option and you didn't dispose of the stock in the same year.
- Any general business credit claimed on Form 3800 if either line 6 (in Part I) or line 25 of Form 3800 is more than zero.
- Qualified electric vehicle credit.
- Alternative fuel vehicle refueling property tax.
- Credit for prior year minimum tax.
- Foreign tax credit.

 Form 6251 should be filled in for certain children who are under age 24 at the end of 2015. See the Instructions for Form 6251 for more information.

For help with the alternative minimum tax, go to *www.irs.gov/AMT*.

Line 46

Excess Advance Premium Tax Credit Repayment

The premium tax credit helps pay premiums for health insurance purchased from the Marketplace. If advance payments were made for coverage for you, your spouse, or your dependent, complete Form 8962. If the advance payments were more than the premium tax credit you can claim, enter the amount from Form 8962, line 29.

You may have to repay excess advance premium tax credit payments even if someone else enrolled you, your spouse, or your dependent. You may also have to repay excess advance premium tax credit payments if you enrolled someone in coverage through the Marketplace whom you do not claim as a dependent on your return. For more information, see the instructions for Form 8962.

Line 48

Foreign Tax Credit

If you paid income tax to a foreign country or U.S. possession, you may be able to take this credit. Generally, you must complete and attach Form 1116 to do so.

Exception. You do not have to complete Form 1116 to take this credit if all of the following apply.

1. All of your foreign source gross income was from interest and dividends and all of that income and the foreign tax paid on it were reported to you on Form 1099-INT, Form 1099-DIV, or Schedule K-1 (or substitute statement).

2. The total of your foreign taxes wasn't more than $300 (not more than $600 if married filing jointly).

3. You held the stock or bonds on which the dividends or interest were paid for at least 16 days and were not obligated to pay these amounts to someone else.

4. You are not filing Form 4563 or excluding income from sources within Puerto Rico.

5. All of your foreign taxes were:

a. Legally owed and not eligible for a refund or reduced tax rate under a tax treaty, and

b. Paid to countries that are recognized by the United States and do not support terrorism.

For more details on these requirements, see the Instructions for Form 1116.

Do you meet all five requirements just listed?

☐ **Yes.** Enter on line 48 the smaller of (a) your total foreign taxes, or (b) the total of the amounts on Form 1040, lines 44 and 46.

☐ **No.** See Form 1116 to find out if you can take the credit and, if you can, if you have to file Form 1116.

Line 49

Credit for Child and Dependent Care Expenses

You may be able to take this credit if you paid someone to care for:

- Your qualifying child under age 13 whom you claim as your dependent,
- Your disabled spouse or any other disabled person who couldn't care for himself or herself, or
- Your child whom you couldn't claim as a dependent because of the rules for *Children of divorced or separated parents* in the instructions for line 6c.

For details, use *Tax Topic 602* or see Form 2441.

Line 50

Education Credits

If you (or your dependent) paid qualified expenses in 2015 for yourself, your spouse, or your dependent to enroll in or attend an eligible educational institution, you may be able to take an education credit. See Form 8863 for details. However, you can't take an education credit if any of the following applies.

- You, or your spouse if filing jointly, are claimed as a dependent on someone else's (such as your parent's) 2015 tax return.
- Your filing status is married filing separately.

Need more information or forms? Visit IRS.gov.

Worksheet To See if You Should Fill in Form 6251—Line 45

Before you begin: ✓ Be sure you have read the **Exception** in the instructions for this line to see if you must fill in Form 6251 instead of using this worksheet.

1. Are you filing **Schedule A?**

  ☐ **No.**   Skip lines 1 through 3; enter on line 4 the amount from Form 1040, line 38, and go to line 5

  ☐ **Yes.**   Enter the amount from Form 1040, line 41 . . . . **1.** _____

2. If you or your spouse was age 65 or older, enter the **smaller** of the amount on Schedule A, line 4, or 2.5% (0.025) of the amount on Form 1040, line 38. If zero or less, enter -0- . . . . **2.** _____

3. Enter the total of the amounts from Schedule A, lines 9 and 27 . . . . **3.** _____

4. Add lines 1 through 3 . . . . **4.** _____

5. Enter any tax refund from Form 1040, lines 10 and 21 . . . . **5.** _____

6. If you completed the Itemized Deductions Worksheet in the Instructions for Schedule A, enter the amount from line 9 of that worksheet . . . . **6.** _____

7. Add lines 5 and 6 . . . . **7.** _____

8. Subtract line 7 from line 4 . . . . **8.** _____

9. Enter the amount shown below for your filing status

  ● Single or head of household—$53,600

  ● Married filing jointly or qualifying widow(er)—$83,400   } . . . .

  ● Married filing separately—$41,700   **9.** _____

10. Is the amount on line 8 more than the amount on line 9?

  ☐ **No.** (STOP) You do not need to fill in Form 6251. Do not complete the rest of this worksheet.

  ☐ **Yes.** Subtract line 9 from line 8 . . . . **10.** _____

11. Enter the amount shown below for your filing status.

  ● Single or head of household—$119,200

  ● Married filing jointly or qualifying widow(er)—$158,900   } . . . .

  ● Married filing separately—$79,450   **11.** _____

12. Is the amount on line 8 more than the amount on line 11?

  ☐ **No.**   Enter -0-. Skip line 13. Enter on line 14 the amount from line 10, and go to line 15.

  ☐ **Yes.** Subtract line 11 from line 8 . . . . **12.** _____

13. Multiply line 12 by 25% (0.25) and enter the **smaller** of the result or line 9 . . . . **13.** _____

14. Add lines 10 and 13 . . . . **14.** _____

15. Is the amount on line 14 more than $185,400 ($92,700 if married filing separately)?

  ☐ **Yes.** (STOP) Fill in Form 6251 to see if you owe the alternative minimum tax.

  ☐ **No.**   Multiply line 14 by 26% (0.26) . . . . **15.** _____

16. Add Form 1040, line 44 (minus any tax from Form 4972), and Form 1040, line 46. (If you used Schedule J to figure your tax on Form 1040, line 44, refigure that tax without using Schedule J before including it in this calculation) . . . . **16.** _____

Next. Is the amount on line 15 more than the amount on line 16?

  ☐ **Yes.** Fill in Form 6251 to see if you owe the alternative minimum tax.

  ☐ **No.**   You do not owe alternative minimum tax and do not need to fill out Form 6251. Leave line 45 blank.

• The amount on Form 1040, line 38, is $90,000 or more ($180,000 or more if married filing jointly).

• You, or your spouse, were a nonresident alien for any part of 2015 unless your filing status is married filing jointly.

You may be able to increase an education credit if the student chooses to include all or part of a Pell grant or certain other scholarships or fellowships in income.

For more information, see Pub. 970, the instructions for line 68, and www.irs.gov/uac/Am-I-Eligible-to-Claim-an-Education-Credit%3F.

Line 51

Retirement Savings Contributions Credit (Saver's Credit)

You may be able to take this credit if you, or your spouse if filing jointly,

made (a) contributions, other than rollover contributions, to a traditional or Roth IRA (including a *my*RA); (b) elective deferrals to a 401(k) or 403(b) plan (including designated Roth contributions) or to a governmental 457, SEP, or SIMPLE plan; (c) voluntary employee contributions to a qualified retirement plan (including the federal Thrift Savings Plan); or (d) contributions to a 501(c)(18)(D) plan.

However, you can't take the credit if either of the following applies.

1. The amount on Form 1040, line 38, is more than $30,500 ($45,750 if head of household; $61,000 if married filing jointly).

2. The person(s) who made the qualified contribution or elective deferral (a) was born after January 1, 1998, (b) is claimed as a dependent on someone else's 2015 tax return, or (c) was a student (defined next).

You were a student if during any part of 5 calendar months of 2015 you:

• Were enrolled as a full-time student at a school, or

• Took a full-time, on-farm training course given by a school or a state, county, or local government agency.

A school includes a technical, trade, or mechanical school. It doesn't include an on-the-job training course, correspondence school, or school offering courses only through the Internet.

For more details, use *Tax Topic 610* or see Form 8880.

Need more information or forms? Visit IRS.gov.

2015 Child Tax Credit Worksheet—Line 52

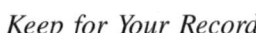

Keep for Your Records

CAUTION

1. To be a qualifying child for the child tax credit, the child must be your dependent, **under age 17** at the end of 2015, and meet all the conditions in Steps 1 through 3 in the instructions for line 6c. Make sure you checked the box on Form 1040, line 6c, column (4), for each qualifying child.

2. If you do not have a qualifying child, you cannot claim the child tax credit.

3. Be sure to see "Social security number" in the instructions for line 6c. If your qualifying child has an ITIN instead of an SSN, file Schedule 8812.

4. Do **not** use this worksheet, but use Pub. 972 instead, if:

   a. You are claiming the adoption credit, mortgage interest credit, District of Columbia first-time homebuyer credit, or residential energy efficient property credit,

   b. You are excluding income from Puerto Rico, or

   c. You are filing Form 2555, 2555-EZ, or 4563.

Part 1

1. Number of qualifying children: _____ × $1,000. Enter the result. | **1** |

2. Enter the amount from Form 1040, line 38. | **2** |

3. Enter the amount shown below for your filing status.

   ● Married filing jointly — $110,000

   ● Single, head of household, or qualifying widow(er) — $75,000

   ● Married filing separately — $55,000

   | **3** |

4. Is the amount on line 2 more than the amount on line 3?

   ☐ **No.** Leave line 4 blank. Enter -0- on line 5, and go to line 6.

   ☐ **Yes.** Subtract line 3 from line 2.
   If the result is not a multiple of $1,000, increase it to the next multiple of $1,000. For example, increase $425 to $1,000, increase $1,025 to $2,000, etc.

   | **4** |

5. Multiply the amount on line 4 by 5% (0.05). Enter the result. | **5** |

6. Is the amount on line 1 more than the amount on line 5?

   ☐ **No.** (STOP)
   You cannot take the child tax credit on Form 1040, line 52. You also cannot take the additional child tax credit on Form 1040, line 67. Complete the rest of your Form 1040.

   ☐ **Yes.** Subtract line 5 from line 1. Enter the result.
   Go to Part 2.

   | **6** |

2015 Child Tax Credit Worksheet—*Continued*

Keep for Your Records

Before you begin Part 2: ✓ Figure the amount of any credits you are claiming on Form 5695, Part II; Form 8910; Form 8936; or Schedule R.

Part 2

7. Enter the amount from Form 1040, line 47.

7 ☐

8. Add any amounts from:

Form 1040, line 48 _____

Form 1040, line 49 + _____

Form 1040, line 50 + _____

Form 1040, line 51 + _____

Form 5695, line 30 + _____

Form 8910, line 15 + _____

Form 8936, line 23 + _____

Schedule R, line 22 + _____

Enter the total. **8** ☐

9. Are the amounts on lines 7 and 8 the same?

☐ **Yes.** (STOP)
You cannot take this credit because there is no tax to reduce. However, you may be able to take the **additional child tax credit.** See the **TIP** below.

☐ **No.** Subtract line 8 from line 7.

9 ☐

10. Is the amount on line 6 more than the amount on line 9?

☐ **Yes.** Enter the amount from line 9.
Also, you may be able to take the **additional child tax credit.** See the **TIP** below.

☐ **No.** Enter the amount from line 6.

} **This is your child tax credit.**

10 ☐

Enter this amount on Form 1040, line 52.

1040

TIP

You may be able to take the **additional child tax credit** on Form 1040, line 67, if you answered "Yes" on line 9 **or** line 10 above.

● First, complete your Form 1040 through lines 66a and 66b.

● Then, use Schedule 8812 to figure any additional child tax credit.

Need more information or forms? Visit IRS.gov.

Line 53

Residential Energy Credits

Residential energy efficient property credit. You may be able to take this credit by completing and attaching Form 5695 if you paid for any of the following during 2015.

• Qualified solar electric property for use in your home located in the United States.

• Qualified solar water heating property for use in your home located in the United States.

• Qualified fuel cell property installed on or in connection with your main home located in the United States.

• Qualified small wind energy property for use in connection with your home located in the United States.

• Qualified geothermal heat pump property installed on or in connection with your home located in the United States.

Nonbusiness energy property credit. You may be able to take this credit by completing and attaching Form 5695 for any of the following improvements to your main home located in the United States in 2015 if they are new and meet certain requirements for energy efficiency.

• Any insulation material or system primarily designed to reduce heat gain or loss in your home.

• Exterior windows (including skylights).

• Exterior doors.

• A metal roof or asphalt roof with pigmented coatings or cooling granules primarily designed to reduce the heat gain in your home.

You may also be able to take this credit for the cost of the following items if the items meet certain performance and quality standards.

• Certain electric heat pump water heaters, electric heat pumps, central air conditioners, and natural gas, propane, or oil water heaters.

• A qualified furnace or hot water boiler that uses natural gas, propane, or oil.

• A stove that burns biomass fuel to heat your home or to heat water for use in your home.

• An advanced main air circulating fan used in a natural gas, propane, or oil furnace.

Condos and co-ops. If you are a member of a condominium management association for a condominium you own or a tenant-stockholder in a cooperative housing corporation, you are treated as having paid your proportionate share of any costs of such association or corporation for purposes of these credits.

More details. For details, see Form 5695.

Line 54

Other Credits

Enter the total of the following credits on line 54 and check the appropriate box(es). Check all boxes that apply. If box c is checked, also enter the applicable form number. To find out if you can take the credit, see the form or publication indicated.

• General business credit. This credit consists of a number of credits that usually apply only to individuals who are partners, shareholders in an S corporation, self-employed, or who have rental property. See Form 3800 or Pub. 334.

• Credit for prior year minimum tax. If you paid alternative minimum tax in a prior year, see Form 8801.

• Mortgage interest credit. If a state or local government gave you a mortgage credit certificate, see Form 8396.

• Credit for the elderly or the disabled. See Schedule R.

• Adoption credit. You may be able to take this credit if you paid expenses to adopt a child or you adopted a child with special needs and the adoption became final in 2015. See the Instructions for Form 8839.

• District of Columbia first-time homebuyer credit. You can't claim this credit for a home you bought after 2011. You can claim it only if you have a credit carryforward from 2014. See Form 8859.

• Qualified plug-in electric drive motor vehicle credit. See Form 8936.

• Qualified electric vehicle credit. You can't claim this credit for a vehicle placed in service after 2006. You can claim this credit only if you have an electric vehicle passive activity credit carried forward from a prior year. See Form 8834.

• Alternative motor vehicle credit. See Form 8910 if you placed a new fuel cell motor vehicle in service during 2015.

• Alternative fuel vehicle refueling property credit. See Form 8911.

• Credit to holders of tax credit bonds. See Form 8912.

Other Taxes

Line 58

Unreported Social Security and Medicare Tax from Forms 4137 and 8919

Enter the total of any taxes from Form 4137 and Form 8919. Check the appropriate box(es).

Form 4137. If you received tips of $20 or more in any month and you didn't report the full amount to your employer, you must pay the social security and Medicare or railroad retirement (RRTA) tax on the unreported tips.

Do not include the value of any noncash tips, such as tickets or passes. You do not pay social security and Medicare taxes or RRTA tax on these noncash tips.

To figure the social security and Medicare tax, use Form 4137. If you owe RRTA tax, contact your employer. Your employer will figure and collect the RRTA tax.

 You may be charged a penalty equal to 50% of the social security and Medicare or RRTA tax due on tips you received but didn't report to your employer.

Form 8919. If you are an employee who received wages from an employer who didn't withhold social security and Medicare tax from your wages, use Form 8919 to figure your share of the unreported tax. Include on line 58 the amount from line 13 of Form 8919. Include the amount from line 6 of Form 8919 on Form 1040, line 7.

Line 59

Additional Tax on IRAs, Other Qualified Retirement Plans, etc.

If any of the following apply, see Form 5329 and its instructions to find out if you owe this tax and if you must file Form 5329. Also see Form 5329 and its instructions for definitions of the terms used here.

1. You received an early distribution from (a) an IRA or other qualified retirement plan, (b) an annuity, or (c) a modified endowment contract entered into after June 20, 1988, and the total distribution wasn't rolled over in a qualified rollover contribution.

2. Excess contributions were made to your IRA, Coverdell education savings account (ESA), Archer MSA, health savings account (HSA), or ABLE account.

3. You received a taxable distribution from a Coverdell ESA, qualified tuition program, or ABLE account.

4. You were born before July 1, 1944, and didn't take the minimum required distribution from your IRA or other qualified retirement plan.

Exception. If only item (1) applies and distribution code 1 is correctly shown in box 7 of all your Forms 1099-R, you do not have to file Form 5329. Instead, multiply the taxable amount of the distribution by 10% (0.10) and enter the result on line 59. The taxable amount of the distribution is the part of the distribution you reported on Form 1040, line 15b or line 16b, or on Form 4972. Also, enter "No" under the heading *Other Taxes* to the left of line 59 to indicate that you do not have to file Form 5329. But you must file Form 5329 if distribution code 1 is incorrectly shown in box 7 of Form 1099-R or you qualify for an exception, such as the exceptions for qualified medical expenses, qualified higher education expenses, qualified first-time homebuyer distributions, or a qualified reservist distribution.

Line 60a

Household Employment Taxes

Enter the household employment taxes you owe for having a household employee. If any of the following apply, see Schedule H and its instructions to find out if you owe these taxes.

1. You paid any one household employee (defined below) cash wages of $1,900 or more in 2015. Cash wages include wages paid by check, money order, etc. But do not count amounts paid to an employee who was under age 18 at any time in 2015 and was a student.

2. You withheld federal income tax during 2015 at the request of any household employee.

3. You paid total cash wages of $1,000 or more in any calendar quarter of 2014 or 2015 to household employees.

Any person who does household work is a household employee if you can control what will be done and how it will be done. Household work includes work done in or around your home by babysitters, nannies, health aides, housekeepers, yard workers, and similar domestic workers.

Line 60b

First-time Homebuyer Credit Repayment

Enter the first-time homebuyer credit you have to repay if:

- You bought the home in 2008, or
- The home you bought was destroyed, condemned, or sold under threat of condemnation in 2013 and that event occurred during the 36-month period that began on the date you bought the home.

If you bought the home in 2008 and owned and used it as your main home for all of 2015, you can enter your 2015 repayment on this line without attaching Form 5405.

See the Form 5405 instructions for details and for exceptions to the repayment rule.

Line 61

Health Care: Individual Responsibility

You must either:

- Have qualifying health care coverage for every month of 2015 for yourself, your spouse (if filing jointly), and anyone you can or do claim as a dependent (you are treated as having coverage for any month in which you have coverage for at least 1 day of the month),
- Qualify for an exemption from the requirement to have health care coverage, or
- Make a shared responsibility payment with your return and enter the amount on this line.

If you had qualifying health care coverage (called minimum essential coverage) for every month of 2015 for yourself, your spouse (if filing jointly), and anyone you can or do claim as a dependent, check the box on this line and leave the entry space blank.

Otherwise, do not check the box on this line. If you, your spouse (if filing jointly), or someone you can or do claim as a dependent didn't have coverage for each month of 2015 you must either claim a coverage exemption on Form 8965 or report a shared responsibility payment on line 61. See the instructions for Form 8965 for information on coverage exemptions and figuring the shared responsibility payment.

You can check the box even if:

- A dependent child who was born or adopted during the year was not covered by your insurance during the month of or months before birth or adoption (but the child must have had minimum essential coverage every month of 2015 following the birth or adoption), or
- A spouse or dependent who died during the year was not covered by your insurance during the month of death and months after death (but he or she must have had minimum essential coverage every month of 2015 he or she was alive).

If you can be claimed as a dependent, do not check the box on this line. Leave the entry space blank. You do not need to attach Form 8965 or see its instructions.

If you or someone in your household had minimum essential coverage in 2015, the provider of that coverage is required to send you a Form 1095-A, 1095-B, or 1095-C (with Part III completed) that lists individuals in your family who were enrolled in the coverage and shows their months of coverage.

• Individuals enrolled in health insurance coverage through the Marketplace generally receive this information on Form 1095-A, Health Insurance Marketplace Statement.

• Individuals enrolled in health insurance coverage provided by their employer generally receive this information on either Form 1095-B, Health Coverage, or on Form 1095-C, Employer-Provided Health Insurance Offer and Coverage.

• Individuals enrolled in a government-sponsored health program or in other types of coverage generally receive this information on Form 1095-B, Health Coverage.

Even if you haven't received one of these forms, you may have had health care coverage and can rely on other information you have about your coverage to complete line 61.

Your health care coverage provider may have asked for your social security number. To understand why, go to *www.irs.gov/ACASSN*.

Minimum essential coverage. Most health care coverage that people have is minimum essential coverage.

Minimum essential coverage includes:

• Most types of health care coverage provided by your employer,

• Many types of government-sponsored health care coverage including Medicare, most Medicaid coverage, and most health care coverage provided to veterans and active duty service members,

• Certain types of health care coverage you buy directly from an insurance company, and

• Health care coverage you buy through the Marketplace.

See the instructions for Form 8965 for more information on what qualifies as minimum essential coverage.

Reminder - health care coverage. If you need health care coverage, go to *www.HealthCare.gov* to learn about health insurance options for you and your family, how to buy health insurance, and how you might qualify to get financial assistance to buy health insurance.

Premium tax credit. If you, your spouse, or a dependent enrolled in health insurance through the Marketplace, you may be able to claim the premium tax credit. See the instructions for line 69 and Form 8962.

Line 62

Other Taxes

Use line 62 to report any taxes not reported elsewhere on your return or other schedules. To find out if you owe the tax, see the form or publication indicated. Enter on line 62 the total of all of the following taxes you owe.

Additional Medicare Tax. See Form 8959 and its instructions if the total of your 2015 wages and any self-employment income was more than:

• $125,000 if married filing separately,

• $250,000 if married filing jointly, or

• $200,000 if single, head of household, or qualifying widow(er).

Also see Form 8959 if you had railroad retirement (RRTA) compensation that was more than the amount just listed that applies to you.

If you are married filing jointly and either you or your spouse had wages or RRTA compensation of more than $200,000, your employer may have withheld Additional Medicare Tax even if you do not owe the tax. In that case, you may be able to get a refund of the tax withheld. See the Instructions for Form 8959 to find out how to report the withheld tax on Form 8959.

Check box a if you owe the tax.

Net Investment Income Tax. See Form 8960 and its instructions if the amount on Form 1040, line 38, is more than:

• $125,000 if married filing separately,

• $250,000 if married filing jointly or qualifying widow(er), or

• $200,000 if single or head of household.

If you file Form 2555 or 2555-EZ, see Form 8960 and its instructions if the amount on Form 1040, line 38, is more than:

• $24,200 if married filing separately,

• $149,200 if married filing jointly or qualifying widow(er), or

• $99,200 if single or head of household.

Check box b if you owe the tax.

Other taxes. For the following taxes, check box c and, in the space next to that box, enter the amount of the tax and the code that identifies it. If you need more room, attach a statement listing the amount of each tax and the code.

1. Additional tax on health savings account (HSA) distributions (see Form 8889, Part II). Identify as "HSA."

2. Additional tax on an HSA because you didn't remain an eligible individual during the testing period (see Form 8889, Part III). Identify as "HDHP."

3. Additional tax on Archer MSA distributions (see Form 8853). Identify as "MSA."

4. Additional tax on Medicare Advantage MSA distributions (see Form 8853). Identify as "Med MSA."

5. Recapture of the following credits.

a. Investment credit (see Form 4255). Identify as "ICR."

b. Low-income housing credit (see Form 8611). Identify as "LIHCR."

c. Indian employment credit (see Form 8845). Identify as "IECR."

d. New markets credit (see Form 8874). Identify as "NMCR."

e. Credit for employer-provided child care facilities (see Form 8882). Identify as "ECCFR."

f. Alternative motor vehicle credit (see Form 8910). Identify as "AMVCR."

g. Alternative fuel vehicle refueling property credit (see Form 8911). Identify as "ARPCR."

h. Qualified plug-in electric drive motor vehicle credit (see Form 8936). Identify as "8936R."

6. Recapture of federal mortgage subsidy. If you sold your home in 2015

and it was financed (in whole or in part) from the proceeds of any tax-exempt qualified mortgage bond or you claimed the mortgage interest credit, see Form 8828. Identify as "FMSR."

7. Section 72(m)(5) excess benefits tax (see Pub. 560). Identify as "Sec. 72(m)(5)."

8. Uncollected social security and Medicare or RRTA tax on tips or group-term life insurance. This tax should be shown in box 12 of Form W-2 with codes A and B or M and N. Identify as "UT."

9. Golden parachute payments. If you received an excess parachute payment (EPP), you must pay a 20% tax on it. This tax should be shown in box 12 of Form W-2 with code K. If you received a Form 1099-MISC, the tax is 20% of the EPP shown in box 13. Identify as "EPP."

10. Tax on accumulation distribution of trusts (see Form 4970). Identify as "ADT."

11. Excise tax on insider stock compensation from an expatriated corporation. See section 4985. Identify as "ISC."

12. Interest on the tax due on installment income from the sale of certain residential lots and timeshares. Identify as "453(l)(3)."

13. Interest on the deferred tax on gain from certain installment sales with a sales price over $150,000. Identify as "453A(c)."

14. Additional tax on recapture of a charitable contribution deduction relating to a fractional interest in tangible personal property. See Pub. 526. Identify as "FITPP."

15. Look-back interest under section 167(g) or 460(b). See Form 8697 or 8866. Identify as "8697" or "8866."

16. Additional tax on income you received from a nonqualified deferred compensation plan that fails to meet the requirements of section 409A. This income should be shown in box 12 of Form W-2 with code Z, or in box 15b of Form 1099-MISC. The tax is 20% of the amount required to be included in income plus an interest amount determined under section 409A(a)(1)(B)(ii).

See section 409A(a)(1)(B) for details. Identify as "NQDC."

17. Additional tax on compensation you received from a nonqualified deferred compensation plan described in section 457A if the compensation would have been includible in your income in an earlier year except that the amount wasn't determinable until 2015. The tax is 20% of the amount required to be included in income plus an interest amount determined under section 457A(c)(2). See section 457A for details. Identify as "457A."

18. Tax on noneffectively connected income for any part of the year you were a nonresident alien (see the Instructions for Form 1040NR). Identify as "1040NR."

19. Any interest amount from Form 8621, line 16f, relating to distributions from, and dispositions of, stock of a section 1291 fund. Identify as "1291INT."

20. Any interest amount from Form 8621, line 24. Identify as "1294INT."

Payments

Line 64

Federal Income Tax Withheld

Add the amounts shown as federal income tax withheld on your Forms W-2, W-2G, and 1099-R. Enter the total on line 64. The amount withheld should be shown in box 2 of Form W-2 and in box 4 of Form W-2G or 1099-R. Attach your Form(s) W-2 to the front of your return. Attach Forms W-2G and 1099-R to the front of your return if federal income tax was withheld.

If you received a 2015 Form 1099 showing federal income tax withheld on dividends, taxable or tax-exempt interest income, unemployment compensation, social security benefits, railroad retirement benefits, or other income you received, include the amount withheld in the total on line 64. This should be shown in box 4 of Form 1099, box 6 of Form SSA-1099, or box 10 of Form RRB-1099.

If you had Additional Medicare Tax withheld, include the amount shown on Form 8959, line 24, in the total on line 64. Attach Form 8959.

Also include on line 64 any federal income tax withheld that is shown on a Schedule K-1.

Line 65

2015 Estimated Tax Payments

Enter any estimated federal income tax payments you made for 2015. Include any overpayment that you applied to your 2015 estimated tax from:
- Your 2014 return, or
- An amended return (Form 1040X).

If you and your spouse paid joint estimated tax but are now filing separate income tax returns, you can divide the amount paid in any way you choose as long as you both agree. If you can't agree, you must divide the payments in proportion to each spouse's individual tax as shown on your separate returns for 2015. For an example and more information, see Pub. 505. Be sure to show both social security numbers (SSNs) in the space provided on the separate returns. If you or your spouse paid separate estimated tax but you are now filing a joint return, add the amounts you each paid. Follow these instructions even if your spouse died in 2015 or in 2016 before filing a 2015 return.

Divorced taxpayers. If you got divorced in 2015 and you made joint estimated tax payments with your former spouse, enter your former spouse's SSN in the space provided on the front of Form 1040. If you were divorced and remarried in 2015, enter your present spouse's SSN in the space provided on the front of Form 1040. Also, under the heading *Payments* to the left of line 65, enter your former spouse's SSN, followed by "DIV."

Name change. If you changed your name and you made estimated tax payments using your former name, attach a statement to the front of Form 1040 that explains all the payments you and your spouse made in 2015 and the name(s) and SSN(s) under which you made them.

Lines 66a and 66b— Earned Income Credit (EIC)

What Is the EIC?

The EIC is a credit for certain people who work. The credit may give you a refund even if you do not owe any tax or did not have any tax withheld.

To Take the EIC:

- Follow the steps below.
- Complete the worksheet that applies to you or let the IRS figure the credit for you.
- If you have a qualifying child, complete and attach Schedule EIC.

For help in determining if you are eligible for the EIC, go to *www.irs.gov/eitc* and click on "EITC Assistant." This service is available in English and Spanish.

 If you take the EIC even though you aren't eligible and it is determined that your error is due to reckless or intentional disregard of the EIC rules, you won't be allowed to take the credit for 2 years even if you are otherwise eligible to do so. If you fraudulently take the EIC, you won't be allowed to take the credit for 10 years. See Form 8862, who must file, later. You may also have to pay penalties.

Step 1 All Filers

1. If, in 2015:
   - 3 or more children lived with you, is the amount on Form 1040, line 38, less than $47,747 ($53,267 if married filing jointly)?
   - 2 children lived with you, is the amount on Form 1040, line 38, less than $44,454 ($49,974 if married filing jointly)?
   - 1 child lived with you, is the amount on Form 1040, line 38, less than $39,131 ($44,651 if married filing jointly)?
   - No children lived with you, is the amount on Form 1040, line 38, less than $14,820 ($20,330 if married filing jointly)?

   ☐ **Yes.** Continue ☐ **No.**
   You can't take the credit.

2. Do you, and your spouse if filing a joint return, have a social security number that allows you to work and is valid for EIC purposes (explained later under *Definitions and Special Rules*)?

   ☐ **Yes.** Continue ☐ **No.**
   You can't take the credit. Enter "No" on the dotted line next to line 66a.

3. Is your filing status married filing separately?

   ☐ **Yes.**   ☐ **No.** Continue
   You can't take the credit.

4. Are you filing Form 2555 or 2555-EZ (relating to foreign earned income)?

   ☐ **Yes.**   ☐ **No.** Continue
   You can't take the credit.

5. Were you or your spouse a nonresident alien for any part of 2015?

   ☐ **Yes.** See *Nonresident aliens,* later, under *Definitions and Special Rules.* ☐ **No.** Go to Step 2.

Step 2 Investment Income

1. Add the amounts from Form 1040:

Line 8a		_____
Line 8b	+	_____
Line 9a	+	_____
Line 13*	+	_____
Investment Income	=	_____

   *If line 13 is a loss, enter -0-.

2. Is your investment income more than $3,400?

   ☐ **Yes.** Continue ☐ **No.** Skip question 3; go to question 4.

3. Are you filing Form 4797 (relating to sales of business property)?

   ☐ **Yes.** See *Form 4797 filers,* later, under *Definitions and Special Rules.* ☐ **No.**
   You can't take the credit.

4. Do any of the following apply for 2015?
   - You are filing Schedule E.
   - You are reporting income from the rental of personal property not used in a trade or business.
   - You are filing Form 8814 (relating to election to report child's interest and dividends on your return).
   - You have income or loss from a passive activity.

   ☐ **Yes.** Use Worksheet 1 in Pub. 596 to see if you can take the credit. ☐ **No.** Go to Step 3.

Step 3   Qualifying Child

A qualifying child for the EIC is a child who is your...

Son, daughter, stepchild, foster child, brother, sister, stepbrother, stepsister, half brother, half sister, or a descendant of any of them (for example, your grandchild, niece, or nephew)

was ...

Under age 19 at the end of 2015 and younger than you
(or your spouse, if filing jointly)

or

Under age 24 at the end of 2015, a student (defined later), and younger than you
(or your spouse, if filing jointly)

or

Any age and permanently and totally disabled (defined later)

Who isn't filing a joint return for 2015
or is filing a joint return for 2015 only to claim a refund of withheld income tax or estimated tax paid (see Pub. 596 for examples)

Who lived with you in the United States for more than half of 2015.

> ⚠️ **CAUTION**
> *You can't take the credit for a child who didn't live with you for more than half the year, even if you paid most of the child's living expenses. The IRS may ask you for documents to show you lived with each qualifying child. Documents you might want to keep for this purpose include school and child care records and other records that show your child's address.*

> 💡 **TIP**
> *If the child didn't live with you for more than half of 2015 because of a temporary absence, birth, death, or kidnapping, see Exception to time lived with you, later.*

> ⚠️ **CAUTION**
> *If the child meets the conditions to be a qualifying child of any other person (other than your spouse if filing a joint return) for 2015, see Qualifying child of more than one person, later. If the child was married, see Married child, later.*

---

1. Do you have at least one child who meets the conditions to be your qualifying child?

   ☐ **Yes.** The child must have a valid social security number (SSN) as defined later, unless the child was born and died in 2015. If at least one qualifying child has a valid SSN (or was born or died in 2015), go to question 2. Otherwise, you can't take the credit.

   ☐ **No.** Skip questions 2 and 3; go to Step 4.

2. Are you filing a joint return for 2015?

   ☐ **Yes.** Skip question 3 and Step 4; go to Step 5.

   ☐ **No.** Continue ➘

3. Could you be a qualifying child of another person for 2015? (Check "No" if the other person isn't required to file, and isn't filing, a 2015 tax return or is filing a 2015 return only to claim a refund of withheld income tax or estimated tax paid (see Pub. 596 for examples).)

   ☐ **Yes.** 🛑
   You can't take the credit. Enter "No" on the dotted line next to line 66a.

   ☐ **No.** Skip Step 4; go to Step 5.

Step 4   Filers Without a Qualifying Child

1. Is the amount on Form 1040, line 38, less than $14,820 ($20,330 if married filing jointly)?

   ☐ **Yes.** Continue ➘

   ☐ **No.** 🛑
   You can't take the credit.

2. Were you, or your spouse if filing a joint return, at least age 25 but under age 65 at the end of 2015? (Check "Yes" if you, or your spouse if filing a joint return, were born after December 31, 1950, and before January 2, 1991.) If your spouse died in 2015 or if you are preparing a return for someone who died in 2015, see Pub. 596 before you answer.

   ☐ **Yes.** Continue ➘

   ☐ **No.** 🛑
   You can't take the credit.

3. Was your main home, and your spouse's if filing a joint return, in the United States for more than half of 2015? Members of the military stationed outside the United States, see *Members of the military,* later, before you answer.

   ☐ **Yes.** Continue ➘

   ☐ **No.** 🛑
   You can't take the credit. Enter "No" on the dotted line next to line 66a.

Need more information or forms? Visit IRS.gov.

4. Are you filing a joint return for 2015?

☐ **Yes.** Skip questions 5 and 6; go to Step 5.   ☐ **No.** Continue ⬎

---

5. Could you be a qualifying child of another person for 2015? (Check "No" if the other person isn't required to file, and isn't filing, a 2015 tax return or is filing a 2015 return only to claim a refund of withheld income tax or estimated tax paid (see Pub. 596 for examples).)

☐ **Yes.** (stop)   ☐ **No.** Continue ⬎

You can't take the credit. Enter "No" on the dotted line next to line 66a.

---

6. Can you be claimed as a dependent on someone else's 2015 tax return?

☐ **Yes.** (stop)   ☐ **No.** Go to Step 5.

You can't take the credit.

Step 5   Earned Income

1. Are you filing Schedule SE because you were a member of the clergy or you had church employee income of $108.28 or more?

☐ **Yes.** See *Clergy* or *Church employees,* whichever applies.   ☐ **No.** Complete the following worksheet.

1. Enter the amount from Form 1040, line 7 . . .   1._____

2. Enter any amount included on Form 1040, line 7, that is a taxable scholarship or fellowship grant not reported on a Form W-2 . . . .   2._____

3. Enter any amount included on Form 1040, line 7, that you received for work performed while an inmate in a penal institution. (Enter "PRI" and the same amount on the dotted line next to Form 1040, line 7) . . . .   3._____

4. Enter any amount included on Form 1040, line 7, that you received as a pension or annuity from a nonqualified deferred compensation plan or a nongovernmental section 457 plan. (Enter "DFC" and the same amount on the dotted line next to Form 1040, line 7.) This amount may be shown in box 11 of Form W-2. If you received such an amount but box 11 is blank, contact your employer for the amount received   4._____

5. Enter any amount included on Form 1040, line 7, that is a Medicaid waiver payment you exclude from income. (See the instructions for line 21) . . . .   5._____

6. Add lines 2, 3, 4, and 5 . . . .   6._____

7. Subtract line 6 from line 1 . . . .   7._____

8. Enter all of your nontaxable combat pay if you elect to include it in earned income. Also enter this amount on Form 1040, line 66b. See *Combat pay, nontaxable,* later . . . .   8._____

⚠ **CAUTION**   *Electing to include nontaxable combat pay may increase or decrease your EIC. Figure the credit with and without your nontaxable combat pay before making the election.*

9. Add lines 7 and 8. **This is your earned income** . . . .   9._____

---

2. Were you self-employed at any time in 2015, or are you filing Schedule SE because you were a member of the clergy or you had church employee income, or are you filing Schedule C or C-EZ as a statutory employee?

☐ **Yes.** Skip question 3 and Step 6; go to Worksheet B.   ☐ **No.** Continue ⬎

3. If you have:
- 3 or more qualifying children, is your earned income less than $47,747 ($53,267 if married filing jointly)?
- 2 qualifying children, is your earned income less than $44,454 ($49,974 if married filing jointly)?
- 1 qualifying child, is your earned income less than $39,131 ($44,651 if married filing jointly)?
- No qualifying children, is your earned income less than $14,820 ($20,330 if married filing jointly)?

☐ **Yes.** Go to Step 6.   ☐ **No.** (stop)

You can't take the credit.

Step 6   How To Figure the Credit

1. Do you want the IRS to figure the credit for you?

☐ **Yes.** See *Credit figured by the IRS*, later.   ☐ **No.** Go to Worksheet A.

Definitions and Special Rules

Adopted child. An adopted child is always treated as your own child. An adopted child includes a child lawfully placed with you for legal adoption.

Church employees. Determine how much of the amount on Form 1040, line 7, was also reported on Schedule SE, Section B, line 5a. Subtract that amount from the amount on Form 1040, line 7, and enter the result on line 1 of the worksheet in Step 5 (instead of entering the actual amount from Form 1040, line 7). Be sure to answer "Yes" to question 2 in Step 5.

Clergy. The following instructions apply to ministers, members of religious orders who have not taken a vow of poverty, and Christian Science practitioners. If you are filing Schedule SE and the amount on line 2 of that schedule includes an amount that was also reported on Form 1040, line 7:

2015 Form 1040—Lines 66a and 66b

1. Enter "Clergy" on the dotted line next to Form 1040, line 66a.

2. Determine how much of the amount on Form 1040, line 7, was also reported on Schedule SE, Section A, line 2, or Section B, line 2.

3. Subtract that amount from the amount on Form 1040, line 7. Enter the result on line 1 of the worksheet in Step 5 (instead of entering the actual amount from Form 1040, line 7).

4. Be sure to answer "Yes" to question 2 in Step 5.

Combat pay, nontaxable. If you were a member of the U.S. Armed Forces who served in a combat zone, certain pay is excluded from your income. See *Combat Zone Exclusion* in Pub. 3. You can elect to include this pay in your earned income when figuring the EIC. The amount of your nontaxable combat pay should be shown in box 12 of Form(s) W-2 with code Q. If you are filing a joint return and both you and your spouse received nontaxable combat pay, you can each make your own election. In other words, if one of you makes the election, the other one can also make it but doesn't have to.

Credit figured by the IRS. To have the IRS figure your EIC:

1. Enter "EIC" on the dotted line next to Form 1040, line 66a.

2. Be sure you enter the nontaxable combat pay you elect to include in earned income on Form 1040, line 66b. See *Combat pay, nontaxable*, earlier.

3. If you have a qualifying child, complete and attach Schedule EIC. If your EIC for a year after 1996 was reduced or disallowed, see *Form 8862, who must file*, later.

Exception to time lived with you. Temporary absences by you or the child for special circumstances, such as school, vacation, business, medical care, military service, or detention in a juvenile facility, count as time the child lived with you. Also see *Kidnapped child* in the instructions for line 6c and *Members of the military*, later. A child is considered to have lived with you for more than half of 2015 if the child was born or died in 2015 and your home was this child's home for more than half the time he or she was alive in 2015.

Form 4797 filers. If the amount on Form 1040, line 13, includes an amount from Form 4797, you must use Worksheet 1 in Pub. 596 to see if you can take the EIC. Otherwise, stop; you can't take the EIC.

Form 8862, who must file. You must file Form 8862 if your EIC for a year after 1996 was reduced or disallowed for any reason other than a math or clerical error. But do not file Form 8862 if either of the following applies.

• You filed Form 8862 for another year, the EIC was allowed for that year, and your EIC hasn't been reduced or disallowed again for any reason other than a math or clerical error.

• You are taking the EIC without a qualifying child and the only reason your EIC was reduced or disallowed in the other year was because it was determined that a child listed on Schedule EIC wasn't your qualifying child.

Also, do not file Form 8862 or take the credit for the:

• 2 years after the most recent tax year for which there was a final determination that your EIC claim was due to reckless or intentional disregard of the EIC rules, or

• 10 years after the most recent tax year for which there was a final determination that your EIC claim was due to fraud.

Foster child. A foster child is any child placed with you by an authorized placement agency or by judgment, decree, or other order of any court of competent jurisdiction. For more details on authorized placement agencies, see Pub. 596.

Married child. A child who was married at the end of 2015 is a qualifying child only if (a) you can claim him or her as your dependent on Form 1040, line 6c, or (b) you could have claimed him or her as your dependent except for the special rule for *Children of divorced or separated parents* in the instructions for line 6c.

Members of the military. If you were on extended active duty outside the United States, your main home is considered to be in the United States during that duty period. Extended active duty is military duty ordered for an indefinite period or for a period of more than 90 days. Once you begin serving extended active duty, you are considered to be on extended active duty even if you do not serve more than 90 days.

Nonresident aliens. If your filing status is married filing jointly, go to Step 2. Otherwise, stop; you can't take the EIC. Enter "No" on the dotted line next to line 66a.

Permanently and totally disabled. A person is permanently and totally disabled if, at any time in 2015, the person couldn't engage in any substantial gainful activity because of a physical or mental condition and a doctor has determined that this condition (a) has lasted or can be expected to last continuously for at least a year, or (b) can be expected to lead to death.

Qualifying child of more than one person. Even if a child meets the conditions to be the qualifying child of more than one person, only one person can claim the child as a qualifying child for all of the following tax benefits, unless the special rule for *Children of divorced or separated parents* in the instructions for line 6c applies.

1. Dependency exemption (line 6c).

2. Child tax credits (lines 52 and 67).

3. Head of household filing status (line 4).

4. Credit for child and dependent care expenses (line 49).

5. Exclusion for dependent care benefits (Form 2441, Part III).

6. Earned income credit (lines 66a and 66b).

No other person can take any of the six tax benefits just listed unless he or she has a different qualifying child. If you and any other person can claim the child as a qualifying child, the following rules apply.

• If only one of the persons is the child's parent, the child is treated as the qualifying child of the parent.

• If the parents file a joint return together and can claim the child as a qualifying child, the child is treated as the qualifying child of the parents.

-57-   *Need more information or forms? Visit IRS.gov.*

- If the parents do not file a joint return together but both parents claim the child as a qualifying child, the IRS will treat the child as the qualifying child of the parent with whom the child lived for the longer period of time in 2015. If the child lived with each parent for the same amount of time, the IRS will treat the child as the qualifying child of the parent who had the higher adjusted gross income (AGI) for 2015.

- If no parent can claim the child as a qualifying child, the child is treated as the qualifying child of the person who had the highest AGI for 2015.

- If a parent can claim the child as a qualifying child but no parent does so claim the child, the child is treated as the qualifying child of the person who had the highest AGI for 2015, but only if that person's AGI is higher than the highest AGI of any parent of the child who can claim the child.

Example. Your daughter meets the conditions to be a qualifying child for both you and your mother. Your daughter doesn't meet the conditions to be a qualifying child of any other person, including her other parent. Under the rules just described, you can claim your daughter as a qualifying child for all of the six tax benefits listed here for which you otherwise qualify. Your mother can't claim any of the six tax benefits listed here unless she has a different qualifying child. However, if your mother's AGI is higher than yours and you do not claim your daughter as a qualifying child, your daughter is the qualifying child of your mother.

For more details and examples, see Pub. 596.

If you won't be taking the EIC with a qualifying child, enter "No" on the dotted line next to line 66a. Otherwise, go to Step 3, question 1.

Social security number (SSN). For the EIC, a valid SSN is a number issued by the Social Security Administration unless "Not Valid for Employment" is printed on the social security card and the number was issued solely to allow the recipient of the SSN to apply for or receive a federally funded benefit. However, if "Valid for Work Only With DHS Authorization" is printed on your social security card, your SSN is valid for EIC purposes only as long as the DHS authorization is still valid.

To find out how to get an SSN, see *Social Security Number (SSN)* near the beginning of these instructions. If you won't have an SSN by the date your return is due, see *What if You Can't File on Time?*

If you didn't have an SSN by the due date of your 2015 return (including extensions), you can't claim the EIC on either your original or an amended 2015 return, even if you later get an SSN. Also, if a child didn't have an SSN by the due date of your return (including extensions), you can't count that child as a qualifying child in figuring the EIC on either your original or an amended 2015 return, even if that child later gets an SSN.

Student. A student is a child who during any part of 5 calendar months of 2015 was enrolled as a full-time student at a school, or took a full-time, on-farm training course given by a school or a state, county, or local government agency. A school includes a technical, trade, or mechanical school. It doesn't include an on-the-job training course, correspondence school, or school offering courses only through the Internet.

Welfare benefits, effect of credit on. Any refund you receive as a result of taking the EIC can't be counted as income when determining if you or anyone else is eligible for benefits or assistance, or how much you or anyone else can receive, under any federal program or under any state or local program financed in whole or in part with federal funds. These programs include Temporary Assistance for Needy Families (TANF), Medicaid, Supplemental Security Income (SSI), and Supplemental Nutrition Assistance Program (food stamps). In addition, when determining eligibility, the refund can't be counted as a resource for at least 12 months after you receive it. Check with your local benefit coordinator to find out if your refund will affect your benefits.

Worksheet A—2015 EIC—Lines 66a and 66b

Keep for Your Records

Before you begin: ✓ Be sure you are using the correct worksheet. Use this worksheet only if you answered "No" to Step 5, question 2. Otherwise, use Worksheet B.

Part 1

All Filers Using Worksheet A

1. Enter your earned income from Step 5.

| 1 | |

2. Look up the amount on line 1 above in the EIC Table (right after Worksheet B) to find the credit. Be sure you use the correct column for your filing status and the number of children you have. Enter the credit here.

   If line 2 is zero, **(STOP)** You cannot take the credit.
   Enter "No" on the dotted line next to line 66a.

| 2 | |

3. Enter the amount from Form 1040, line 38.

| 3 | |

4. Are the amounts on lines 3 and 1 the same?

   ☐ **Yes.** Skip line 5; enter the amount from line 2 on line 6.

   ☐ **No.** Go to line 5.

Part 2

Filers Who Answered "No" on Line 4

5. If you have:
   - No qualifying children, is the amount on line 3 less than $8,250 ($13,750 if married filing jointly)?
   - 1 or more qualifying children, is the amount on line 3 less than $18,150 ($23,650 if married filing jointly)?

   ☐ **Yes.** Leave line 5 blank; enter the amount from line 2 on line 6.

   ☐ **No.** Look up the amount on line 3 in the EIC Table to find the credit. Be sure you use the correct column for your filing status and the number of children you have. Enter the credit here.
   Look at the amounts on lines 5 and 2.
   Then, enter the **smaller** amount on line 6.

| 5 | |

Part 3

Your Earned Income Credit

6. **This is your earned income credit.**

| 6 | |

   Enter this amount on
   Form 1040, line 66a.

Reminder—

✓ If you have a qualifying child, complete and attach Schedule EIC.

> ⚠ **CAUTION**
> *If your EIC for a year after 1996 was reduced or disallowed, see Form 8862, who must file, earlier, to find out if you must file Form 8862 to take the credit for 2015.*

Need more information or forms? Visit IRS.gov.

Worksheet B—2015 EIC—Lines 66a and 66b

Keep for Your Records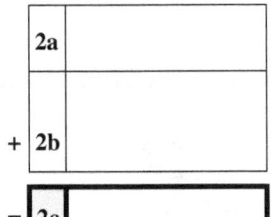

Use this worksheet if you answered "Yes" to Step 5, question 2.

✓ Complete the parts below (Parts 1 through 3) that apply to you. Then, continue to Part 4.

✓ If you are married filing a joint return, include your spouse's amounts, if any, with yours to figure the amounts to enter in Parts 1 through 3.

Part 1 **Self-Employed, Members of the Clergy, and People With Church Employee Income Filing Schedule SE**	**1a.** Enter the amount from Schedule SE, Section A, line 3, or Section B, line 3, whichever applies.	**1a**
	b. Enter any amount from Schedule SE, Section B, line 4b, and line 5a.	+ **1b**
	c. Combine lines 1a and 1b.	= **1c**
	d. Enter the amount from Schedule SE, Section A, line 6, or Section B, line 13, whichever applies.	− **1d**
	e. Subtract line 1d from 1c.	= **1e**

Part 2 **Self-Employed NOT Required To File Schedule SE** For example, your net earnings from self-employment were less than $400.	**2.** Do not include on these lines any statutory employee income, any net profit from services performed as a notary public, any amount exempt from self-employment tax as the result of the filing and approval of Form 4029 or Form 4361, or any other amounts exempt from self-employment tax.	
	a. Enter any net farm profit or (loss) from Schedule F, line 34, and from farm partnerships, Schedule K-1 (Form 1065), box 14, code A*.	**2a**
	b. Enter any net profit or (loss) from Schedule C, line 31; Schedule C-EZ, line 3; Schedule K-1 (Form 1065), box 14, code A (other than farming); and Schedule K-1 (Form 1065-B), box 9, code J1*.	+ **2b**
	c. Combine lines 2a and 2b.	= **2c**
	If you have any Schedule K-1 amounts, complete the appropriate line(s) of Schedule SE, Section A. Reduce the Schedule K-1 amounts as described in the Partner's Instructions for Schedule K-1. Enter your name and social security number on Schedule SE and attach it to your return.	

Part 3 **Statutory Employees Filing Schedule C or C-EZ**	**3.** Enter the amount from Schedule C, line 1, or Schedule C-EZ, line 1, that you are filing as a statutory employee.	**3**

Part 4 **All Filers Using Worksheet B** **Note.** If line 4b includes income on which you should have paid self-employment tax but didn't, we may reduce your credit by the amount of self-employment tax not paid.	**4a.** Enter your earned income from Step 5.	**4a**
	b. Combine lines 1e, 2c, 3, and 4a. **This is your total earned income.**	**4b**
	If line 4b is zero or less, (STOP) You cannot take the credit. Enter "No" on the dotted line next to line 66a.	
	5. If you have:	
	● 3 or more qualifying children, is line 4b less than $47,747 ($53,267 if married filing jointly)?	
	● 2 qualifying children, is line 4b less than $44,454 ($49,974 if married filing jointly)?	
	● 1 qualifying child, is line 4b less than $39,131 ($44,651 if married filing jointly)?	
	● No qualifying children, is line 4b less than $14,820 ($20,330 if married filing jointly)?	
	☐ **Yes.** If you want the IRS to figure your credit, see *Credit figured by the IRS*, earlier. If you want to figure the credit yourself, enter the amount from line 4b on line 6 of this worksheet.	
	☐ **No.** (STOP) You cannot take the credit. Enter "No" on the dotted line next to line 66a.	

2015 Form 1040—Lines 66a and 66b

Worksheet B—2015 EIC—Lines 66a and 66b—*Continued*   *Keep for Your Records*

Part 5

All Filers Using Worksheet B

6. Enter your total earned income from Part 4, line 4b.   **6** [ ]

7. Look up the amount on line 6 above in the EIC Table to find the credit. Be sure you use the correct column for your filing status and the number of children you have. Enter the credit here.   **7** [ ]

   If line 7 is zero, (STOP) You cannot take the credit. Enter "No" on the dotted line next to line 66a.

8. Enter the amount from Form 1040, line 38.   **8** [ ]

9. Are the amounts on lines 8 and 6 the same?

   ☐ **Yes.** Skip line 10; enter the amount from line 7 on line 11.

   ☐ **No.** Go to line 10.

Part 6

Filers Who Answered "No" on Line 9

10. If you have:
    ● No qualifying children, is the amount on line 8 less than $8,250 ($13,750 if married filing jointly)?
    ● 1 or more qualifying children, is the amount on line 8 less than $18,150 ($23,650 if married filing jointly)?

    ☐ **Yes.** Leave line 10 blank; enter the amount from line 7 on line 11.

    ☐ **No.** Look up the amount on line 8 in the EIC Table to find the credit. Be sure you use the correct column for your filing status and the number of children you have. Enter the credit here.   **10** [ ]
    Look at the amounts on lines 10 and 7.
    Then, enter the **smaller** amount on line 11.

Part 7

Your Earned Income Credit

11. **This is your earned income credit.**   **11** [ ]

    Reminder—

    √ If you have a qualifying child, complete and attach Schedule EIC.

    Enter this amount on Form 1040, line 66a.

     If your EIC for a year after 1996 was reduced or disallowed, see Form 8862, who must file, earlier, to find out if you must file Form 8862 to take the credit for 2015.

2015 Earned Income Credit (EIC) Table
Caution. This is **not** a tax table.

1. To find your credit, read down the "At least - But less than" columns and find the line that includes the amount you were told to look up from your EIC Worksheet.

2. Then, go to the column that includes your filing status and the number of qualifying children you have. Enter the credit from that column on your EIC Worksheet.

Example. If your filing status is single, you have one qualifying child, and the amount you are looking up from your EIC Worksheet is $2,455, you would enter $842.

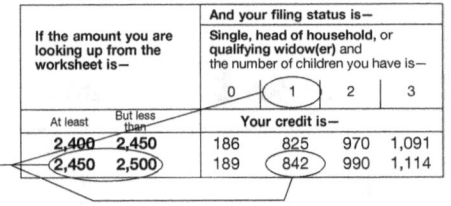

If the amount you are looking up from the worksheet is—		And your filing status is— Single, head of household, or qualifying widow(er) and the number of children you have is—			
At least	But less than	0	1	2	3
		Your credit is—			
2,400	2,450	186	825	970	1,091
2,450	2,500	189	842	990	1,114

If the amount you are looking up from the worksheet is—		Single, head of household, or qualifying widow(er) and the number of children you have is—				Married filing jointly and the number of children you have is—			
At least	But less than	0	1	2	3	0	1	2	3
		Your credit is—				Your credit is—			
$1	$50	$2	$9	$10	$11	$2	$9	$10	$11
50	100	6	26	30	34	6	26	30	34
100	150	10	43	50	56	10	43	50	56
150	200	13	60	70	79	13	60	70	79
200	250	17	77	90	101	17	77	90	101
250	300	21	94	110	124	21	94	110	124
300	350	25	111	130	146	25	111	130	146
350	400	29	128	150	169	29	128	150	169
400	450	33	145	170	191	33	145	170	191
450	500	36	162	190	214	36	162	190	214
500	550	40	179	210	236	40	179	210	236
550	600	44	196	230	259	44	196	230	259
600	650	48	213	250	281	48	213	250	281
650	700	52	230	270	304	52	230	270	304
700	750	55	247	290	326	55	247	290	326
750	800	59	264	310	349	59	264	310	349
800	850	63	281	330	371	63	281	330	371
850	900	67	298	350	394	67	298	350	394
900	950	71	315	370	416	71	315	370	416
950	1,000	75	332	390	439	75	332	390	439
1,000	1,050	78	349	410	461	78	349	410	461
1,050	1,100	82	366	430	484	82	366	430	484
1,100	1,150	86	383	450	506	86	383	450	506
1,150	1,200	90	400	470	529	90	400	470	529
1,200	1,250	94	417	490	551	94	417	490	551
1,250	1,300	98	434	510	574	98	434	510	574
1,300	1,350	101	451	530	596	101	451	530	596
1,350	1,400	105	468	550	619	105	468	550	619
1,400	1,450	109	485	570	641	109	485	570	641
1,450	1,500	113	502	590	664	113	502	590	664
1,500	1,550	117	519	610	686	117	519	610	686
1,550	1,600	120	536	630	709	120	536	630	709
1,600	1,650	124	553	650	731	124	553	650	731
1,650	1,700	128	570	670	754	128	570	670	754
1,700	1,750	132	587	690	776	132	587	690	776
1,750	1,800	136	604	710	799	136	604	710	799
1,800	1,850	140	621	730	821	140	621	730	821
1,850	1,900	143	638	750	844	143	638	750	844
1,900	1,950	147	655	770	866	147	655	770	866
1,950	2,000	151	672	790	889	151	672	790	889
2,000	2,050	155	689	810	911	155	689	810	911
2,050	2,100	159	706	830	934	159	706	830	934
2,100	2,150	163	723	850	956	163	723	850	956
2,150	2,200	166	740	870	979	166	740	870	979
2,200	2,250	170	757	890	1,001	170	757	890	1,001
2,250	2,300	174	774	910	1,024	174	774	910	1,024
2,300	2,350	178	791	930	1,046	178	791	930	1,046
2,350	2,400	182	808	950	1,069	182	808	950	1,069
2,400	2,450	186	825	970	1,091	186	825	970	1,091
2,450	2,500	189	842	990	1,114	189	842	990	1,114
2,500	2,550	193	859	1,010	1,136	193	859	1,010	1,136
2,550	2,600	197	876	1,030	1,159	197	876	1,030	1,159
2,600	2,650	201	893	1,050	1,181	201	893	1,050	1,181
2,650	2,700	205	910	1,070	1,204	205	910	1,070	1,204
2,700	2,750	208	927	1,090	1,226	208	927	1,090	1,226
2,750	2,800	212	944	1,110	1,249	212	944	1,110	1,249
2,800	2,850	216	961	1,130	1,271	216	961	1,130	1,271
2,850	2,900	220	978	1,150	1,294	220	978	1,150	1,294
2,900	2,950	224	995	1,170	1,316	224	995	1,170	1,316
2,950	3,000	228	1,012	1,190	1,339	228	1,012	1,190	1,339
3,000	3,050	231	1,029	1,210	1,361	231	1,029	1,210	1,361
3,050	3,100	235	1,046	1,230	1,384	235	1,046	1,230	1,384
3,100	3,150	239	1,063	1,250	1,406	239	1,063	1,250	1,406
3,150	3,200	243	1,080	1,270	1,429	243	1,080	1,270	1,429
3,200	3,250	247	1,097	1,290	1,451	247	1,097	1,290	1,451
3,250	3,300	251	1,114	1,310	1,474	251	1,114	1,310	1,474
3,300	3,350	254	1,131	1,330	1,496	254	1,131	1,330	1,496
3,350	3,400	258	1,148	1,350	1,519	258	1,148	1,350	1,519
3,400	3,450	262	1,165	1,370	1,541	262	1,165	1,370	1,541
3,450	3,500	266	1,182	1,390	1,564	266	1,182	1,390	1,564
3,500	3,550	270	1,199	1,410	1,586	270	1,199	1,410	1,586
3,550	3,600	273	1,216	1,430	1,609	273	1,216	1,430	1,609
3,600	3,650	277	1,233	1,450	1,631	277	1,233	1,450	1,631
3,650	3,700	281	1,250	1,470	1,654	281	1,250	1,470	1,654
3,700	3,750	285	1,267	1,490	1,676	285	1,267	1,490	1,676
3,750	3,800	289	1,284	1,510	1,699	289	1,284	1,510	1,699
3,800	3,850	293	1,301	1,530	1,721	293	1,301	1,530	1,721
3,850	3,900	296	1,318	1,550	1,744	296	1,318	1,550	1,744
3,900	3,950	300	1,335	1,570	1,766	300	1,335	1,570	1,766
3,950	4,000	304	1,352	1,590	1,789	304	1,352	1,590	1,789
4,000	4,050	308	1,369	1,610	1,811	308	1,369	1,610	1,811
4,050	4,100	312	1,386	1,630	1,834	312	1,386	1,630	1,834
4,100	4,150	316	1,403	1,650	1,856	316	1,403	1,650	1,856
4,150	4,200	319	1,420	1,670	1,879	319	1,420	1,670	1,879
4,200	4,250	323	1,437	1,690	1,901	323	1,437	1,690	1,901
4,250	4,300	327	1,454	1,710	1,924	327	1,454	1,710	1,924
4,300	4,350	331	1,471	1,730	1,946	331	1,471	1,730	1,946
4,350	4,400	335	1,488	1,750	1,969	335	1,488	1,750	1,969
4,400	4,450	339	1,505	1,770	1,991	339	1,505	1,770	1,991
4,450	4,500	342	1,522	1,790	2,014	342	1,522	1,790	2,014
4,500	4,550	346	1,539	1,810	2,036	346	1,539	1,810	2,036
4,550	4,600	350	1,556	1,830	2,059	350	1,556	1,830	2,059
4,600	4,650	354	1,573	1,850	2,081	354	1,573	1,850	2,081
4,650	4,700	358	1,590	1,870	2,104	358	1,590	1,870	2,104
4,700	4,750	361	1,607	1,890	2,126	361	1,607	1,890	2,126
4,750	4,800	365	1,624	1,910	2,149	365	1,624	1,910	2,149
4,800	4,850	369	1,641	1,930	2,171	369	1,641	1,930	2,171
4,850	4,900	373	1,658	1,950	2,194	373	1,658	1,950	2,194
4,900	4,950	377	1,675	1,970	2,216	377	1,675	1,970	2,216
4,950	5,000	381	1,692	1,990	2,239	381	1,692	1,990	2,239
5,000	5,050	384	1,709	2,010	2,261	384	1,709	2,010	2,261
5,050	5,100	388	1,726	2,030	2,284	388	1,726	2,030	2,284
5,100	5,150	392	1,743	2,050	2,306	392	1,743	2,050	2,306
5,150	5,200	396	1,760	2,070	2,329	396	1,760	2,070	2,329
5,200	5,250	400	1,777	2,090	2,351	400	1,777	2,090	2,351
5,250	5,300	404	1,794	2,110	2,374	404	1,794	2,110	2,374
5,300	5,350	407	1,811	2,130	2,396	407	1,811	2,130	2,396
5,350	5,400	411	1,828	2,150	2,419	411	1,828	2,150	2,419
5,400	5,450	415	1,845	2,170	2,441	415	1,845	2,170	2,441
5,450	5,500	419	1,862	2,190	2,464	419	1,862	2,190	2,464
5,500	5,550	423	1,879	2,210	2,486	423	1,879	2,210	2,486
5,550	5,600	426	1,896	2,230	2,509	426	1,896	2,230	2,509

(Continued)

Need more information or forms? Visit IRS.gov.

Earned Income Credit (EIC) Table - *Continued* (**Caution.** This is **not** a tax table.)

If the amount you are looking up from the worksheet is–		And your filing status is– **Single, head of household,** or **qualifying widow(er)** and the number of children you have is–				**Married filing jointly** and the number of children you have is–			
		0	1	2	3	0	1	2	3
At least	But less than	Your credit is–				Your credit is–			
5,600	**5,650**	430	1,913	2,250	2,531	430	1,913	2,250	2,531
5,650	**5,700**	434	1,930	2,270	2,554	434	1,930	2,270	2,554
5,700	**5,750**	438	1,947	2,290	2,576	438	1,947	2,290	2,576
5,750	**5,800**	442	1,964	2,310	2,599	442	1,964	2,310	2,599
5,800	**5,850**	446	1,981	2,330	2,621	446	1,981	2,330	2,621
5,850	**5,900**	449	1,998	2,350	2,644	449	1,998	2,350	2,644
5,900	**5,950**	453	2,015	2,370	2,666	453	2,015	2,370	2,666
5,950	**6,000**	457	2,032	2,390	2,689	457	2,032	2,390	2,689
6,000	**6,050**	461	2,049	2,410	2,711	461	2,049	2,410	2,711
6,050	**6,100**	465	2,066	2,430	2,734	465	2,066	2,430	2,734
6,100	**6,150**	469	2,083	2,450	2,756	469	2,083	2,450	2,756
6,150	**6,200**	472	2,100	2,470	2,779	472	2,100	2,470	2,779
6,200	**6,250**	476	2,117	2,490	2,801	476	2,117	2,490	2,801
6,250	**6,300**	480	2,134	2,510	2,824	480	2,134	2,510	2,824
6,300	**6,350**	484	2,151	2,530	2,846	484	2,151	2,530	2,846
6,350	**6,400**	488	2,168	2,550	2,869	488	2,168	2,550	2,869
6,400	**6,450**	492	2,185	2,570	2,891	492	2,185	2,570	2,891
6,450	**6,500**	495	2,202	2,590	2,914	495	2,202	2,590	2,914
6,500	**6,550**	499	2,219	2,610	2,936	499	2,219	2,610	2,936
6,550	**6,600**	503	2,236	2,630	2,959	503	2,236	2,630	2,959
6,600	**6,650**	503	2,253	2,650	2,981	503	2,253	2,650	2,981
6,650	**6,700**	503	2,270	2,670	3,004	503	2,270	2,670	3,004
6,700	**6,750**	503	2,287	2,690	3,026	503	2,287	2,690	3,026
6,750	**6,800**	503	2,304	2,710	3,049	503	2,304	2,710	3,049
6,800	**6,850**	503	2,321	2,730	3,071	503	2,321	2,730	3,071
6,850	**6,900**	503	2,338	2,750	3,094	503	2,338	2,750	3,094
6,900	**6,950**	503	2,355	2,770	3,116	503	2,355	2,770	3,116
6,950	**7,000**	503	2,372	2,790	3,139	503	2,372	2,790	3,139
7,000	**7,050**	503	2,389	2,810	3,161	503	2,389	2,810	3,161
7,050	**7,100**	503	2,406	2,830	3,184	503	2,406	2,830	3,184
7,100	**7,150**	503	2,423	2,850	3,206	503	2,423	2,850	3,206
7,150	**7,200**	503	2,440	2,870	3,229	503	2,440	2,870	3,229
7,200	**7,250**	503	2,457	2,890	3,251	503	2,457	2,890	3,251
7,250	**7,300**	503	2,474	2,910	3,274	503	2,474	2,910	3,274
7,300	**7,350**	503	2,491	2,930	3,296	503	2,491	2,930	3,296
7,350	**7,400**	503	2,508	2,950	3,319	503	2,508	2,950	3,319
7,400	**7,450**	503	2,525	2,970	3,341	503	2,525	2,970	3,341
7,450	**7,500**	503	2,542	2,990	3,364	503	2,542	2,990	3,364
7,500	**7,550**	503	2,559	3,010	3,386	503	2,559	3,010	3,386
7,550	**7,600**	503	2,576	3,030	3,409	503	2,576	3,030	3,409
7,600	**7,650**	503	2,593	3,050	3,431	503	2,593	3,050	3,431
7,650	**7,700**	503	2,610	3,070	3,454	503	2,610	3,070	3,454
7,700	**7,750**	503	2,627	3,090	3,476	503	2,627	3,090	3,476
7,750	**7,800**	503	2,644	3,110	3,499	503	2,644	3,110	3,499
7,800	**7,850**	503	2,661	3,130	3,521	503	2,661	3,130	3,521
7,850	**7,900**	503	2,678	3,150	3,544	503	2,678	3,150	3,544
7,900	**7,950**	503	2,695	3,170	3,566	503	2,695	3,170	3,566
7,950	**8,000**	503	2,712	3,190	3,589	503	2,712	3,190	3,589
8,000	**8,050**	503	2,729	3,210	3,611	503	2,729	3,210	3,611
8,050	**8,100**	503	2,746	3,230	3,634	503	2,746	3,230	3,634
8,100	**8,150**	503	2,763	3,250	3,656	503	2,763	3,250	3,656
8,150	**8,200**	503	2,780	3,270	3,679	503	2,780	3,270	3,679
8,200	**8,250**	503	2,797	3,290	3,701	503	2,797	3,290	3,701
8,250	**8,300**	501	2,814	3,310	3,724	503	2,814	3,310	3,724
8,300	**8,350**	497	2,831	3,330	3,746	503	2,831	3,330	3,746
8,350	**8,400**	493	2,848	3,350	3,769	503	2,848	3,350	3,769
8,400	**8,450**	489	2,865	3,370	3,791	503	2,865	3,370	3,791
8,450	**8,500**	485	2,882	3,390	3,814	503	2,882	3,390	3,814
8,500	**8,550**	482	2,899	3,410	3,836	503	2,899	3,410	3,836
8,550	**8,600**	478	2,916	3,430	3,859	503	2,916	3,430	3,859
8,600	**8,650**	474	2,933	3,450	3,881	503	2,933	3,450	3,881
8,650	**8,700**	470	2,950	3,470	3,904	503	2,950	3,470	3,904
8,700	**8,750**	466	2,967	3,490	3,926	503	2,967	3,490	3,926
8,750	**8,800**	462	2,984	3,510	3,949	503	2,984	3,510	3,949
8,800	**8,850**	459	3,001	3,530	3,971	503	3,001	3,530	3,971
8,850	**8,900**	455	3,018	3,550	3,994	503	3,018	3,550	3,994
8,900	**8,950**	451	3,035	3,570	4,016	503	3,035	3,570	4,016
8,950	**9,000**	447	3,052	3,590	4,039	503	3,052	3,590	4,039
9,000	**9,050**	443	3,069	3,610	4,061	503	3,069	3,610	4,061
9,050	**9,100**	439	3,086	3,630	4,084	503	3,086	3,630	4,084
9,100	**9,150**	436	3,103	3,650	4,106	503	3,103	3,650	4,106
9,150	**9,200**	432	3,120	3,670	4,129	503	3,120	3,670	4,129

If the amount you are looking up from the worksheet is–		And your filing status is– **Single, head of household,** or **qualifying widow(er)** and the number of children you have is–				**Married filing jointly** and the number of children you have is–			
		0	1	2	3	0	1	2	3
At least	But less than	Your credit is–				Your credit is–			
9,200	**9,250**	428	3,137	3,690	4,151	503	3,137	3,690	4,151
9,250	**9,300**	424	3,154	3,710	4,174	503	3,154	3,710	4,174
9,300	**9,350**	420	3,171	3,730	4,196	503	3,171	3,730	4,196
9,350	**9,400**	417	3,188	3,750	4,219	503	3,188	3,750	4,219
9,400	**9,450**	413	3,205	3,770	4,241	503	3,205	3,770	4,241
9,450	**9,500**	409	3,222	3,790	4,264	503	3,222	3,790	4,264
9,500	**9,550**	405	3,239	3,810	4,286	503	3,239	3,810	4,286
9,550	**9,600**	401	3,256	3,830	4,309	503	3,256	3,830	4,309
9,600	**9,650**	397	3,273	3,850	4,331	503	3,273	3,850	4,331
9,650	**9,700**	394	3,290	3,870	4,354	503	3,290	3,870	4,354
9,700	**9,750**	390	3,307	3,890	4,376	503	3,307	3,890	4,376
9,750	**9,800**	386	3,324	3,910	4,399	503	3,324	3,910	4,399
9,800	**9,850**	382	3,341	3,930	4,421	503	3,341	3,930	4,421
9,850	**9,900**	378	3,359	3,950	4,444	503	3,359	3,950	4,444
9,900	**9,950**	374	3,359	3,970	4,466	503	3,359	3,970	4,466
9,950	**10,000**	371	3,359	3,990	4,489	503	3,359	3,990	4,489
10,000	**10,050**	367	3,359	4,010	4,511	503	3,359	4,010	4,511
10,050	**10,100**	363	3,359	4,030	4,534	503	3,359	4,030	4,534
10,100	**10,150**	359	3,359	4,050	4,556	503	3,359	4,050	4,556
10,150	**10,200**	355	3,359	4,070	4,579	503	3,359	4,070	4,579
10,200	**10,250**	352	3,359	4,090	4,601	503	3,359	4,090	4,601
10,250	**10,300**	348	3,359	4,110	4,624	503	3,359	4,110	4,624
10,300	**10,350**	344	3,359	4,130	4,646	503	3,359	4,130	4,646
10,350	**10,400**	340	3,359	4,150	4,669	503	3,359	4,150	4,669
10,400	**10,450**	336	3,359	4,170	4,691	503	3,359	4,170	4,691
10,450	**10,500**	332	3,359	4,190	4,714	503	3,359	4,190	4,714
10,500	**10,550**	329	3,359	4,210	4,736	503	3,359	4,210	4,736
10,550	**10,600**	325	3,359	4,230	4,759	503	3,359	4,230	4,759
10,600	**10,650**	321	3,359	4,250	4,781	503	3,359	4,250	4,781
10,650	**10,700**	317	3,359	4,270	4,804	503	3,359	4,270	4,804
10,700	**10,750**	313	3,359	4,290	4,826	503	3,359	4,290	4,826
10,750	**10,800**	309	3,359	4,310	4,849	503	3,359	4,310	4,849
10,800	**10,850**	306	3,359	4,330	4,871	503	3,359	4,330	4,871
10,850	**10,900**	302	3,359	4,350	4,894	503	3,359	4,350	4,894
10,900	**10,950**	298	3,359	4,370	4,916	503	3,359	4,370	4,916
10,950	**11,000**	294	3,359	4,390	4,939	503	3,359	4,390	4,939
11,000	**11,050**	290	3,359	4,410	4,961	503	3,359	4,410	4,961
11,050	**11,100**	286	3,359	4,430	4,984	503	3,359	4,430	4,984
11,100	**11,150**	283	3,359	4,450	5,006	503	3,359	4,450	5,006
11,150	**11,200**	279	3,359	4,470	5,029	503	3,359	4,470	5,029
11,200	**11,250**	275	3,359	4,490	5,051	503	3,359	4,490	5,051
11,250	**11,300**	271	3,359	4,510	5,074	503	3,359	4,510	5,074
11,300	**11,350**	267	3,359	4,530	5,096	503	3,359	4,530	5,096
11,350	**11,400**	264	3,359	4,550	5,119	503	3,359	4,550	5,119
11,400	**11,450**	260	3,359	4,570	5,141	503	3,359	4,570	5,141
11,450	**11,500**	256	3,359	4,590	5,164	503	3,359	4,590	5,164
11,500	**11,550**	252	3,359	4,610	5,186	503	3,359	4,610	5,186
11,550	**11,600**	248	3,359	4,630	5,209	503	3,359	4,630	5,209
11,600	**11,650**	244	3,359	4,650	5,231	503	3,359	4,650	5,231
11,650	**11,700**	241	3,359	4,670	5,254	503	3,359	4,670	5,254
11,700	**11,750**	237	3,359	4,690	5,276	503	3,359	4,690	5,276
11,750	**11,800**	233	3,359	4,710	5,299	503	3,359	4,710	5,299
11,800	**11,850**	229	3,359	4,730	5,321	503	3,359	4,730	5,321
11,850	**11,900**	225	3,359	4,750	5,344	503	3,359	4,750	5,344
11,900	**11,950**	221	3,359	4,770	5,366	503	3,359	4,770	5,366
11,950	**12,000**	218	3,359	4,790	5,389	503	3,359	4,790	5,389
12,000	**12,050**	214	3,359	4,810	5,411	503	3,359	4,810	5,411
12,050	**12,100**	210	3,359	4,830	5,434	503	3,359	4,830	5,434
12,100	**12,150**	206	3,359	4,850	5,456	503	3,359	4,850	5,456
12,150	**12,200**	202	3,359	4,870	5,479	503	3,359	4,870	5,479
12,200	**12,250**	199	3,359	4,890	5,501	503	3,359	4,890	5,501
12,250	**12,300**	195	3,359	4,910	5,524	503	3,359	4,910	5,524
12,300	**12,350**	191	3,359	4,930	5,546	503	3,359	4,930	5,546
12,350	**12,400**	187	3,359	4,950	5,569	503	3,359	4,950	5,569
12,400	**12,450**	183	3,359	4,970	5,591	503	3,359	4,970	5,591
12,450	**12,500**	179	3,359	4,990	5,614	503	3,359	4,990	5,614
12,500	**12,550**	176	3,359	5,010	5,636	503	3,359	5,010	5,636
12,550	**12,600**	172	3,359	5,030	5,659	503	3,359	5,030	5,659
12,600	**12,650**	168	3,359	5,050	5,681	503	3,359	5,050	5,681
12,650	**12,700**	164	3,359	5,070	5,704	503	3,359	5,070	5,704
12,700	**12,750**	160	3,359	5,090	5,726	503	3,359	5,090	5,726
12,750	**12,800**	156	3,359	5,110	5,749	503	3,359	5,110	5,749

(Continued)

If the amount you are looking up from the worksheet is—		Single, head of household, or qualifying widow(er) and the number of children you have is—				Married filing jointly and the number of children you have is—			
At least	But less than	0	1	2	3	0	1	2	3
		Your credit is—				Your credit is—			
12,800	12,850	153	3,359	5,130	5,771	503	3,359	5,130	5,771
12,850	12,900	149	3,359	5,150	5,794	503	3,359	5,150	5,794
12,900	12,950	145	3,359	5,170	5,816	503	3,359	5,170	5,816
12,950	13,000	141	3,359	5,190	5,839	503	3,359	5,190	5,839
13,000	13,050	137	3,359	5,210	5,861	503	3,359	5,210	5,861
13,050	13,100	133	3,359	5,230	5,884	503	3,359	5,230	5,884
13,100	13,150	130	3,359	5,250	5,906	503	3,359	5,250	5,906
13,150	13,200	126	3,359	5,270	5,929	503	3,359	5,270	5,929
13,200	13,250	122	3,359	5,290	5,951	503	3,359	5,290	5,951
13,250	13,300	118	3,359	5,310	5,974	503	3,359	5,310	5,974
13,300	13,350	114	3,359	5,330	5,996	503	3,359	5,330	5,996
13,350	13,400	111	3,359	5,350	6,019	503	3,359	5,350	6,019
13,400	13,450	107	3,359	5,370	6,041	503	3,359	5,370	6,041
13,450	13,500	103	3,359	5,390	6,064	503	3,359	5,390	6,064
13,500	13,550	99	3,359	5,410	6,086	503	3,359	5,410	6,086
13,550	13,600	95	3,359	5,430	6,109	503	3,359	5,430	6,109
13,600	13,650	91	3,359	5,450	6,131	503	3,359	5,450	6,131
13,650	13,700	88	3,359	5,470	6,154	503	3,359	5,470	6,154
13,700	13,750	84	3,359	5,490	6,176	503	3,359	5,490	6,176
13,750	13,800	80	3,359	5,510	6,199	501	3,359	5,510	6,199
13,800	13,850	76	3,359	5,530	6,221	498	3,359	5,530	6,221
13,850	13,900	72	3,359	5,548	6,242	494	3,359	5,548	6,242
13,900	13,950	68	3,359	5,548	6,242	490	3,359	5,548	6,242
13,950	14,000	65	3,359	5,548	6,242	486	3,359	5,548	6,242
14,000	14,050	61	3,359	5,548	6,242	482	3,359	5,548	6,242
14,050	14,100	57	3,359	5,548	6,242	479	3,359	5,548	6,242
14,100	14,150	53	3,359	5,548	6,242	475	3,359	5,548	6,242
14,150	14,200	49	3,359	5,548	6,242	471	3,359	5,548	6,242
14,200	14,250	46	3,359	5,548	6,242	467	3,359	5,548	6,242
14,250	14,300	42	3,359	5,548	6,242	463	3,359	5,548	6,242
14,300	14,350	38	3,359	5,548	6,242	459	3,359	5,548	6,242
14,350	14,400	34	3,359	5,548	6,242	456	3,359	5,548	6,242
14,400	14,450	30	3,359	5,548	6,242	452	3,359	5,548	6,242
14,450	14,500	26	3,359	5,548	6,242	448	3,359	5,548	6,242
14,500	14,550	23	3,359	5,548	6,242	444	3,359	5,548	6,242
14,550	14,600	19	3,359	5,548	6,242	440	3,359	5,548	6,242
14,600	14,650	15	3,359	5,548	6,242	436	3,359	5,548	6,242
14,650	14,700	11	3,359	5,548	6,242	433	3,359	5,548	6,242
14,700	14,750	7	3,359	5,548	6,242	429	3,359	5,548	6,242
14,750	14,800	3	3,359	5,548	6,242	425	3,359	5,548	6,242
14,800	14,850	*	3,359	5,548	6,242	421	3,359	5,548	6,242
14,850	14,900	0	3,359	5,548	6,242	417	3,359	5,548	6,242
14,900	14,950	0	3,359	5,548	6,242	413	3,359	5,548	6,242
14,950	15,000	0	3,359	5,548	6,242	410	3,359	5,548	6,242
15,000	15,050	0	3,359	5,548	6,242	406	3,359	5,548	6,242
15,050	15,100	0	3,359	5,548	6,242	402	3,359	5,548	6,242
15,100	15,150	0	3,359	5,548	6,242	398	3,359	5,548	6,242
15,150	15,200	0	3,359	5,548	6,242	394	3,359	5,548	6,242
15,200	15,250	0	3,359	5,548	6,242	391	3,359	5,548	6,242
15,250	15,300	0	3,359	5,548	6,242	387	3,359	5,548	6,242
15,300	15,350	0	3,359	5,548	6,242	383	3,359	5,548	6,242
15,350	15,400	0	3,359	5,548	6,242	379	3,359	5,548	6,242
15,400	15,450	0	3,359	5,548	6,242	375	3,359	5,548	6,242
15,450	15,500	0	3,359	5,548	6,242	371	3,359	5,548	6,242
15,500	15,550	0	3,359	5,548	6,242	368	3,359	5,548	6,242
15,550	15,600	0	3,359	5,548	6,242	364	3,359	5,548	6,242
15,600	15,650	0	3,359	5,548	6,242	360	3,359	5,548	6,242
15,650	15,700	0	3,359	5,548	6,242	356	3,359	5,548	6,242
15,700	15,750	0	3,359	5,548	6,242	352	3,359	5,548	6,242
15,750	15,800	0	3,359	5,548	6,242	348	3,359	5,548	6,242
15,800	15,850	0	3,359	5,548	6,242	345	3,359	5,548	6,242
15,850	15,900	0	3,359	5,548	6,242	341	3,359	5,548	6,242
15,900	15,950	0	3,359	5,548	6,242	337	3,359	5,548	6,242
15,950	16,000	0	3,359	5,548	6,242	333	3,359	5,548	6,242
16,000	16,050	0	3,359	5,548	6,242	329	3,359	5,548	6,242
16,050	16,100	0	3,359	5,548	6,242	326	3,359	5,548	6,242
16,100	16,150	0	3,359	5,548	6,242	322	3,359	5,548	6,242
16,150	16,200	0	3,359	5,548	6,242	318	3,359	5,548	6,242
16,200	16,250	0	3,359	5,548	6,242	314	3,359	5,548	6,242
16,250	16,300	0	3,359	5,548	6,242	310	3,359	5,548	6,242
16,300	16,350	0	3,359	5,548	6,242	306	3,359	5,548	6,242
16,350	16,400	0	3,359	5,548	6,242	303	3,359	5,548	6,242
16,400	16,450	0	3,359	5,548	6,242	299	3,359	5,548	6,242
16,450	16,500	0	3,359	5,548	6,242	295	3,359	5,548	6,242
16,500	16,550	0	3,359	5,548	6,242	291	3,359	5,548	6,242
16,550	16,600	0	3,359	5,548	6,242	287	3,359	5,548	6,242
16,600	16,650	0	3,359	5,548	6,242	283	3,359	5,548	6,242
16,650	16,700	0	3,359	5,548	6,242	280	3,359	5,548	6,242
16,700	16,750	0	3,359	5,548	6,242	276	3,359	5,548	6,242
16,750	16,800	0	3,359	5,548	6,242	272	3,359	5,548	6,242
16,800	16,850	0	3,359	5,548	6,242	268	3,359	5,548	6,242
16,850	16,900	0	3,359	5,548	6,242	264	3,359	5,548	6,242
16,900	16,950	0	3,359	5,548	6,242	260	3,359	5,548	6,242
16,950	17,000	0	3,359	5,548	6,242	257	3,359	5,548	6,242
17,000	17,050	0	3,359	5,548	6,242	253	3,359	5,548	6,242
17,050	17,100	0	3,359	5,548	6,242	249	3,359	5,548	6,242
17,100	17,150	0	3,359	5,548	6,242	245	3,359	5,548	6,242
17,150	17,200	0	3,359	5,548	6,242	241	3,359	5,548	6,242
17,200	17,250	0	3,359	5,548	6,242	238	3,359	5,548	6,242
17,250	17,300	0	3,359	5,548	6,242	234	3,359	5,548	6,242
17,300	17,350	0	3,359	5,548	6,242	230	3,359	5,548	6,242
17,350	17,400	0	3,359	5,548	6,242	226	3,359	5,548	6,242
17,400	17,450	0	3,359	5,548	6,242	222	3,359	5,548	6,242
17,450	17,500	0	3,359	5,548	6,242	218	3,359	5,548	6,242
17,500	17,550	0	3,359	5,548	6,242	215	3,359	5,548	6,242
17,550	17,600	0	3,359	5,548	6,242	211	3,359	5,548	6,242
17,600	17,650	0	3,359	5,548	6,242	207	3,359	5,548	6,242
17,650	17,700	0	3,359	5,548	6,242	203	3,359	5,548	6,242
17,700	17,750	0	3,359	5,548	6,242	199	3,359	5,548	6,242
17,750	17,800	0	3,359	5,548	6,242	195	3,359	5,548	6,242
17,800	17,850	0	3,359	5,548	6,242	192	3,359	5,548	6,242
17,850	17,900	0	3,359	5,548	6,242	188	3,359	5,548	6,242
17,900	17,950	0	3,359	5,548	6,242	184	3,359	5,548	6,242
17,950	18,000	0	3,359	5,548	6,242	180	3,359	5,548	6,242
18,000	18,050	0	3,359	5,548	6,242	176	3,359	5,548	6,242
18,050	18,100	0	3,359	5,548	6,242	173	3,359	5,548	6,242
18,100	18,150	0	3,359	5,548	6,242	169	3,359	5,548	6,242
18,150	18,200	0	3,349	5,534	6,228	165	3,359	5,548	6,242
18,200	18,250	0	3,341	5,524	6,217	161	3,359	5,548	6,242
18,250	18,300	0	3,333	5,513	6,207	157	3,359	5,548	6,242
18,300	18,350	0	3,325	5,503	6,196	153	3,359	5,548	6,242
18,350	18,400	0	3,317	5,492	6,186	150	3,359	5,548	6,242
18,400	18,450	0	3,309	5,482	6,175	146	3,359	5,548	6,242
18,450	18,500	0	3,301	5,471	6,165	142	3,359	5,548	6,242
18,500	18,550	0	3,293	5,461	6,154	138	3,359	5,548	6,242
18,550	18,600	0	3,285	5,450	6,144	134	3,359	5,548	6,242
18,600	18,650	0	3,277	5,440	6,133	130	3,359	5,548	6,242
18,650	18,700	0	3,269	5,429	6,123	127	3,359	5,548	6,242
18,700	18,750	0	3,261	5,418	6,112	123	3,359	5,548	6,242
18,750	18,800	0	3,253	5,408	6,101	119	3,359	5,548	6,242
18,800	18,850	0	3,245	5,397	6,091	115	3,359	5,548	6,242
18,850	18,900	0	3,237	5,387	6,080	111	3,359	5,548	6,242
18,900	18,950	0	3,229	5,376	6,070	107	3,359	5,548	6,242
18,950	19,000	0	3,221	5,366	6,059	104	3,359	5,548	6,242
19,000	19,050	0	3,213	5,355	6,049	100	3,359	5,548	6,242
19,050	19,100	0	3,205	5,345	6,038	96	3,359	5,548	6,242
19,100	19,150	0	3,197	5,334	6,028	92	3,359	5,548	6,242
19,150	19,200	0	3,189	5,324	6,017	88	3,359	5,548	6,242

* If the amount you are looking up from the worksheet is at least $14,800 but less than $14,820, and you have no qualifying children, your credit is $1. If the amount you are looking up from the worksheet is $14,820 or more, and you have no qualifying children, you can't take the credit.

(Continued)

Need more information or forms? Visit IRS.gov.

Earned Income Credit (EIC) Table - Continued

(**Caution.** This is **not** a tax table.)

If the amount you are looking up from the worksheet is—		Single, head of household, or qualifying widow(er) and the number of children you have is—				Married filing jointly and the number of children you have is—			
At least	But less than	0	1	2	3	0	1	2	3
		Your credit is—				Your credit is—			
19,200	19,250	0	3,181	5,313	6,007	85	3,359	5,548	6,242
19,250	19,300	0	3,173	5,303	5,996	81	3,359	5,548	6,242
19,300	19,350	0	3,165	5,292	5,986	77	3,359	5,548	6,242
19,350	19,400	0	3,157	5,282	5,975	73	3,359	5,548	6,242
19,400	19,450	0	3,149	5,271	5,965	69	3,359	5,548	6,242
19,450	19,500	0	3,141	5,261	5,954	65	3,359	5,548	6,242
19,500	19,550	0	3,133	5,250	5,944	62	3,359	5,548	6,242
19,550	19,600	0	3,125	5,239	5,933	58	3,359	5,548	6,242
19,600	19,650	0	3,117	5,229	5,922	54	3,359	5,548	6,242
19,650	19,700	0	3,109	5,218	5,912	50	3,359	5,548	6,242
19,700	19,750	0	3,101	5,208	5,901	46	3,359	5,548	6,242
19,750	19,800	0	3,093	5,197	5,891	42	3,359	5,548	6,242
19,800	19,850	0	3,085	5,187	5,880	39	3,359	5,548	6,242
19,850	19,900	0	3,077	5,176	5,870	35	3,359	5,548	6,242
19,900	19,950	0	3,069	5,166	5,859	31	3,359	5,548	6,242
19,950	20,000	0	3,061	5,155	5,849	27	3,359	5,548	6,242
20,000	20,050	0	3,053	5,145	5,838	23	3,359	5,548	6,242
20,050	20,100	0	3,045	5,134	5,828	20	3,359	5,548	6,242
20,100	20,150	0	3,037	5,124	5,817	16	3,359	5,548	6,242
20,150	20,200	0	3,029	5,113	5,807	12	3,359	5,548	6,242
20,200	20,250	0	3,021	5,103	5,796	8	3,359	5,548	6,242
20,250	20,300	0	3,013	5,092	5,786	4	3,359	5,548	6,242
20,300	20,350	0	3,005	5,082	5,775	*	3,359	5,548	6,242
20,350	20,400	0	2,997	5,071	5,764	0	3,359	5,548	6,242
20,400	20,450	0	2,989	5,060	5,754	0	3,359	5,548	6,242
20,450	20,500	0	2,981	5,050	5,743	0	3,359	5,548	6,242
20,500	20,550	0	2,973	5,039	5,733	0	3,359	5,548	6,242
20,550	20,600	0	2,965	5,029	5,722	0	3,359	5,548	6,242
20,600	20,650	0	2,957	5,018	5,712	0	3,359	5,548	6,242
20,650	20,700	0	2,949	5,008	5,701	0	3,359	5,548	6,242
20,700	20,750	0	2,941	4,997	5,691	0	3,359	5,548	6,242
20,750	20,800	0	2,933	4,987	5,680	0	3,359	5,548	6,242
20,800	20,850	0	2,925	4,976	5,670	0	3,359	5,548	6,242
20,850	20,900	0	2,917	4,966	5,659	0	3,359	5,548	6,242
20,900	20,950	0	2,909	4,955	5,649	0	3,359	5,548	6,242
20,950	21,000	0	2,901	4,945	5,638	0	3,359	5,548	6,242
21,000	21,050	0	2,893	4,934	5,628	0	3,359	5,548	6,242
21,050	21,100	0	2,885	4,924	5,617	0	3,359	5,548	6,242
21,100	21,150	0	2,877	4,913	5,607	0	3,359	5,548	6,242
21,150	21,200	0	2,869	4,903	5,596	0	3,359	5,548	6,242
21,200	21,250	0	2,861	4,892	5,585	0	3,359	5,548	6,242
21,250	21,300	0	2,853	4,881	5,575	0	3,359	5,548	6,242
21,300	21,350	0	2,845	4,871	5,564	0	3,359	5,548	6,242
21,350	21,400	0	2,837	4,860	5,554	0	3,359	5,548	6,242
21,400	21,450	0	2,829	4,850	5,543	0	3,359	5,548	6,242
21,450	21,500	0	2,821	4,839	5,533	0	3,359	5,548	6,242
21,500	21,550	0	2,813	4,829	5,522	0	3,359	5,548	6,242
21,550	21,600	0	2,805	4,818	5,512	0	3,359	5,548	6,242
21,600	21,650	0	2,798	4,808	5,501	0	3,359	5,548	6,242
21,650	21,700	0	2,790	4,797	5,491	0	3,359	5,548	6,242
21,700	21,750	0	2,782	4,787	5,480	0	3,359	5,548	6,242
21,750	21,800	0	2,774	4,776	5,470	0	3,359	5,548	6,242
21,800	21,850	0	2,766	4,766	5,459	0	3,359	5,548	6,242
21,850	21,900	0	2,758	4,755	5,449	0	3,359	5,548	6,242
21,900	21,950	0	2,750	4,745	5,438	0	3,359	5,548	6,242
21,950	22,000	0	2,742	4,734	5,428	0	3,359	5,548	6,242
22,000	22,050	0	2,734	4,724	5,417	0	3,359	5,548	6,242
22,050	22,100	0	2,726	4,713	5,406	0	3,359	5,548	6,242
22,100	22,150	0	2,718	4,702	5,396	0	3,359	5,548	6,242
22,150	22,200	0	2,710	4,692	5,385	0	3,359	5,548	6,242
22,200	22,250	0	2,702	4,681	5,375	0	3,359	5,548	6,242
22,250	22,300	0	2,694	4,671	5,364	0	3,359	5,548	6,242
22,300	22,350	0	2,686	4,660	5,354	0	3,359	5,548	6,242
22,350	22,400	0	2,678	4,650	5,343	0	3,359	5,548	6,242
22,400	22,450	0	2,670	4,639	5,333	0	3,359	5,548	6,242
22,450	22,500	0	2,662	4,629	5,322	0	3,359	5,548	6,242
22,500	22,550	0	2,654	4,618	5,312	0	3,359	5,548	6,242
22,550	22,600	0	2,646	4,608	5,301	0	3,359	5,548	6,242
22,600	22,650	0	2,638	4,597	5,291	0	3,359	5,548	6,242
22,650	22,700	0	2,630	4,587	5,280	0	3,359	5,548	6,242
22,700	22,750	0	2,622	4,576	5,270	0	3,359	5,548	6,242
22,750	22,800	0	2,614	4,566	5,259	0	3,359	5,548	6,242
22,800	22,850	0	2,606	4,555	5,249	0	3,359	5,548	6,242
22,850	22,900	0	2,598	4,544	5,238	0	3,359	5,548	6,242
22,900	22,950	0	2,590	4,534	5,227	0	3,359	5,548	6,242
22,950	23,000	0	2,582	4,523	5,217	0	3,359	5,548	6,242
23,000	23,050	0	2,574	4,513	5,206	0	3,359	5,548	6,242
23,050	23,100	0	2,566	4,502	5,196	0	3,359	5,548	6,242
23,100	23,150	0	2,558	4,492	5,185	0	3,359	5,548	6,242
23,150	23,200	0	2,550	4,481	5,175	0	3,359	5,548	6,242
23,200	23,250	0	2,542	4,471	5,164	0	3,359	5,548	6,242
23,250	23,300	0	2,534	4,460	5,154	0	3,359	5,548	6,242
23,300	23,350	0	2,526	4,450	5,143	0	3,359	5,548	6,242
23,350	23,400	0	2,518	4,439	5,133	0	3,359	5,548	6,242
23,400	23,450	0	2,510	4,429	5,122	0	3,359	5,548	6,242
23,450	23,500	0	2,502	4,418	5,112	0	3,359	5,548	6,242
23,500	23,550	0	2,494	4,408	5,101	0	3,359	5,548	6,242
23,550	23,600	0	2,486	4,397	5,091	0	3,359	5,548	6,242
23,600	23,650	0	2,478	4,387	5,080	0	3,359	5,548	6,242
23,650	23,700	0	2,470	4,376	5,070	0	3,352	5,539	6,232
23,700	23,750	0	2,462	4,365	5,059	0	3,344	5,528	6,221
23,750	23,800	0	2,454	4,355	5,048	0	3,336	5,517	6,211
23,800	23,850	0	2,446	4,344	5,038	0	3,328	5,507	6,200
23,850	23,900	0	2,438	4,334	5,027	0	3,320	5,496	6,190
23,900	23,950	0	2,430	4,323	5,017	0	3,312	5,486	6,179
23,950	24,000	0	2,422	4,313	5,006	0	3,304	5,475	6,169
24,000	24,050	0	2,414	4,302	4,996	0	3,296	5,465	6,158
24,050	24,100	0	2,406	4,292	4,985	0	3,288	5,454	6,148
24,100	24,150	0	2,398	4,281	4,975	0	3,280	5,444	6,137
24,150	24,200	0	2,390	4,271	4,964	0	3,272	5,433	6,127
24,200	24,250	0	2,382	4,260	4,954	0	3,264	5,423	6,116
24,250	24,300	0	2,374	4,250	4,943	0	3,256	5,412	6,106
24,300	24,350	0	2,366	4,239	4,933	0	3,248	5,402	6,095
24,350	24,400	0	2,358	4,229	4,922	0	3,240	5,391	6,085
24,400	24,450	0	2,350	4,218	4,912	0	3,232	5,381	6,074
24,450	24,500	0	2,342	4,208	4,901	0	3,224	5,370	6,064
24,500	24,550	0	2,334	4,197	4,891	0	3,216	5,360	6,053
24,550	24,600	0	2,326	4,186	4,880	0	3,208	5,349	6,042
24,600	24,650	0	2,318	4,176	4,869	0	3,200	5,338	6,032
24,650	24,700	0	2,310	4,165	4,859	0	3,192	5,328	6,021
24,700	24,750	0	2,302	4,155	4,848	0	3,184	5,317	6,011
24,750	24,800	0	2,294	4,144	4,838	0	3,176	5,307	6,000
24,800	24,850	0	2,286	4,134	4,827	0	3,168	5,296	5,990
24,850	24,900	0	2,278	4,123	4,817	0	3,160	5,286	5,979
24,900	24,950	0	2,270	4,113	4,806	0	3,152	5,275	5,969
24,950	25,000	0	2,262	4,102	4,796	0	3,144	5,265	5,958
25,000	25,050	0	2,254	4,092	4,785	0	3,136	5,254	5,948
25,050	25,100	0	2,246	4,081	4,775	0	3,128	5,244	5,937
25,100	25,150	0	2,238	4,071	4,764	0	3,120	5,233	5,927
25,150	25,200	0	2,230	4,060	4,754	0	3,112	5,223	5,916
25,200	25,250	0	2,222	4,050	4,743	0	3,104	5,212	5,906
25,250	25,300	0	2,214	4,039	4,733	0	3,096	5,202	5,895
25,300	25,350	0	2,206	4,029	4,722	0	3,088	5,191	5,885
25,350	25,400	0	2,198	4,018	4,711	0	3,080	5,181	5,874
25,400	25,450	0	2,190	4,007	4,701	0	3,072	5,170	5,863
25,450	25,500	0	2,182	3,997	4,690	0	3,064	5,159	5,853
25,500	25,550	0	2,174	3,986	4,680	0	3,056	5,149	5,842
25,550	25,600	0	2,166	3,976	4,669	0	3,048	5,138	5,832

* If the amount you are looking up from the worksheet is at least $20,300 but less than $20,330, and you have no qualifying children, your credit is $1. If the amount you are looking up from the worksheet is $20,330 or more, and you have no qualifying children, you can't take the credit.

(Continued)

If the amount you are looking up from the worksheet is—		Single, head of household, or qualifying widow(er) and the number of children you have is—				Married filing jointly and the number of children you have is—			
At least	But less than	0	1	2	3	0	1	2	3
25,600	25,650	0	2,158	3,965	4,659	0	3,040	5,128	5,821
25,650	25,700	0	2,150	3,955	4,648	0	3,032	5,117	5,811
25,700	25,750	0	2,142	3,944	4,638	0	3,024	5,107	5,800
25,750	25,800	0	2,134	3,934	4,627	0	3,016	5,096	5,790
25,800	25,850	0	2,126	3,923	4,617	0	3,008	5,086	5,779
25,850	25,900	0	2,118	3,913	4,606	0	3,000	5,075	5,769
25,900	25,950	0	2,110	3,902	4,596	0	2,992	5,065	5,758
25,950	26,000	0	2,102	3,892	4,585	0	2,984	5,054	5,748
26,000	26,050	0	2,094	3,881	4,575	0	2,976	5,044	5,737
26,050	26,100	0	2,086	3,871	4,564	0	2,968	5,033	5,727
26,100	26,150	0	2,078	3,860	4,554	0	2,960	5,023	5,716
26,150	26,200	0	2,070	3,850	4,543	0	2,953	5,012	5,706
26,200	26,250	0	2,062	3,839	4,532	0	2,945	5,001	5,695
26,250	26,300	0	2,054	3,828	4,522	0	2,937	4,991	5,684
26,300	26,350	0	2,046	3,818	4,511	0	2,929	4,980	5,674
26,350	26,400	0	2,038	3,807	4,501	0	2,921	4,970	5,663
26,400	26,450	0	2,030	3,797	4,490	0	2,913	4,959	5,653
26,450	26,500	0	2,022	3,786	4,480	0	2,905	4,949	5,642
26,500	26,550	0	2,014	3,776	4,469	0	2,897	4,938	5,632
26,550	26,600	0	2,006	3,765	4,459	0	2,889	4,928	5,621
26,600	26,650	0	1,999	3,755	4,448	0	2,881	4,917	5,611
26,650	26,700	0	1,991	3,744	4,438	0	2,873	4,907	5,600
26,700	26,750	0	1,983	3,734	4,427	0	2,865	4,896	5,590
26,750	26,800	0	1,975	3,723	4,417	0	2,857	4,886	5,579
26,800	26,850	0	1,967	3,713	4,406	0	2,849	4,875	5,569
26,850	26,900	0	1,959	3,702	4,396	0	2,841	4,865	5,558
26,900	26,950	0	1,951	3,692	4,385	0	2,833	4,854	5,548
26,950	27,000	0	1,943	3,681	4,375	0	2,825	4,844	5,537
27,000	27,050	0	1,935	3,671	4,364	0	2,817	4,833	5,527
27,050	27,100	0	1,927	3,660	4,353	0	2,809	4,822	5,516
27,100	27,150	0	1,919	3,649	4,343	0	2,801	4,812	5,505
27,150	27,200	0	1,911	3,639	4,332	0	2,793	4,801	5,495
27,200	27,250	0	1,903	3,628	4,322	0	2,785	4,791	5,484
27,250	27,300	0	1,895	3,618	4,311	0	2,777	4,780	5,474
27,300	27,350	0	1,887	3,607	4,301	0	2,769	4,770	5,463
27,350	27,400	0	1,879	3,597	4,290	0	2,761	4,759	5,453
27,400	27,450	0	1,871	3,586	4,280	0	2,753	4,749	5,442
27,450	27,500	0	1,863	3,576	4,269	0	2,745	4,738	5,432
27,500	27,550	0	1,855	3,565	4,259	0	2,737	4,728	5,421
27,550	27,600	0	1,847	3,555	4,248	0	2,729	4,717	5,411
27,600	27,650	0	1,839	3,544	4,238	0	2,721	4,707	5,400
27,650	27,700	0	1,831	3,534	4,227	0	2,713	4,696	5,390
27,700	27,750	0	1,823	3,523	4,217	0	2,705	4,686	5,379
27,750	27,800	0	1,815	3,513	4,206	0	2,697	4,675	5,369
27,800	27,850	0	1,807	3,502	4,196	0	2,689	4,665	5,358
27,850	27,900	0	1,799	3,491	4,185	0	2,681	4,654	5,348
27,900	27,950	0	1,791	3,481	4,174	0	2,673	4,643	5,337
27,950	28,000	0	1,783	3,470	4,164	0	2,665	4,633	5,326
28,000	28,050	0	1,775	3,460	4,153	0	2,657	4,622	5,316
28,050	28,100	0	1,767	3,449	4,143	0	2,649	4,612	5,305
28,100	28,150	0	1,759	3,439	4,132	0	2,641	4,601	5,295
28,150	28,200	0	1,751	3,428	4,122	0	2,633	4,591	5,284
28,200	28,250	0	1,743	3,418	4,111	0	2,625	4,580	5,274
28,250	28,300	0	1,735	3,407	4,101	0	2,617	4,570	5,263
28,300	28,350	0	1,727	3,397	4,090	0	2,609	4,559	5,253
28,350	28,400	0	1,719	3,386	4,080	0	2,601	4,549	5,242
28,400	28,450	0	1,711	3,376	4,069	0	2,593	4,538	5,232
28,450	28,500	0	1,703	3,365	4,059	0	2,585	4,528	5,221
28,500	28,550	0	1,695	3,355	4,048	0	2,577	4,517	5,211
28,550	28,600	0	1,687	3,344	4,038	0	2,569	4,507	5,200
28,600	28,650	0	1,679	3,334	4,027	0	2,561	4,496	5,190
28,650	28,700	0	1,671	3,323	4,017	0	2,553	4,486	5,179
28,700	28,750	0	1,663	3,312	4,006	0	2,545	4,475	5,168
28,750	28,800	0	1,655	3,302	3,995	0	2,537	4,464	5,158
28,800	28,850	0	1,647	3,291	3,985	0	2,529	4,454	5,147
28,850	28,900	0	1,639	3,281	3,974	0	2,521	4,443	5,137
28,900	28,950	0	1,631	3,270	3,964	0	2,513	4,433	5,126
28,950	29,000	0	1,623	3,260	3,953	0	2,505	4,422	5,116
29,000	29,050	0	1,615	3,249	3,943	0	2,497	4,412	5,105
29,050	29,100	0	1,607	3,239	3,932	0	2,489	4,401	5,095
29,100	29,150	0	1,599	3,228	3,922	0	2,481	4,391	5,084
29,150	29,200	0	1,591	3,218	3,911	0	2,473	4,380	5,074
29,200	29,250	0	1,583	3,207	3,901	0	2,465	4,370	5,063
29,250	29,300	0	1,575	3,197	3,890	0	2,457	4,359	5,053
29,300	29,350	0	1,567	3,186	3,880	0	2,449	4,349	5,042
29,350	29,400	0	1,559	3,176	3,869	0	2,441	4,338	5,032
29,400	29,450	0	1,551	3,165	3,859	0	2,433	4,328	5,021
29,450	29,500	0	1,543	3,155	3,848	0	2,425	4,317	5,011
29,500	29,550	0	1,535	3,144	3,838	0	2,417	4,307	5,000
29,550	29,600	0	1,527	3,133	3,827	0	2,409	4,296	4,989
29,600	29,650	0	1,519	3,123	3,816	0	2,401	4,285	4,979
29,650	29,700	0	1,511	3,112	3,806	0	2,393	4,275	4,968
29,700	29,750	0	1,503	3,102	3,795	0	2,385	4,264	4,958
29,750	29,800	0	1,495	3,091	3,785	0	2,377	4,254	4,947
29,800	29,850	0	1,487	3,081	3,774	0	2,369	4,243	4,937
29,850	29,900	0	1,479	3,070	3,764	0	2,361	4,233	4,926
29,900	29,950	0	1,471	3,060	3,753	0	2,353	4,222	4,916
29,950	30,000	0	1,463	3,049	3,743	0	2,345	4,212	4,905
30,000	30,050	0	1,455	3,039	3,732	0	2,337	4,201	4,895
30,050	30,100	0	1,447	3,028	3,722	0	2,329	4,191	4,884
30,100	30,150	0	1,439	3,018	3,711	0	2,321	4,180	4,874
30,150	30,200	0	1,431	3,007	3,701	0	2,313	4,170	4,863
30,200	30,250	0	1,423	2,997	3,690	0	2,305	4,159	4,853
30,250	30,300	0	1,415	2,986	3,680	0	2,297	4,149	4,842
30,300	30,350	0	1,407	2,976	3,669	0	2,289	4,138	4,832
30,350	30,400	0	1,399	2,965	3,658	0	2,281	4,128	4,821
30,400	30,450	0	1,391	2,954	3,648	0	2,273	4,117	4,810
30,450	30,500	0	1,383	2,944	3,637	0	2,265	4,106	4,800
30,500	30,550	0	1,375	2,933	3,627	0	2,257	4,096	4,789
30,550	30,600	0	1,367	2,923	3,616	0	2,249	4,085	4,779
30,600	30,650	0	1,359	2,912	3,606	0	2,241	4,075	4,768
30,650	30,700	0	1,351	2,902	3,595	0	2,233	4,064	4,758
30,700	30,750	0	1,343	2,891	3,585	0	2,225	4,054	4,747
30,750	30,800	0	1,335	2,881	3,574	0	2,217	4,043	4,737
30,800	30,850	0	1,327	2,870	3,564	0	2,209	4,033	4,726
30,850	30,900	0	1,319	2,860	3,553	0	2,201	4,022	4,716
30,900	30,950	0	1,311	2,849	3,543	0	2,193	4,012	4,705
30,950	31,000	0	1,303	2,839	3,532	0	2,185	4,001	4,695
31,000	31,050	0	1,295	2,828	3,522	0	2,177	3,991	4,684
31,050	31,100	0	1,287	2,818	3,511	0	2,169	3,980	4,674
31,100	31,150	0	1,279	2,807	3,501	0	2,161	3,970	4,663
31,150	31,200	0	1,271	2,797	3,490	0	2,154	3,959	4,653
31,200	31,250	0	1,263	2,786	3,479	0	2,146	3,948	4,642
31,250	31,300	0	1,255	2,775	3,469	0	2,138	3,938	4,631
31,300	31,350	0	1,247	2,765	3,458	0	2,130	3,927	4,621
31,350	31,400	0	1,239	2,754	3,448	0	2,122	3,917	4,610
31,400	31,450	0	1,231	2,744	3,437	0	2,114	3,906	4,600
31,450	31,500	0	1,223	2,733	3,427	0	2,106	3,896	4,589
31,500	31,550	0	1,215	2,723	3,416	0	2,098	3,885	4,579
31,550	31,600	0	1,207	2,712	3,406	0	2,090	3,875	4,568
31,600	31,650	0	1,200	2,702	3,395	0	2,082	3,864	4,558
31,650	31,700	0	1,192	2,691	3,385	0	2,074	3,854	4,547
31,700	31,750	0	1,184	2,681	3,374	0	2,066	3,843	4,537
31,750	31,800	0	1,176	2,670	3,364	0	2,058	3,833	4,526
31,800	31,850	0	1,168	2,660	3,353	0	2,050	3,822	4,516
31,850	31,900	0	1,160	2,649	3,343	0	2,042	3,812	4,505
31,900	31,950	0	1,152	2,639	3,332	0	2,034	3,801	4,495
31,950	32,000	0	1,144	2,628	3,322	0	2,026	3,791	4,484
32,000	32,050	0	1,136	2,618	3,311	0	2,018	3,780	4,474
32,050	32,100	0	1,128	2,607	3,300	0	2,010	3,769	4,463
32,100	32,150	0	1,120	2,596	3,290	0	2,002	3,759	4,452
32,150	32,200	0	1,112	2,586	3,279	0	1,994	3,748	4,442
32,200	32,250	0	1,104	2,575	3,269	0	1,986	3,738	4,431
32,250	32,300	0	1,096	2,565	3,258	0	1,978	3,727	4,421
32,300	32,350	0	1,088	2,554	3,248	0	1,970	3,717	4,410
32,350	32,400	0	1,080	2,544	3,237	0	1,962	3,706	4,400
32,400	32,450	0	1,072	2,533	3,227	0	1,954	3,696	4,389
32,450	32,500	0	1,064	2,523	3,216	0	1,946	3,685	4,379
32,500	32,550	0	1,056	2,512	3,206	0	1,938	3,675	4,368
32,550	32,600	0	1,048	2,502	3,195	0	1,930	3,664	4,358
32,600	32,650	0	1,040	2,491	3,185	0	1,922	3,654	4,347
32,650	32,700	0	1,032	2,481	3,174	0	1,914	3,643	4,337
32,700	32,750	0	1,024	2,470	3,164	0	1,906	3,633	4,326
32,750	32,800	0	1,016	2,460	3,153	0	1,898	3,622	4,316

(Continued)

Need more information or forms? Visit IRS.gov.

Earned Income Credit (EIC) Table - *Continued*

(Caution. This is not a tax table.)

If the amount you are looking up from the worksheet is—		Single, head of household, or qualifying widow(er) and the number of children you have is—				Married filing jointly and the number of children you have is—			
At least	But less than	0	1	2	3	0	1	2	3
		Your credit is—				Your credit is—			
32,800	32,850	0	1,008	2,449	3,143	0	1,890	3,612	4,305
32,850	32,900	0	1,000	2,438	3,132	0	1,882	3,601	4,295
32,900	32,950	0	992	2,428	3,121	0	1,874	3,590	4,284
32,950	33,000	0	984	2,417	3,111	0	1,866	3,580	4,273
33,000	33,050	0	976	2,407	3,100	0	1,858	3,569	4,263
33,050	33,100	0	968	2,396	3,090	0	1,850	3,559	4,252
33,100	33,150	0	960	2,386	3,079	0	1,842	3,548	4,242
33,150	33,200	0	952	2,375	3,069	0	1,834	3,538	4,231
33,200	33,250	0	944	2,365	3,058	0	1,826	3,527	4,221
33,250	33,300	0	936	2,354	3,048	0	1,818	3,517	4,210
33,300	33,350	0	928	2,344	3,037	0	1,810	3,506	4,200
33,350	33,400	0	920	2,333	3,027	0	1,802	3,496	4,189
33,400	33,450	0	912	2,323	3,016	0	1,794	3,485	4,179
33,450	33,500	0	904	2,312	3,006	0	1,786	3,475	4,168
33,500	33,550	0	896	2,302	2,995	0	1,778	3,464	4,158
33,550	33,600	0	888	2,291	2,985	0	1,770	3,454	4,147
33,600	33,650	0	880	2,281	2,974	0	1,762	3,443	4,137
33,650	33,700	0	872	2,270	2,964	0	1,754	3,433	4,126
33,700	33,750	0	864	2,259	2,953	0	1,746	3,422	4,115
33,750	33,800	0	856	2,249	2,942	0	1,738	3,411	4,105
33,800	33,850	0	848	2,238	2,932	0	1,730	3,401	4,094
33,850	33,900	0	840	2,228	2,921	0	1,722	3,390	4,084
33,900	33,950	0	832	2,217	2,911	0	1,714	3,380	4,073
33,950	34,000	0	824	2,207	2,900	0	1,706	3,369	4,063
34,000	34,050	0	816	2,196	2,890	0	1,698	3,359	4,052
34,050	34,100	0	808	2,186	2,879	0	1,690	3,348	4,042
34,100	34,150	0	800	2,175	2,869	0	1,682	3,338	4,031
34,150	34,200	0	792	2,165	2,858	0	1,674	3,327	4,021
34,200	34,250	0	784	2,154	2,848	0	1,666	3,317	4,010
34,250	34,300	0	776	2,144	2,837	0	1,658	3,306	4,000
34,300	34,350	0	768	2,133	2,827	0	1,650	3,296	3,989
34,350	34,400	0	760	2,123	2,816	0	1,642	3,285	3,979
34,400	34,450	0	752	2,112	2,806	0	1,634	3,275	3,968
34,450	34,500	0	744	2,102	2,795	0	1,626	3,264	3,958
34,500	34,550	0	736	2,091	2,785	0	1,618	3,254	3,947
34,550	34,600	0	728	2,080	2,774	0	1,610	3,243	3,936
34,600	34,650	0	720	2,070	2,763	0	1,602	3,232	3,926
34,650	34,700	0	712	2,059	2,753	0	1,594	3,222	3,915
34,700	34,750	0	704	2,049	2,742	0	1,586	3,211	3,905
34,750	34,800	0	696	2,038	2,732	0	1,578	3,201	3,894
34,800	34,850	0	688	2,028	2,721	0	1,570	3,190	3,884
34,850	34,900	0	680	2,017	2,711	0	1,562	3,180	3,873
34,900	34,950	0	672	2,007	2,700	0	1,554	3,169	3,863
34,950	35,000	0	664	1,996	2,690	0	1,546	3,159	3,852
35,000	35,050	0	656	1,986	2,679	0	1,538	3,148	3,842
35,050	35,100	0	648	1,975	2,669	0	1,530	3,138	3,831
35,100	35,150	0	640	1,965	2,658	0	1,522	3,127	3,821
35,150	35,200	0	632	1,954	2,648	0	1,514	3,117	3,810
35,200	35,250	0	624	1,944	2,637	0	1,506	3,106	3,800
35,250	35,300	0	616	1,933	2,627	0	1,498	3,096	3,789
35,300	35,350	0	608	1,923	2,616	0	1,490	3,085	3,779
35,350	35,400	0	600	1,912	2,605	0	1,482	3,075	3,768
35,400	35,450	0	592	1,901	2,595	0	1,474	3,064	3,757
35,450	35,500	0	584	1,891	2,584	0	1,466	3,053	3,747
35,500	35,550	0	576	1,880	2,574	0	1,458	3,043	3,736
35,550	35,600	0	568	1,870	2,563	0	1,450	3,032	3,726
35,600	35,650	0	560	1,859	2,553	0	1,442	3,022	3,715
35,650	35,700	0	552	1,849	2,542	0	1,434	3,011	3,705
35,700	35,750	0	544	1,838	2,532	0	1,426	3,001	3,694
35,750	35,800	0	536	1,828	2,521	0	1,418	2,990	3,684
35,800	35,850	0	528	1,817	2,511	0	1,410	2,980	3,673
35,850	35,900	0	520	1,807	2,500	0	1,402	2,969	3,663
35,900	35,950	0	512	1,796	2,490	0	1,394	2,959	3,652
35,950	36,000	0	504	1,786	2,479	0	1,386	2,948	3,642
36,000	36,050	0	496	1,775	2,469	0	1,378	2,938	3,631
36,050	36,100	0	488	1,765	2,458	0	1,370	2,927	3,621
36,100	36,150	0	480	1,754	2,448	0	1,362	2,917	3,610
36,150	36,200	0	472	1,744	2,437	0	1,355	2,906	3,600
36,200	36,250	0	464	1,733	2,426	0	1,347	2,895	3,589
36,250	36,300	0	456	1,722	2,416	0	1,339	2,885	3,578
36,300	36,350	0	448	1,712	2,405	0	1,331	2,874	3,568
36,350	36,400	0	440	1,701	2,395	0	1,323	2,864	3,557
36,400	36,450	0	432	1,691	2,384	0	1,315	2,853	3,547
36,450	36,500	0	424	1,680	2,374	0	1,307	2,843	3,536
36,500	36,550	0	416	1,670	2,363	0	1,299	2,832	3,526
36,550	36,600	0	408	1,659	2,353	0	1,291	2,822	3,515
36,600	36,650	0	401	1,649	2,342	0	1,283	2,811	3,505
36,650	36,700	0	393	1,638	2,332	0	1,275	2,801	3,494
36,700	36,750	0	385	1,628	2,321	0	1,267	2,790	3,484
36,750	36,800	0	377	1,617	2,311	0	1,259	2,780	3,473
36,800	36,850	0	369	1,607	2,300	0	1,251	2,769	3,463
36,850	36,900	0	361	1,596	2,290	0	1,243	2,759	3,452
36,900	36,950	0	353	1,586	2,279	0	1,235	2,748	3,442
36,950	37,000	0	345	1,575	2,269	0	1,227	2,738	3,431
37,000	37,050	0	337	1,565	2,258	0	1,219	2,727	3,421
37,050	37,100	0	329	1,554	2,247	0	1,211	2,716	3,410
37,100	37,150	0	321	1,543	2,237	0	1,203	2,706	3,399
37,150	37,200	0	313	1,533	2,226	0	1,195	2,695	3,389
37,200	37,250	0	305	1,522	2,216	0	1,187	2,685	3,378
37,250	37,300	0	297	1,512	2,205	0	1,179	2,674	3,368
37,300	37,350	0	289	1,501	2,195	0	1,171	2,664	3,357
37,350	37,400	0	281	1,491	2,184	0	1,163	2,653	3,347
37,400	37,450	0	273	1,480	2,174	0	1,155	2,643	3,336
37,450	37,500	0	265	1,470	2,163	0	1,147	2,632	3,326
37,500	37,550	0	257	1,459	2,153	0	1,139	2,622	3,315
37,550	37,600	0	249	1,449	2,142	0	1,131	2,611	3,305
37,600	37,650	0	241	1,438	2,132	0	1,123	2,601	3,294
37,650	37,700	0	233	1,428	2,121	0	1,115	2,590	3,284
37,700	37,750	0	225	1,417	2,111	0	1,107	2,580	3,273
37,750	37,800	0	217	1,407	2,100	0	1,099	2,569	3,263
37,800	37,850	0	209	1,396	2,090	0	1,091	2,559	3,252
37,850	37,900	0	201	1,385	2,079	0	1,083	2,548	3,242
37,900	37,950	0	193	1,375	2,068	0	1,075	2,537	3,231
37,950	38,000	0	185	1,364	2,058	0	1,067	2,527	3,220
38,000	38,050	0	177	1,354	2,047	0	1,059	2,516	3,210
38,050	38,100	0	169	1,343	2,037	0	1,051	2,506	3,199
38,100	38,150	0	161	1,333	2,026	0	1,043	2,495	3,189
38,150	38,200	0	153	1,322	2,016	0	1,035	2,485	3,178
38,200	38,250	0	145	1,312	2,005	0	1,027	2,474	3,168
38,250	38,300	0	137	1,301	1,995	0	1,019	2,464	3,157
38,300	38,350	0	129	1,291	1,984	0	1,011	2,453	3,147
38,350	38,400	0	121	1,280	1,974	0	1,003	2,443	3,136
38,400	38,450	0	113	1,270	1,963	0	995	2,432	3,126
38,450	38,500	0	105	1,259	1,953	0	987	2,422	3,115
38,500	38,550	0	97	1,249	1,942	0	979	2,411	3,105
38,550	38,600	0	89	1,238	1,932	0	971	2,401	3,094
38,600	38,650	0	81	1,228	1,921	0	963	2,390	3,084
38,650	38,700	0	73	1,217	1,911	0	955	2,380	3,073
38,700	38,750	0	65	1,206	1,900	0	947	2,369	3,062
38,750	38,800	0	57	1,196	1,889	0	939	2,358	3,052
38,800	38,850	0	49	1,185	1,879	0	931	2,348	3,041
38,850	38,900	0	41	1,175	1,868	0	923	2,337	3,031
38,900	38,950	0	33	1,164	1,858	0	915	2,327	3,020
38,950	39,000	0	25	1,154	1,847	0	907	2,316	3,010
39,000	39,050	0	17	1,143	1,837	0	899	2,306	2,999
39,050	39,100	0	9	1,133	1,826	0	891	2,295	2,989
39,100	39,150	0	*	1,122	1,816	0	883	2,285	2,978
39,150	39,200	0	0	1,112	1,805	0	875	2,274	2,968

* If the amount you are looking up from the worksheet is at least $39,100 but less than $39,131, and you have one qualifying child, your credit is $3.
If the amount you are looking up from the worksheet is $39,131 or more, and you have one qualifying child, you can't take the credit.

(Continued)

Earned Income Credit (EIC) Table - Continued

If the amount you are looking up from the worksheet is—		Single, head of household, or qualifying widow(er) and the number of children you have—				Married filing jointly and the number of children you have—			
At least	But less than	0	1	2	3	0	1	2	3
		Your credit is—				Your credit is—			
39,200	39,250	0	0	1,101	1,795	0	867	2,264	2,957
39,250	39,300	0	0	1,091	1,784	0	859	2,253	2,947
39,300	39,350	0	0	1,080	1,774	0	851	2,243	2,936
39,350	39,400	0	0	1,070	1,763	0	843	2,232	2,926
39,400	39,450	0	0	1,059	1,753	0	835	2,222	2,915
39,450	39,500	0	0	1,049	1,742	0	827	2,211	2,905
39,500	39,550	0	0	1,038	1,732	0	819	2,201	2,894
39,550	39,600	0	0	1,027	1,721	0	811	2,190	2,883
39,600	39,650	0	0	1,017	1,710	0	803	2,179	2,873
39,650	39,700	0	0	1,006	1,700	0	795	2,169	2,862
39,700	39,750	0	0	996	1,689	0	787	2,158	2,852
39,750	39,800	0	0	985	1,679	0	779	2,148	2,841
39,800	39,850	0	0	975	1,668	0	771	2,137	2,831
39,850	39,900	0	0	964	1,658	0	763	2,127	2,820
39,900	39,950	0	0	954	1,647	0	755	2,116	2,810
39,950	40,000	0	0	943	1,637	0	747	2,106	2,799
40,000	40,050	0	0	933	1,626	0	739	2,095	2,789
40,050	40,100	0	0	922	1,616	0	731	2,085	2,778
40,100	40,150	0	0	912	1,605	0	723	2,074	2,768
40,150	40,200	0	0	901	1,595	0	715	2,064	2,757
40,200	40,250	0	0	891	1,584	0	707	2,053	2,747
40,250	40,300	0	0	880	1,574	0	699	2,043	2,736
40,300	40,350	0	0	870	1,563	0	691	2,032	2,726
40,350	40,400	0	0	859	1,552	0	683	2,022	2,715
40,400	40,450	0	0	848	1,542	0	675	2,011	2,704
40,450	40,500	0	0	838	1,531	0	667	2,000	2,694
40,500	40,550	0	0	827	1,521	0	659	1,990	2,683
40,550	40,600	0	0	817	1,510	0	651	1,979	2,673
40,600	40,650	0	0	806	1,500	0	643	1,969	2,662
40,650	40,700	0	0	796	1,489	0	635	1,958	2,652
40,700	40,750	0	0	785	1,479	0	627	1,948	2,641
40,750	40,800	0	0	775	1,468	0	619	1,937	2,631
40,800	40,850	0	0	764	1,458	0	611	1,927	2,620
40,850	40,900	0	0	754	1,447	0	603	1,916	2,610
40,900	40,950	0	0	743	1,437	0	595	1,906	2,599
40,950	41,000	0	0	733	1,426	0	587	1,895	2,589
41,000	41,050	0	0	722	1,416	0	579	1,885	2,578
41,050	41,100	0	0	712	1,405	0	571	1,874	2,568
41,100	41,150	0	0	701	1,395	0	563	1,864	2,557
41,150	41,200	0	0	691	1,384	0	556	1,853	2,547
41,200	41,250	0	0	680	1,373	0	548	1,842	2,536
41,250	41,300	0	0	669	1,363	0	540	1,832	2,525
41,300	41,350	0	0	659	1,352	0	532	1,821	2,515
41,350	41,400	0	0	648	1,342	0	524	1,811	2,504
41,400	41,450	0	0	638	1,331	0	516	1,800	2,494
41,450	41,500	0	0	627	1,321	0	508	1,790	2,483
41,500	41,550	0	0	617	1,310	0	500	1,779	2,473
41,550	41,600	0	0	606	1,300	0	492	1,769	2,462
41,600	41,650	0	0	596	1,289	0	484	1,758	2,452
41,650	41,700	0	0	585	1,279	0	476	1,748	2,441
41,700	41,750	0	0	575	1,268	0	468	1,737	2,431
41,750	41,800	0	0	564	1,258	0	460	1,727	2,420
41,800	41,850	0	0	554	1,247	0	452	1,716	2,410
41,850	41,900	0	0	543	1,237	0	444	1,706	2,399
41,900	41,950	0	0	533	1,226	0	436	1,695	2,389
41,950	42,000	0	0	522	1,216	0	428	1,685	2,378
42,000	42,050	0	0	512	1,205	0	420	1,674	2,368
42,050	42,100	0	0	501	1,194	0	412	1,663	2,357
42,100	42,150	0	0	490	1,184	0	404	1,653	2,346
42,150	42,200	0	0	480	1,173	0	396	1,642	2,336
42,200	42,250	0	0	469	1,163	0	388	1,632	2,325
42,250	42,300	0	0	459	1,152	0	380	1,621	2,315
42,300	42,350	0	0	448	1,142	0	372	1,611	2,304
42,350	42,400	0	0	438	1,131	0	364	1,600	2,294
42,400	42,450	0	0	427	1,121	0	356	1,590	2,283
42,450	42,500	0	0	417	1,110	0	348	1,579	2,273
42,500	42,550	0	0	406	1,100	0	340	1,569	2,262
42,550	42,600	0	0	396	1,089	0	332	1,558	2,252
42,600	42,650	0	0	385	1,079	0	324	1,548	2,241
42,650	42,700	0	0	375	1,068	0	316	1,537	2,231
42,700	42,750	0	0	364	1,058	0	308	1,527	2,220
42,750	42,800	0	0	354	1,047	0	300	1,516	2,210
42,800	42,850	0	0	343	1,037	0	292	1,506	2,199
42,850	42,900	0	0	332	1,026	0	284	1,495	2,189
42,900	42,950	0	0	322	1,015	0	276	1,484	2,178
42,950	43,000	0	0	311	1,005	0	268	1,474	2,167
43,000	43,050	0	0	301	994	0	260	1,463	2,157
43,050	43,100	0	0	290	984	0	252	1,453	2,146
43,100	43,150	0	0	280	973	0	244	1,442	2,136
43,150	43,200	0	0	269	963	0	236	1,432	2,125
43,200	43,250	0	0	259	952	0	228	1,421	2,115
43,250	43,300	0	0	248	942	0	220	1,411	2,104
43,300	43,350	0	0	238	931	0	212	1,400	2,094
43,350	43,400	0	0	227	921	0	204	1,390	2,083
43,400	43,450	0	0	217	910	0	196	1,379	2,073
43,450	43,500	0	0	206	900	0	188	1,369	2,062
43,500	43,550	0	0	196	889	0	180	1,358	2,052
43,550	43,600	0	0	185	879	0	172	1,348	2,041
43,600	43,650	0	0	175	868	0	164	1,337	2,031
43,650	43,700	0	0	164	858	0	156	1,327	2,020
43,700	43,750	0	0	153	847	0	148	1,316	2,009
43,750	43,800	0	0	143	836	0	140	1,305	1,999
43,800	43,850	0	0	132	826	0	132	1,295	1,988
43,850	43,900	0	0	122	815	0	124	1,284	1,978
43,900	43,950	0	0	111	805	0	116	1,274	1,967
43,950	44,000	0	0	101	794	0	108	1,263	1,957
44,000	44,050	0	0	90	784	0	100	1,253	1,946
44,050	44,100	0	0	80	773	0	92	1,242	1,936
44,100	44,150	0	0	69	763	0	84	1,232	1,925
44,150	44,200	0	0	59	752	0	76	1,221	1,915
44,200	44,250	0	0	48	742	0	68	1,211	1,904
44,250	44,300	0	0	38	731	0	60	1,200	1,894
44,300	44,350	0	0	27	721	0	52	1,190	1,883
44,350	44,400	0	0	17	710	0	44	1,179	1,873
44,400	44,450	0	0	6	700	0	36	1,169	1,862
44,450	44,500	0	0	0	689	0	28	1,158	1,852
44,500	44,550	0	0	0	679	0	20	1,148	1,841
44,550	44,600	0	0	0	668	0	12	1,137	1,830
44,600	44,650	0	0	0	657	0	4	1,126	1,820
44,650	44,700	0	0	0	647	0	0	1,116	1,809
44,700	44,750	0	0	0	636	0	0	1,105	1,799
44,750	44,800	0	0	0	626	0	0	1,095	1,788
44,800	44,850	0	0	0	615	0	0	1,084	1,778
44,850	44,900	0	0	0	605	0	0	1,074	1,767
44,900	44,950	0	0	0	594	0	0	1,063	1,757
44,950	45,000	0	0	0	584	0	0	1,053	1,746
45,000	45,050	0	0	0	573	0	0	1,042	1,736
45,050	45,100	0	0	0	563	0	0	1,032	1,725
45,100	45,150	0	0	0	552	0	0	1,021	1,715
45,150	45,200	0	0	0	542	0	0	1,011	1,704
45,200	45,250	0	0	0	531	0	0	1,000	1,694
45,250	45,300	0	0	0	521	0	0	990	1,683
45,300	45,350	0	0	0	510	0	0	979	1,673
45,350	45,400	0	0	0	499	0	0	969	1,662
45,400	45,450	0	0	0	489	0	0	958	1,651
45,450	45,500	0	0	0	478	0	0	947	1,641
45,500	45,550	0	0	0	468	0	0	937	1,630
45,550	45,600	0	0	0	457	0	0	926	1,620
45,600	45,650	0	0	0	447	0	0	916	1,609
45,650	45,700	0	0	0	436	0	0	905	1,599
45,700	45,750	0	0	0	426	0	0	895	1,588
45,750	45,800	0	0	0	415	0	0	884	1,578
45,800	45,850	0	0	0	405	0	0	874	1,567
45,850	45,900	0	0	0	394	0	0	863	1,557
45,900	45,950	0	0	0	384	0	0	853	1,546
45,950	46,000	0	0	0	373	0	0	842	1,536
46,000	46,050	0	0	0	363	0	0	832	1,525
46,050	46,100	0	0	0	352	0	0	821	1,515
46,100	46,150	0	0	0	342	0	0	811	1,504
46,150	46,200	0	0	0	331	0	0	800	1,494
46,200	46,250	0	0	0	320	0	0	789	1,483
46,250	46,300	0	0	0	310	0	0	779	1,472
46,300	46,350	0	0	0	299	0	0	768	1,462
46,350	46,400	0	0	0	289	0	0	758	1,451

(Continued)

Need more information or forms? Visit IRS.gov.

If the amount you are looking up from the worksheet is—		Single, head of household, or qualifying widow(er) and the number of children you have is—				Married filing jointly and the number of children you have is—			
At least	But less than	0	1	2	3	0	1	2	3
		Your credit is—				Your credit is—			
46,400	46,450	0	0	0	278	0	0	747	1,441
46,450	46,500	0	0	0	268	0	0	737	1,430
46,500	46,550	0	0	0	257	0	0	726	1,420
46,550	46,600	0	0	0	247	0	0	716	1,409
46,600	46,650	0	0	0	236	0	0	705	1,399
46,650	46,700	0	0	0	226	0	0	695	1,388
46,700	46,750	0	0	0	215	0	0	684	1,378
46,750	46,800	0	0	0	205	0	0	674	1,367
46,800	46,850	0	0	0	194	0	0	663	1,357
46,850	46,900	0	0	0	184	0	0	653	1,346
46,900	46,950	0	0	0	173	0	0	642	1,336
46,950	47,000	0	0	0	163	0	0	632	1,325
47,000	47,050	0	0	0	152	0	0	621	1,315
47,050	47,100	0	0	0	141	0	0	610	1,304
47,100	47,150	0	0	0	131	0	0	600	1,293
47,150	47,200	0	0	0	120	0	0	589	1,283
47,200	47,250	0	0	0	110	0	0	579	1,272
47,250	47,300	0	0	0	99	0	0	568	1,262
47,300	47,350	0	0	0	89	0	0	558	1,251
47,350	47,400	0	0	0	78	0	0	547	1,241
47,400	47,450	0	0	0	68	0	0	537	1,230
47,450	47,500	0	0	0	57	0	0	526	1,220
47,500	47,550	0	0	0	47	0	0	516	1,209
47,550	47,600	0	0	0	36	0	0	505	1,199
47,600	47,650	0	0	0	26	0	0	495	1,188
47,650	47,700	0	0	0	15	0	0	484	1,178
47,700	47,750	0	0	0	*	0	0	474	1,167
47,750	47,800	0	0	0	0	0	0	463	1,157
47,800	47,850	0	0	0	0	0	0	453	1,146
47,850	47,900	0	0	0	0	0	0	442	1,136
47,900	47,950	0	0	0	0	0	0	431	1,125
47,950	48,000	0	0	0	0	0	0	421	1,114
48,000	48,050	0	0	0	0	0	0	410	1,104
48,050	48,100	0	0	0	0	0	0	400	1,093
48,100	48,150	0	0	0	0	0	0	389	1,083
48,150	48,200	0	0	0	0	0	0	379	1,072
48,200	48,250	0	0	0	0	0	0	368	1,062
48,250	48,300	0	0	0	0	0	0	358	1,051
48,300	48,350	0	0	0	0	0	0	347	1,041
48,350	48,400	0	0	0	0	0	0	337	1,030
48,400	48,450	0	0	0	0	0	0	326	1,020
48,450	48,500	0	0	0	0	0	0	316	1,009
48,500	48,550	0	0	0	0	0	0	305	999
48,550	48,600	0	0	0	0	0	0	295	988
48,600	48,650	0	0	0	0	0	0	284	978
48,650	48,700	0	0	0	0	0	0	274	967
48,700	48,750	0	0	0	0	0	0	263	956
48,750	48,800	0	0	0	0	0	0	252	946
48,800	48,850	0	0	0	0	0	0	242	935
48,850	48,900	0	0	0	0	0	0	231	925
48,900	48,950	0	0	0	0	0	0	221	914
48,950	49,000	0	0	0	0	0	0	210	904
49,000	49,050	0	0	0	0	0	0	200	893
49,050	49,100	0	0	0	0	0	0	189	883
49,100	49,150	0	0	0	0	0	0	179	872
49,150	49,200	0	0	0	0	0	0	168	862
49,200	49,250	0	0	0	0	0	0	158	851
49,250	49,300	0	0	0	0	0	0	147	841
49,300	49,350	0	0	0	0	0	0	137	830
49,350	49,400	0	0	0	0	0	0	126	820
49,400	49,450	0	0	0	0	0	0	116	809
49,450	49,500	0	0	0	0	0	0	105	799
49,500	49,550	0	0	0	0	0	0	95	788
49,550	49,600	0	0	0	0	0	0	84	777
49,600	49,650	0	0	0	0	0	0	73	767
49,650	49,700	0	0	0	0	0	0	63	756
49,700	49,750	0	0	0	0	0	0	52	746
49,750	49,800	0	0	0	0	0	0	42	735
49,800	49,850	0	0	0	0	0	0	31	725
49,850	49,900	0	0	0	0	0	0	21	714
49,900	49,950	0	0	0	0	0	0	10	704
49,950	50,000	0	0	0	0	0	0	**	693
50,000	50,050	0	0	0	0	0	0	0	683
50,050	50,100	0	0	0	0	0	0	0	672
50,100	50,150	0	0	0	0	0	0	0	662
50,150	50,200	0	0	0	0	0	0	0	651
50,200	50,250	0	0	0	0	0	0	0	641
50,250	50,300	0	0	0	0	0	0	0	630
50,300	50,350	0	0	0	0	0	0	0	620
50,350	50,400	0	0	0	0	0	0	0	609
50,400	50,450	0	0	0	0	0	0	0	598
50,450	50,500	0	0	0	0	0	0	0	588
50,500	50,550	0	0	0	0	0	0	0	577
50,550	50,600	0	0	0	0	0	0	0	567
50,600	50,650	0	0	0	0	0	0	0	556
50,650	50,700	0	0	0	0	0	0	0	546
50,700	50,750	0	0	0	0	0	0	0	535
50,750	50,800	0	0	0	0	0	0	0	525
50,800	50,850	0	0	0	0	0	0	0	514
50,850	50,900	0	0	0	0	0	0	0	504
50,900	50,950	0	0	0	0	0	0	0	493
50,950	51,000	0	0	0	0	0	0	0	483
51,000	51,050	0	0	0	0	0	0	0	472
51,050	51,100	0	0	0	0	0	0	0	462
51,100	51,150	0	0	0	0	0	0	0	451
51,150	51,200	0	0	0	0	0	0	0	441
51,200	51,250	0	0	0	0	0	0	0	430
51,250	51,300	0	0	0	0	0	0	0	419
51,300	51,350	0	0	0	0	0	0	0	409
51,350	51,400	0	0	0	0	0	0	0	398
51,400	51,450	0	0	0	0	0	0	0	388
51,450	51,500	0	0	0	0	0	0	0	377
51,500	51,550	0	0	0	0	0	0	0	367
51,550	51,600	0	0	0	0	0	0	0	356
51,600	51,650	0	0	0	0	0	0	0	346
51,650	51,700	0	0	0	0	0	0	0	335
51,700	51,750	0	0	0	0	0	0	0	325
51,750	51,800	0	0	0	0	0	0	0	314
51,800	51,850	0	0	0	0	0	0	0	304
51,850	51,900	0	0	0	0	0	0	0	293
51,900	51,950	0	0	0	0	0	0	0	283
51,950	52,000	0	0	0	0	0	0	0	272
52,000	52,050	0	0	0	0	0	0	0	262
52,050	52,100	0	0	0	0	0	0	0	251
52,100	52,150	0	0	0	0	0	0	0	240
52,150	52,200	0	0	0	0	0	0	0	230
52,200	52,250	0	0	0	0	0	0	0	219
52,250	52,300	0	0	0	0	0	0	0	209
52,300	52,350	0	0	0	0	0	0	0	198
52,350	52,400	0	0	0	0	0	0	0	188
52,400	52,450	0	0	0	0	0	0	0	177
52,450	52,500	0	0	0	0	0	0	0	167
52,500	52,550	0	0	0	0	0	0	0	156
52,550	52,600	0	0	0	0	0	0	0	146
52,600	52,650	0	0	0	0	0	0	0	135
52,650	52,700	0	0	0	0	0	0	0	125
52,700	52,750	0	0	0	0	0	0	0	114
52,750	52,800	0	0	0	0	0	0	0	104

* If the amount you are looking up from the worksheet is at least $47,700 but less than $47,747, and you have three qualifying children, your credit is $5.

If the amount you are looking up from the worksheet is $47,747 or more, and you have three qualifying children, you can't take the credit.

** If the amount you are looking up from the worksheet is at least $49,950 but less than $49,974, and you have two qualifying children, your credit is $2.

If the amount you are looking up from the worksheet is $49,974 or more, and you have two qualifying children, you can't take the credit.

(Continued)

Earned Income Credit (EIC) Table - *Continued*

(**Caution.** This is **not** a tax table.)

If the amount you are looking up from the worksheet is–		Single, head of household, or qualifying widow(er) and the number of children you have is–				Married filing jointly and the number of children you have is–				If the amount you are looking up from the worksheet is–		Single, head of household, or qualifying widow(er) and the number of children you have is–				Married filing jointly and the number of children you have is–			
		0	1	2	3	0	1	2	3			0	1	2	3	0	1	2	3
At least	But less than	Your credit is–				Your credit is–				At least	But less than	Your credit is–				Your credit is–			
52,800	52,850	0	0	0	0	0	0	0	93	53,200	53,250	0	0	0	0	0	0	0	9
52,850	52,900	0	0	0	0	0	0	0	83	53,250	53,267	0	0	0	0	0	0	0	2
52,900	52,950	0	0	0	0	0	0	0	72										
52,950	53,000	0	0	0	0	0	0	0	61										
53,000	53,050	0	0	0	0	0	0	0	51										
53,050	53,100	0	0	0	0	0	0	0	40										
53,100	53,150	0	0	0	0	0	0	0	30										
53,150	53,200	0	0	0	0	0	0	0	19										

Need more information or forms? Visit IRS.gov.

Line 67

Additional Child Tax Credit

What Is the Additional Child Tax Credit?

This credit is for certain people who have at least one qualifying child for the child tax credit (as defined in Steps 1, 2, and 3 of the instructions for line 6c). The additional child tax credit may give you a refund even if you do not owe any tax or didn't have any tax withheld.

Two Steps To Take the Additional Child Tax Credit!

Step 1. Be sure you figured the amount, if any, of your child tax credit. See the instructions for line 52.

Step 2. Read the TIP at the end of your Child Tax Credit Worksheet. Use Schedule 8812 to see if you can take the additional child tax credit, but only if you meet the condition given in that TIP.

Line 68

American Opportunity Credit

If you meet the requirements to claim an education credit (see the instructions for line 50), enter on line 68 the amount, if any, from Form 8863, line 8. You may be able to increase an education credit and reduce your total tax or increase your tax refund if the student chooses to include all or part of a Pell grant or certain other scholarships or fellowships in income. See Pub. 970 and the instructions for Form 8863 for more information.

Line 69

Net Premium Tax Credit

You may be eligible to claim the premium tax credit if you, your spouse, or a dependent enrolled in health insurance through the Marketplace. The premium tax credit helps pay for this health insurance. Complete Form 8962 to determine the amount of your premium tax credit, if any. Enter the amount, if any, from Form 8962, line 26. See Pub. 974 and the instructions for Form 8962 for more information.

Line 70

Amount Paid With Request for Extension To File

If you got an automatic extension of time to file Form 1040 by filing Form 4868 or by making a payment, enter the amount of the payment or any amount you paid with Form 4868. If you paid by debit or credit card, do not include on line 70 the convenience fee you were charged. Also, include any amounts paid with Form 2350.

 You may be able to deduct any credit or debit card convenience fees on your 2016 Schedule A.

Line 71

Excess Social Security and Tier 1 RRTA Tax Withheld

If you, or your spouse if filing a joint return, had more than one employer for 2015 and total wages of more than $118,500, too much social security or tier 1 railroad retirement (RRTA) tax may have been withheld. You can take a credit on this line for the amount withheld in excess of $7,347. But if any one employer withheld more than $7,347, you can't claim the excess on your return. The employer should adjust the tax for you. If the employer doesn't adjust the overcollection, you can file a claim for refund using Form 843. Figure this amount separately for you and your spouse.

You can't claim a refund for excess tier 2 RRTA tax on Form 1040. Instead, use Form 843.

For more details, see Pub. 505.

Line 72

Credit for Federal Tax on Fuels

Enter any credit for federal excise taxes paid on fuels that are ultimately used for a nontaxable purpose (for example, an off-highway business use). Attach Form 4136.

Line 73

Check the box(es) on line 73 to report any credit from Form 2439 or 8885.

If you are claiming a credit for repayment of amounts you included in your income in an earlier year because it appeared you had a right to the income, include the credit on line 73. Check box d and enter "I.R.C. 1341" in the space next to that box. See Pub. 525 for details about this credit.

If you made a tax payment that doesn't belong on any other line, include the payment on line 73. Check box d and enter "Tax" in the space next to that box.

If you check more than one box, enter the total of the line 73 credits and payments.

Refund

Line 75

Amount Overpaid

If line 75 is under $1, we will send a refund only on written request.

 If the amount you overpaid is large, you may want to decrease the amount of income tax withheld from your pay by filing a new Form W-4. See Income Tax Withholding and Estimated Tax Payments for 2016 under General Information, later.

Refund Offset

If you owe past-due federal tax, state income tax, state unemployment compensation debts, child support, spousal support, or certain federal nontax debts, such as student loans, all or part of the overpayment on line 75 may be used (offset) to pay the past-due amount. Offsets for federal taxes are made by the IRS. All other offsets are made by the Treasury Department's Bureau of the Fiscal Service. For federal tax offsets, you will receive a notice from the IRS. For all other offsets, you will receive a notice from the Fiscal Service. To find out if you may have an offset or if you have any questions about it, contact the agency to which you owe the debt.

Need more information or forms? Visit IRS.gov.

Injured Spouse

If you file a joint return and your spouse has not paid past-due federal tax, state income tax, state unemployment compensation debts, child support, spousal support, or a federal nontax debt, such as a student loan, part or all of the overpayment on line 75 may be used (offset) to pay the past-due amount. But your part of the overpayment may be refunded to you if certain conditions apply and you complete Form 8379. For details, use *Tax Topic 203* or see Form 8379.

Lines 76a Through 76d

Amount Refunded to You

If you want to check the status of your refund, just use the IRS2Go app or go to IRS.gov and click on *Where's My Refund*. See *Refund Information,* later. Information about your return will generally be available within 24 hours after the IRS receives your e-filed return, or 4 weeks after you mail your paper return. If you filed Form 8379 with your return, wait 14 weeks (11 weeks if you filed electronically). Have your 2015 tax return handy so you can enter your social security number, your filing status, and the exact whole dollar amount of your refund.

Where's My Refund? will provide an actual personalized refund date as soon as the IRS processes your tax return and approves your refund.

Effect of refund on benefits. Any refund you receive can't be counted as income when determining if you or anyone else is eligible for benefits or assistance, or how much you or anyone else can receive, under any federal program or under any state or local program financed in whole or in part with federal funds. These programs include Temporary Assistance for Needy Families (TANF), Medicaid, Supplemental Security Income (SSI), and Supplemental Nutrition Assistance Program (food stamps). In addition, when determining eligibility, the refund can't be counted as a resource for at least 12 months after you receive it. Check with your local benefit coordinator to find out if your refund will affect your benefits.

DIRECT DEPOSIT
Simple. Safe. Secure.

Fast Refunds! Join the eight in 10 taxpayers who choose direct deposit—a fast, simple, safe, secure way to have your refund deposited automatically to your checking or savings account, including an individual retirement arrangement (IRA). See the information about IRAs later.

If you want us to directly deposit the amount shown on line 76a to your checking or savings account, including an IRA, at a bank or other financial institution (such as a mutual fund, brokerage firm, or credit union) in the United States:

- Complete lines 76b through 76d (if you want your refund deposited to only one account), or
- Check the box on line 76a and attach Form 8888 if you want to split the direct deposit of your refund into more than one account or use all or part of your refund to buy paper series I savings bonds.

If you do not want your refund directly deposited to your account, do not check the box on line 76a. Draw a line through the boxes on lines 76b and 76d. We will send you a check instead.

Account must be in your name. Do not request a deposit of your refund to an account that isn't in your name, such as your tax return preparer's account. Although you may owe your tax return preparer a fee for preparing your return, do not have any part of your refund deposited into the preparer's account to pay the fee.

The number of refunds that can be directly deposited to a single account or prepaid debit card is limited to three a year. After this limit is reached, paper checks will be sent instead. Learn more at *IRS.gov*.

Why Use Direct Deposit?

- You get your refund faster by direct deposit than you do by check.
- Payment is more secure. There is no check that can get lost or stolen.
- It is more convenient. You do not have to make a trip to the bank to deposit your check.

- It saves tax dollars. It costs the government less to refund by direct deposit.
- It's proven itself. Nearly 98% of social security and veterans' benefits are sent electronically using direct deposit.

 If you file a joint return and check the box on line 76a and attach Form 8888 or fill in lines 76b through 76d, your spouse may get at least part of the refund.

IRA. You can have your refund (or part of it) directly deposited to a traditional IRA, Roth IRA (including a *my*RA), or SEP-IRA, but not a SIMPLE IRA. You must establish the IRA at a bank or other financial institution before you request direct deposit. Make sure your direct deposit will be accepted. You must also notify the trustee or custodian of your account of the year to which the deposit is to be applied (unless the trustee or custodian won't accept a deposit for 2015). If you do not, the trustee or custodian can assume the deposit is for the year during which you are filing the return. For example, if you file your 2015 return during 2016 and do not notify the trustee or custodian in advance, the trustee or custodian can assume the deposit to your IRA is for 2016. If you designate your deposit to be for 2015, you must verify that the deposit was actually made to the account by the due date of the return (not counting extensions). If the deposit isn't made by that date, the deposit isn't an IRA contribution for 2015. In that case, you must file an amended 2015 return and reduce any IRA deduction and any retirement savings contributions credit you claimed.

You and your spouse, if filing jointly, each may be able to contribute up to $5,500 ($6,500 if age 50 or older at the end of 2015) to a traditional IRA or Roth IRA (including a myRA), for 2015. You may owe a penalty if your contributions exceed these limits, and the limits may be lower depending on your compensation and income. For more information on IRA contributions, see Pub. 590-A. If the limits on IRA contributions change for 2016, Pub. 590-A will have the new 2016 limits.

For more information on IRAs, see Pub. 590-A and Pub. 590-B.

myRA® . If you already have a *myRA®* account, you can request a deposit of your refund (or part of it) to your *myRA* account. A *myRA* is a starter retirement account offered by the Department of the Treasury. For more information on *myRA* and to open a *myRA* account on-line, visit *www.myRA.gov*.

TreasuryDirect®. You can request a deposit of your refund (or part of it) to a TreasuryDirect® online account to buy U.S. Treasury marketable securities and savings bonds. For more information, go to *www.publicdebt.treas.gov/index1.htm*.

Form 8888. You can have your refund directly deposited into more than one account or use it to buy up to $5,000 in paper series I savings bonds. You do not need a TreasuryDirect® account to do this. For more information, see the Form 8888 instructions.

Line 76a

You can't file Form 8888 to split your refund into more than one account or buy paper series I savings bonds if Form 8379 is filed with your return.

Line 76b

The routing number must be nine digits. The first two digits must be 01 through 12 or 21 through 32. On the sample check shown here, the routing number is 250250025. Charles and Mary Ellen Keys would use that routing number un-less their financial institution instructed them to use a different routing number for direct deposits.

Ask your financial institution for the correct routing number to enter on line 76b if:
- The routing number on a deposit slip is different from the routing number on your checks,
- Your deposit is to a savings ac-count that doesn't allow you to write checks,
- Your checks state they are payable through a financial institution different from the one at which you have your checking account, or
- Your deposit is to a *myRA*.

Line 76c

Check the appropriate box for the type of account. Do not check more than one

Sample Check—Lines 76b Through 76d

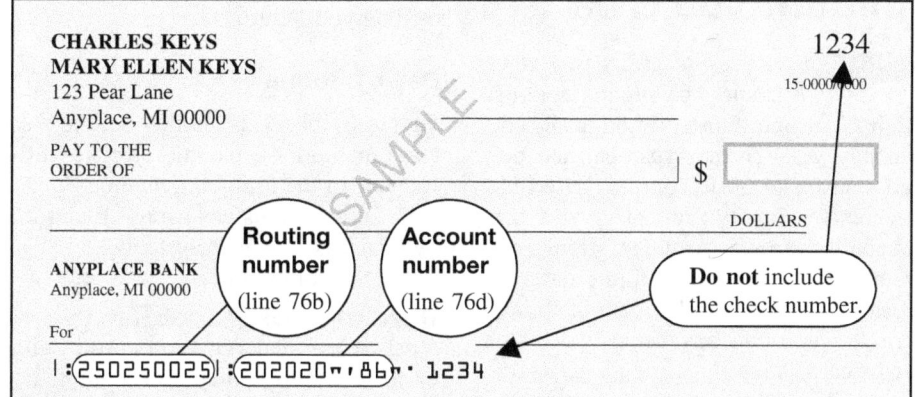

 The routing and account numbers may be in different places on your check.

box. If the deposit is to an account such as an IRA, health savings account, bro-kerage account, or other similar account, ask your financial institution whether you should check the "Checking" or "Savings" box. You must check the cor-rect box to ensure your deposit is accep-ted. If your deposit is to a *myRA* or a TreasuryDirect® online account, check the "Savings" box.

Line 76d

The account number can be up to 17 characters (both numbers and letters). Include hyphens but omit spaces and special symbols. Enter the number from left to right and leave any unused boxes blank. On the sample check shown here, the account number is 20202086. Do not include the check number.

If the direct deposit to your ac-count(s) is different from the amount you expected, you will receive an ex-planation in the mail about 2 weeks after your refund is deposited.

Reasons Your Direct Deposit Request Will Be Rejected

If any of the following apply, your direct deposit request will be rejected and a check will be sent instead.
- You are asking to have a joint re-fund deposited to an individual account, and your financial institution(s) won't al-low this. The IRS isn't responsible if a financial institution rejects a direct de-posit.
- The name on your account doesn't match the name on the refund, and your

financial institution(s) won't allow a re-fund to be deposited unless the name on the refund matches the name on the ac-count.
- Three direct deposits of tax refunds have already been made to the same ac-count or prepaid debit card.
- You haven't given a valid account number.
- You file your 2015 return after De-cember 31, 2016.
- Any numbers or letters on lines 76b through 76d are crossed out or whi-ted out.

 The IRS isn't responsible for a lost refund if you enter the wrong account information. Check with your financial institution to get the correct routing and account numbers and to make sure your direct deposit will be accepted.

Line 77

Applied to Your 2016 Estimated Tax

Enter on line 77 the amount, if any, of the overpayment on line 75 you want applied to your 2016 estimated tax. We will apply this amount to your account unless you include a statement request-ing us to apply it to your spouse's ac-count. Include your spouse's social se-curity number in the statement.

 This election to apply part or all of the amount overpaid to your 2016 estimated tax can't be changed later.

Amount You Owe

 IRS *e-file* offers two electronic payment options. With Electronic Funds Withdrawal, you can pay your current year balance due and also make up to four estimated tax payments. If you file early, you can schedule your payment for withdrawal from your account on a future date, up to and including the due date of the return. Or you can pay using a debit or credit card. Visit *www.irs.gov/payments* for details on both options.

Line 78

Amount You Owe

TIP *To save interest and penalties, pay your taxes in full by the due date of your return (not counting extensions)–April 18, 2016, for most people. You do not have to pay if line 78 is under $1.*

Include any estimated tax penalty from line 79 in the amount you enter on line 78.

You can pay online, by phone, or by check or money order. Do not include any estimated tax payment for 2016 in this payment. Instead, make the estimated tax payment separately.

Bad check or payment. The penalty for writing a bad check to the IRS is $25 or 2% of the check, whichever is more. However, if the amount of the check is less than $25, the penalty equals the amount of the check. This penalty also applies to other forms of payment if the IRS doesn't receive the funds. Use *Tax Topic 206.*

Pay Online

Paying online is convenient and secure and helps make sure we get your payments on time. To pay your taxes online or for more information, go to *www.irs.gov/payments*. You can pay using either of the following methods.
* *IRS Direct Pay* for online transfers from your checking or savings account.
* Debit or credit card. Click on "Pay by Card."

Also see the *e-file* information under *Amount You Owe*, earlier, for information about the Electronic Funds Withdrawal payment option offered when e-filing your return.

Pay by Phone

Paying by phone is another safe and secure method of paying electronically. Use one of the following methods.
* Direct transfer using Electronic Federal Tax Payment System (EFTPS).
* Debit or credit card.

Direct transfer. To use EFTPS, you must be enrolled. You can enroll online or have an enrollment form mailed to you. To make a payment using EFTPS, call 1-800-555-4477 (English) or 1-800-244-4829 (Español). People who are deaf, hard of hearing, or have a speech disability and who have access to TTY/TDD equipment can call 1-800-733-4829. For more information about EFTPS, go to *www.irs.gov/payments*.

Debit or credit card. To pay using a debit or credit card, you can call one of the following service providers. There is a convenience fee charged by these providers that varies by provider, card type, and payment amount.

> Official Payments Corporation
> 1-888-UPAY-TAX™
> (1-888-872-9829)
> *www.officialpayments.com*
>
> Link2Gov Corporation
> 1-888-PAY-1040™
> (1-888-729-1040)
> *www.PAY1040.com*
>
> WorldPay US, Inc.
> 1-844-729-8298
> (1-844-PAY-TAX-8™)
> *www.payUSAtax.com*

For the latest details on how to pay by phone, go to *www.irs.gov/payments*.

Pay by Check or Money Order

Make your check or money order payable to "United States Treasury" for the full amount due. Do not send cash. Do not attach the payment to your return. Write "2015 Form 1040" and your name, address, daytime phone number, and social security number (SSN) on your payment. If you are filing a joint return, enter the SSN shown first on your tax return.

To help us process your payment, enter the amount on the right side of the check like this: $ XXX.XX. Do not use dashes or lines (for example, do not enter "$ XXX–" or "$ XXX$^{xx}/_{100}$").

Then, complete Form 1040-V following the instructions on that form and enclose it in the envelope with your tax return and payment.

 You may need to (a) increase the amount of income tax withheld from your pay by filing a new Form W-4, (b) increase the tax withheld from other income by filing Form W-4P or W-4V, or (c) make estimated tax payments for 2016. See Income Tax Withholding and Estimated Tax Payments for 2016 under General Information, later.

What If You Can't Pay?

If you can't pay the full amount shown on line 78 when you file, you can ask for:
* An installment agreement, or
* An extension of time to pay.

Installment agreement. Under an installment agreement, you can pay all or part of the tax you owe in monthly installments. However, even if your request to pay in installments is granted, you will be charged interest and may be charged a late payment penalty on the tax not paid by the due date of your return (not counting extensions)–April 18, 2016, for most people. You must also pay a fee. To limit the interest and penalty charges, pay as much of the tax as possible when you file. But before requesting an installment agreement, you should consider other less costly alternatives, such as a bank loan or credit card payment.

To ask for an installment agreement, you can apply online or use Form 9465. To apply online, go to IRS.gov and click on *Apply for an Online Payment Plan*.

Extension of time to pay. If paying the tax when it is due would cause you an undue hardship, you can ask for an extension of time to pay by filing Form 1127 by the due date of your return (not counting extensions)–April 18, 2016, for most people. An extension generally won't be granted for more than 6 months. If you pay after that date, you will be charged interest on the tax not paid by April 15, 2016. You must pay the tax before the extension runs out. If you do not, penalties may be imposed.

Line 79

Estimated Tax Penalty

You may owe this penalty if:

- Line 78 is at least $1,000 and it is more than 10% of the tax shown on your return, or
- You didn't pay enough estimated tax by any of the due dates. This is true even if you are due a refund.

For most people, the "tax shown on your return" is the amount on your 2015 Form 1040, line 63, minus the total of any amounts shown on lines 61, 66a, 67, 68, 69, and 72 and Forms 8828, 4137, 5329 (Parts III through IX only), 8885, and 8919. Also subtract from line 63 any:

- Tax on an excess parachute payment,
- Excise tax on insider stock compensation of an expatriated corporation,
- Uncollected social security and Medicare or RRTA tax on tips or group-term life insurance, and
- Look-back interest due under section 167(g) or 460(b).

When figuring the amount on line 63, include household employment taxes only if line 64 is more than zero or you would owe the penalty even if you didn't include those taxes.

Exception. You won't owe the penalty if your 2014 tax return was for a tax year of 12 full months and either of the following applies.

1. You had no tax shown on your 2014 return and you were a U.S. citizen or resident for all of 2014.

2. The total of lines 64, 65, and 71 on your 2015 return is at least 100% of the tax shown on your 2014 return (110% of that amount if you aren't a farmer or fisherman, and your adjusted gross income (AGI) shown on your 2014 return was more than $150,000 (more than $75,000 if married filing separately for 2015)). Your estimated tax payments for 2015 must have been

made on time and for the required amount.

For most people, the "tax shown on your 2014 return" is the amount on your 2014 Form 1040, line 63, minus the total of any amounts shown on lines 61, 66a, 67, 68, 69, and 72 and Forms 8828, 4137, 5329 (Parts III through VIII only), and 8919. Also subtract from line 63 any:

- Tax on an excess parachute payment,
- Excise tax on insider stock compensation of an expatriated corporation,
- Uncollected social security and Medicare or RRTA tax on tips or group-term life insurance, and
- Look-back interest due under section 167(g) or 460(b).

When figuring the amount on line 63, include household employment taxes only if line 64 is more than zero or you would have owed the estimated tax penalty for 2014 even if you didn't include those taxes.

Figuring the Penalty

If the *Exception* just described doesn't apply and you choose to figure the penalty yourself, use Form 2210 (or 2210-F for farmers and fishermen).

Enter any penalty on line 79. Add the penalty to any tax due and enter the total on line 78.

However, if you have an overpayment on line 75, subtract the penalty from the amount you would otherwise enter on line 76a or line 77. Lines 76a, 77, and 79 must equal line 75.

If the penalty is more than the overpayment on line 75, enter -0- on lines 76a and 77. Then subtract line 75 from line 79 and enter the result on line 78.

Do not file Form 2210 with your return unless Form 2210 indicates that you must do so. Instead, keep it for your records.

 Because Form 2210 is complicated, you can leave line 79 blank and the IRS will figure the penalty and send you a bill. We won't charge you interest on the penalty if you pay by the date specified on the bill. If your income varied during the year, the annualized income installment method may reduce the amount of your

penalty. But you must file Form 2210 because the IRS can't figure your penalty under this method. See the Instructions for Form 2210 for other situations in which you may be able to lower your penalty by filing Form 2210.

Third Party Designee

If you want to allow your preparer, a friend, a family member, or any other person you choose to discuss your 2015 tax return with the IRS, check the "Yes" box in the "Third Party Designee" area of your return. Also, enter the designee's name, phone number, and any five digits the designee chooses as his or her personal identification number (PIN).

If you check the "Yes" box, you, and your spouse if filing a joint return, are authorizing the IRS to call the designee to answer any questions that may arise during the processing of your return. You are also authorizing the designee to:

- Give the IRS any information that is missing from your return,
- Call the IRS for information about the processing of your return or the status of your refund or payment(s),
- Receive copies of notices or transcripts related to your return, upon request, and
- Respond to certain IRS notices about math errors, offsets, and return preparation.

You aren't authorizing the designee to receive any refund check, bind you to anything (including any additional tax liability), or otherwise represent you before the IRS. If you want to expand the designee's authorization, see Pub. 947.

The authorization will automatically end no later than the due date (not counting extensions) for filing your 2016 tax return. This is April 18, 2017, for most people.

Sign Your Return

Form 1040 isn't considered a valid return unless you sign it. If you are filing a joint return, your spouse must also sign. If your spouse can't sign the return, see Pub. 501. Be sure to date your return and enter your occupation(s). If you

Need more information or forms? Visit IRS.gov.

have someone prepare your return, you are still responsible for the correctness of the return. If your return is signed by a representative for you, you must have a power of attorney attached that specifically authorizes the representative to sign your return. To do this, you can use Form 2848. If you are filing a joint return as a surviving spouse, see *Death of a Taxpayer,* later.

Court-Appointed Conservator, Guardian, or Other Fiduciary

If you are a court-appointed conservator, guardian, or other fiduciary for a mentally or physically incompetent individual who has to file Form 1040, sign your name for the individual and file Form 56.

Child's Return

If your child can't sign his or her return, either parent can sign the child's name in the space provided. Then, enter "By (your signature), parent for minor child."

Daytime Phone Number

Providing your daytime phone number may help speed the processing of your return. We may have questions about items on your return, such as the earned income credit or the credit for child and dependent care expenses. If you answer our questions over the phone, we may be able to continue processing your return without mailing you a letter. If you are filing a joint return, you can enter either your or your spouse's daytime phone number.

Electronic Return Signatures!

To file your return electronically, you must sign the return electronically using a personal identification number (PIN). If you are filing online using software, you must use a Self-Select PIN. If you are filing electronically using a tax practitioner, you can use a Self-Select PIN or a Practitioner PIN.

Self-Select PIN. The Self-Select PIN method allows you to create your own PIN. If you are married filing jointly, you and your spouse will each need to create a PIN and enter these PINs as your electronic signatures.

A PIN is any combination of five digits you choose except five zeros. If you use a PIN, there is nothing to sign and nothing to mail—not even your Forms W-2.

To verify your identity, you will be prompted to enter your adjusted gross income (AGI) from your originally filed 2014 federal income tax return, if applicable. Do not use your AGI from an amended return (Form 1040X) or a math error correction made by IRS. AGI is the amount shown on your 2014 Form 1040, line 38; Form 1040A, line 22; or Form 1040EZ, line 4. If you do not have your 2014 income tax return, call the IRS at 1-800-908-9946 to get a free transcript of your return or visit *www.irs.gov/ Individuals/Get-Transcript*. (If you filed electronically last year, you may use your prior year PIN to verify your identity instead of your prior year AGI. The prior year PIN is the five digit PIN you used to electronically sign your 2014 return.) You will also be prompted to enter your date of birth (DOB).

 You can't use the Self-Select PIN method if you are a first-time filer under age 16 at the end of 2015.

 If you can't locate your prior year AGI or prior year PIN, use the Electronic Filing PIN Request. *This can be found at* IRS.gov. *Click on* Request an Electronic Filing PIN. *Or you can call 1-866-704-7388.*

Practitioner PIN. The Practitioner PIN method allows you to authorize your tax practitioner to enter or generate your PIN. The practitioner can provide you with details.

Form 8453. You must send in a paper Form 8453 if you have to attach certain forms or other documents that can't be electronically filed. See Form 8453.

Identity Protection PIN

For 2015, if you received an Identity Protection Personal Identification Number (IP PIN) from the IRS, enter it in the IP PIN spaces provided below your day-

time phone number. You must correctly enter all six numbers of your IP PIN. If you didn't receive an IP PIN, leave these spaces blank.

 New IP PINs are issued every year. Enter the latest IP PIN you received. IP PINs for 2015 tax returns generally were sent in December 2015.

If you are filing a joint return and both taxpayers receive an IP PIN, only the taxpayer whose social security number (SSN) appears first on the tax return should enter his or her IP PIN. However, if you are filing electronically, both taxpayers must enter their IP PINs.

If you need more information, go to *www.irs.gov/Individuals/Understanding-Your-CP01A-Notice*. If you received an IP PIN but misplaced it, call 1-800-908-4490.

Paid Preparer Must Sign Your Return

Generally, anyone you pay to prepare your return must sign it and include their Preparer Tax Identification Number (PTIN) in the space provided. The preparer must give you a copy of the return for your records. Someone who prepares your return but doesn't charge you should not sign your return.

Assemble Your Return

Assemble any schedules and forms behind Form 1040 in order of the "Attachment Sequence No." shown in the upper right corner of the schedule or form. If you have supporting statements, arrange them in the same order as the schedules or forms they support and attach them last. Do not attach correspondence or other items unless required to do so. Attach Forms W-2 and 2439 to the front of Form 1040. If you received a Form W-2c (a corrected Form W-2), attach your original Forms W-2 and any Forms W-2c. Attach Forms W-2G and 1099-R to the front of Form 1040 if tax was withheld.

2015 Tax Table

 CAUTION

See the instructions for line 44 to see if you must use the Tax Table below to figure your tax.

Example. Mr. and Mrs. Brown are filing a joint return. Their taxable income on Form 1040, line 43, is $25,300. First, they find the $25,300-25,350 taxable income line. Next, they find the column for married filing jointly and read down the column. The amount shown where the taxable income line and filing status column meet is $2,876. This is the tax amount they should enter on Form 1040, line 44.

Sample Table

At Least	But Less Than	Single	Married filing jointly*	Married filing separately	Head of a household
			Your tax is—		
25,200	25,250	3,323	2,861	3,323	3,126
25,250	25,300	3,330	2,869	3,330	3,134
25,300	25,350	3,338	(2,876)	3,338	3,141
25,350	25,400	3,345	2,884	3,345	3,149

If line 43 (taxable income) is— At least	But less than	Single	Married filing jointly *	Married filing sepa-rately	Head of a house-hold
			Your tax is—		
0	5	0	0	0	0
5	15	1	1	1	1
15	25	2	2	2	2
25	50	4	4	4	4
50	75	6	6	6	6
75	100	9	9	9	9
100	125	11	11	11	11
125	150	14	14	14	14
150	175	16	16	16	16
175	200	19	19	19	19
200	225	21	21	21	21
225	250	24	24	24	24
250	275	26	26	26	26
275	300	29	29	29	29
300	325	31	31	31	31
325	350	34	34	34	34
350	375	36	36	36	36
375	400	39	39	39	39
400	425	41	41	41	41
425	450	44	44	44	44
450	475	46	46	46	46
475	500	49	49	49	49
500	525	51	51	51	51
525	550	54	54	54	54
550	575	56	56	56	56
575	600	59	59	59	59
600	625	61	61	61	61
625	650	64	64	64	64
650	675	66	66	66	66
675	700	69	69	69	69
700	725	71	71	71	71
725	750	74	74	74	74
750	775	76	76	76	76
775	800	79	79	79	79
800	825	81	81	81	81
825	850	84	84	84	84
850	875	86	86	86	86
875	900	89	89	89	89
900	925	91	91	91	91
925	950	94	94	94	94
950	975	96	96	96	96
975	1,000	99	99	99	99

1,000

At least	But less than	Single	Married filing jointly *	Married filing sepa-rately	Head of a house-hold
1,000	1,025	101	101	101	101
1,025	1,050	104	104	104	104
1,050	1,075	106	106	106	106
1,075	1,100	109	109	109	109
1,100	1,125	111	111	111	111
1,125	1,150	114	114	114	114
1,150	1,175	116	116	116	116
1,175	1,200	119	119	119	119
1,200	1,225	121	121	121	121
1,225	1,250	124	124	124	124
1,250	1,275	126	126	126	126
1,275	1,300	129	129	129	129
1,300	1,325	131	131	131	131
1,325	1,350	134	134	134	134
1,350	1,375	136	136	136	136
1,375	1,400	139	139	139	139
1,400	1,425	141	141	141	141
1,425	1,450	144	144	144	144
1,450	1,475	146	146	146	146
1,475	1,500	149	149	149	149
1,500	1,525	151	151	151	151
1,525	1,550	154	154	154	154
1,550	1,575	156	156	156	156
1,575	1,600	159	159	159	159
1,600	1,625	161	161	161	161
1,625	1,650	164	164	164	164
1,650	1,675	166	166	166	166
1,675	1,700	169	169	169	169
1,700	1,725	171	171	171	171
1,725	1,750	174	174	174	174
1,750	1,775	176	176	176	176
1,775	1,800	179	179	179	179
1,800	1,825	181	181	181	181
1,825	1,850	184	184	184	184
1,850	1,875	186	186	186	186
1,875	1,900	189	189	189	189
1,900	1,925	191	191	191	191
1,925	1,950	194	194	194	194
1,950	1,975	196	196	196	196
1,975	2,000	199	199	199	199

2,000

At least	But less than	Single	Married filing jointly *	Married filing sepa-rately	Head of a house-hold
2,000	2,025	201	201	201	201
2,025	2,050	204	204	204	204
2,050	2,075	206	206	206	206
2,075	2,100	209	209	209	209
2,100	2,125	211	211	211	211
2,125	2,150	214	214	214	214
2,150	2,175	216	216	216	216
2,175	2,200	219	219	219	219
2,200	2,225	221	221	221	221
2,225	2,250	224	224	224	224
2,250	2,275	226	226	226	226
2,275	2,300	229	229	229	229
2,300	2,325	231	231	231	231
2,325	2,350	234	234	234	234
2,350	2,375	236	236	236	236
2,375	2,400	239	239	239	239
2,400	2,425	241	241	241	241
2,425	2,450	244	244	244	244
2,450	2,475	246	246	246	246
2,475	2,500	249	249	249	249
2,500	2,525	251	251	251	251
2,525	2,550	254	254	254	254
2,550	2,575	256	256	256	256
2,575	2,600	259	259	259	259
2,600	2,625	261	261	261	261
2,625	2,650	264	264	264	264
2,650	2,675	266	266	266	266
2,675	2,700	269	269	269	269
2,700	2,725	271	271	271	271
2,725	2,750	274	274	274	274
2,750	2,775	276	276	276	276
2,775	2,800	279	279	279	279
2,800	2,825	281	281	281	281
2,825	2,850	284	284	284	284
2,850	2,875	286	286	286	286
2,875	2,900	289	289	289	289
2,900	2,925	291	291	291	291
2,925	2,950	294	294	294	294
2,950	2,975	296	296	296	296
2,975	3,000	299	299	299	299

(Continued)

* This column must also be used by a qualifying widow(er).

Need more information or forms? Visit IRS.gov.

If line 43 (taxable income) is— / And you are—

3,000

At least	But less than	Single	Married filing jointly *	Married filing separately	Head of a household
3,000	3,050	303	303	303	303
3,050	3,100	308	308	308	308
3,100	3,150	313	313	313	313
3,150	3,200	318	318	318	318
3,200	3,250	323	323	323	323
3,250	3,300	328	328	328	328
3,300	3,350	333	333	333	333
3,350	3,400	338	338	338	338
3,400	3,450	343	343	343	343
3,450	3,500	348	348	348	348
3,500	3,550	353	353	353	353
3,550	3,600	358	358	358	358
3,600	3,650	363	363	363	363
3,650	3,700	368	368	368	368
3,700	3,750	373	373	373	373
3,750	3,800	378	378	378	378
3,800	3,850	383	383	383	383
3,850	3,900	388	388	388	388
3,900	3,950	393	393	393	393
3,950	4,000	398	398	398	398

4,000

At least	But less than	Single	Married filing jointly *	Married filing separately	Head of a household
4,000	4,050	403	403	403	403
4,050	4,100	408	408	408	408
4,100	4,150	413	413	413	413
4,150	4,200	418	418	418	418
4,200	4,250	423	423	423	423
4,250	4,300	428	428	428	428
4,300	4,350	433	433	433	433
4,350	4,400	438	438	438	438
4,400	4,450	443	443	443	443
4,450	4,500	448	448	448	448
4,500	4,550	453	453	453	453
4,550	4,600	458	458	458	458
4,600	4,650	463	463	463	463
4,650	4,700	468	468	468	468
4,700	4,750	473	473	473	473
4,750	4,800	478	478	478	478
4,800	4,850	483	483	483	483
4,850	4,900	488	488	488	488
4,900	4,950	493	493	493	493
4,950	5,000	498	498	498	498

5,000

At least	But less than	Single	Married filing jointly *	Married filing separately	Head of a household
5,000	5,050	503	503	503	503
5,050	5,100	508	508	508	508
5,100	5,150	513	513	513	513
5,150	5,200	518	518	518	518
5,200	5,250	523	523	523	523
5,250	5,300	528	528	528	528
5,300	5,350	533	533	533	533
5,350	5,400	538	538	538	538
5,400	5,450	543	543	543	543
5,450	5,500	548	548	548	548
5,500	5,550	553	553	553	553
5,550	5,600	558	558	558	558
5,600	5,650	563	563	563	563
5,650	5,700	568	568	568	568
5,700	5,750	573	573	573	573
5,750	5,800	578	578	578	578
5,800	5,850	583	583	583	583
5,850	5,900	588	588	588	588
5,900	5,950	593	593	593	593
5,950	6,000	598	598	598	598

6,000

At least	But less than	Single	Married filing jointly *	Married filing separately	Head of a household
6,000	6,050	603	603	603	603
6,050	6,100	608	608	608	608
6,100	6,150	613	613	613	613
6,150	6,200	618	618	618	618
6,200	6,250	623	623	623	623
6,250	6,300	628	628	628	628
6,300	6,350	633	633	633	633
6,350	6,400	638	638	638	638
6,400	6,450	643	643	643	643
6,450	6,500	648	648	648	648
6,500	6,550	653	653	653	653
6,550	6,600	658	658	658	658
6,600	6,650	663	663	663	663
6,650	6,700	668	668	668	668
6,700	6,750	673	673	673	673
6,750	6,800	678	678	678	678
6,800	6,850	683	683	683	683
6,850	6,900	688	688	688	688
6,900	6,950	693	693	693	693
6,950	7,000	698	698	698	698

7,000

At least	But less than	Single	Married filing jointly *	Married filing separately	Head of a household
7,000	7,050	703	703	703	703
7,050	7,100	708	708	708	708
7,100	7,150	713	713	713	713
7,150	7,200	718	718	718	718
7,200	7,250	723	723	723	723
7,250	7,300	728	728	728	728
7,300	7,350	733	733	733	733
7,350	7,400	738	738	738	738
7,400	7,450	743	743	743	743
7,450	7,500	748	748	748	748
7,500	7,550	753	753	753	753
7,550	7,600	758	758	758	758
7,600	7,650	763	763	763	763
7,650	7,700	768	768	768	768
7,700	7,750	773	773	773	773
7,750	7,800	778	778	778	778
7,800	7,850	783	783	783	783
7,850	7,900	788	788	788	788
7,900	7,950	793	793	793	793
7,950	8,000	798	798	798	798

8,000

At least	But less than	Single	Married filing jointly *	Married filing separately	Head of a household
8,000	8,050	803	803	803	803
8,050	8,100	808	808	808	808
8,100	8,150	813	813	813	813
8,150	8,200	818	818	818	818
8,200	8,250	823	823	823	823
8,250	8,300	828	828	828	828
8,300	8,350	833	833	833	833
8,350	8,400	838	838	838	838
8,400	8,450	843	843	843	843
8,450	8,500	848	848	848	848
8,500	8,550	853	853	853	853
8,550	8,600	858	858	858	858
8,600	8,650	863	863	863	863
8,650	8,700	868	868	868	868
8,700	8,750	873	873	873	873
8,750	8,800	878	878	878	878
8,800	8,850	883	883	883	883
8,850	8,900	888	888	888	888
8,900	8,950	893	893	893	893
8,950	9,000	898	898	898	898

9,000

At least	But less than	Single	Married filing jointly *	Married filing separately	Head of a household
9,000	9,050	903	903	903	903
9,050	9,100	908	908	908	908
9,100	9,150	913	913	913	913
9,150	9,200	918	918	918	918
9,200	9,250	923	923	923	923
9,250	9,300	930	928	930	928
9,300	9,350	938	933	938	933
9,350	9,400	945	938	945	938
9,400	9,450	953	943	953	943
9,450	9,500	960	948	960	948
9,500	9,550	968	953	968	953
9,550	9,600	975	958	975	958
9,600	9,650	983	963	983	963
9,650	9,700	990	968	990	968
9,700	9,750	998	973	998	973
9,750	9,800	1,005	978	1,005	978
9,800	9,850	1,013	983	1,013	983
9,850	9,900	1,020	988	1,020	988
9,900	9,950	1,028	993	1,028	993
9,950	10,000	1,035	998	1,035	998

10,000

At least	But less than	Single	Married filing jointly *	Married filing separately	Head of a household
10,000	10,050	1,043	1,003	1,043	1,003
10,050	10,100	1,050	1,008	1,050	1,008
10,100	10,150	1,058	1,013	1,058	1,013
10,150	10,200	1,065	1,018	1,065	1,018
10,200	10,250	1,073	1,023	1,073	1,023
10,250	10,300	1,080	1,028	1,080	1,028
10,300	10,350	1,088	1,033	1,088	1,033
10,350	10,400	1,095	1,038	1,095	1,038
10,400	10,450	1,103	1,043	1,103	1,043
10,450	10,500	1,110	1,048	1,110	1,048
10,500	10,550	1,118	1,053	1,118	1,053
10,550	10,600	1,125	1,058	1,125	1,058
10,600	10,650	1,133	1,063	1,133	1,063
10,650	10,700	1,140	1,068	1,140	1,068
10,700	10,750	1,148	1,073	1,148	1,073
10,750	10,800	1,155	1,078	1,155	1,078
10,800	10,850	1,163	1,083	1,163	1,083
10,850	10,900	1,170	1,088	1,170	1,088
10,900	10,950	1,178	1,093	1,178	1,093
10,950	11,000	1,185	1,098	1,185	1,098

11,000

At least	But less than	Single	Married filing jointly *	Married filing separately	Head of a household
11,000	11,050	1,193	1,103	1,193	1,103
11,050	11,100	1,200	1,108	1,200	1,108
11,100	11,150	1,208	1,113	1,208	1,113
11,150	11,200	1,215	1,118	1,215	1,118
11,200	11,250	1,223	1,123	1,223	1,123
11,250	11,300	1,230	1,128	1,230	1,128
11,300	11,350	1,238	1,133	1,238	1,133
11,350	11,400	1,245	1,138	1,245	1,138
11,400	11,450	1,253	1,143	1,253	1,143
11,450	11,500	1,260	1,148	1,260	1,148
11,500	11,550	1,268	1,153	1,268	1,153
11,550	11,600	1,275	1,158	1,275	1,158
11,600	11,650	1,283	1,163	1,283	1,163
11,650	11,700	1,290	1,168	1,290	1,168
11,700	11,750	1,298	1,173	1,298	1,173
11,750	11,800	1,305	1,178	1,305	1,178
11,800	11,850	1,313	1,183	1,313	1,183
11,850	11,900	1,320	1,188	1,320	1,188
11,900	11,950	1,328	1,193	1,328	1,193
11,950	12,000	1,335	1,198	1,335	1,198

(Continued)

* This column must also be used by a qualifying widow(er).

Need more information or forms? Visit IRS.gov.

If line 43 (taxable income) is—		And you are—			
At least	But less than	Single	Married filing jointly *	Married filing separately	Head of a household
		Your tax is—			

12,000

At least	But less than	Single	Married filing jointly *	Married filing separately	Head of a household
12,000	12,050	1,343	1,203	1,343	1,203
12,050	12,100	1,350	1,208	1,350	1,208
12,100	12,150	1,358	1,213	1,358	1,213
12,150	12,200	1,365	1,218	1,365	1,218
12,200	12,250	1,373	1,223	1,373	1,223
12,250	12,300	1,380	1,228	1,380	1,228
12,300	12,350	1,388	1,233	1,388	1,233
12,350	12,400	1,395	1,238	1,395	1,238
12,400	12,450	1,403	1,243	1,403	1,243
12,450	12,500	1,410	1,248	1,410	1,248
12,500	12,550	1,418	1,253	1,418	1,253
12,550	12,600	1,425	1,258	1,425	1,258
12,600	12,650	1,433	1,263	1,433	1,263
12,650	12,700	1,440	1,268	1,440	1,268
12,700	12,750	1,448	1,273	1,448	1,273
12,750	12,800	1,455	1,278	1,455	1,278
12,800	12,850	1,463	1,283	1,463	1,283
12,850	12,900	1,470	1,288	1,470	1,288
12,900	12,950	1,478	1,293	1,478	1,293
12,950	13,000	1,485	1,298	1,485	1,298

13,000

At least	But less than	Single	Married filing jointly *	Married filing separately	Head of a household
13,000	13,050	1,493	1,303	1,493	1,303
13,050	13,100	1,500	1,308	1,500	1,308
13,100	13,150	1,508	1,313	1,508	1,313
13,150	13,200	1,515	1,318	1,515	1,319
13,200	13,250	1,523	1,323	1,523	1,326
13,250	13,300	1,530	1,328	1,530	1,334
13,300	13,350	1,538	1,333	1,538	1,341
13,350	13,400	1,545	1,338	1,545	1,349
13,400	13,450	1,553	1,343	1,553	1,356
13,450	13,500	1,560	1,348	1,560	1,364
13,500	13,550	1,568	1,353	1,568	1,371
13,550	13,600	1,575	1,358	1,575	1,379
13,600	13,650	1,583	1,363	1,583	1,386
13,650	13,700	1,590	1,368	1,590	1,394
13,700	13,750	1,598	1,373	1,598	1,401
13,750	13,800	1,605	1,378	1,605	1,409
13,800	13,850	1,613	1,383	1,613	1,416
13,850	13,900	1,620	1,388	1,620	1,424
13,900	13,950	1,628	1,393	1,628	1,431
13,950	14,000	1,635	1,398	1,635	1,439

14,000

At least	But less than	Single	Married filing jointly *	Married filing separately	Head of a household
14,000	14,050	1,643	1,403	1,643	1,446
14,050	14,100	1,650	1,408	1,650	1,454
14,100	14,150	1,658	1,413	1,658	1,461
14,150	14,200	1,665	1,418	1,665	1,469
14,200	14,250	1,673	1,423	1,673	1,476
14,250	14,300	1,680	1,428	1,680	1,484
14,300	14,350	1,688	1,433	1,688	1,491
14,350	14,400	1,695	1,438	1,695	1,499
14,400	14,450	1,703	1,443	1,703	1,506
14,450	14,500	1,710	1,448	1,710	1,514
14,500	14,550	1,718	1,453	1,718	1,521
14,550	14,600	1,725	1,458	1,725	1,529
14,600	14,650	1,733	1,463	1,733	1,536
14,650	14,700	1,740	1,468	1,740	1,544
14,700	14,750	1,748	1,473	1,748	1,551
14,750	14,800	1,755	1,478	1,755	1,559
14,800	14,850	1,763	1,483	1,763	1,566
14,850	14,900	1,770	1,488	1,770	1,574
14,900	14,950	1,778	1,493	1,778	1,581
14,950	15,000	1,785	1,498	1,785	1,589

15,000

At least	But less than	Single	Married filing jointly *	Married filing separately	Head of a household
15,000	15,050	1,793	1,503	1,793	1,596
15,050	15,100	1,800	1,508	1,800	1,604
15,100	15,150	1,808	1,513	1,808	1,611
15,150	15,200	1,815	1,518	1,815	1,619
15,200	15,250	1,823	1,523	1,823	1,626
15,250	15,300	1,830	1,528	1,830	1,634
15,300	15,350	1,838	1,533	1,838	1,641
15,350	15,400	1,845	1,538	1,845	1,649
15,400	15,450	1,853	1,543	1,853	1,656
15,450	15,500	1,860	1,548	1,860	1,664
15,500	15,550	1,868	1,553	1,868	1,671
15,550	15,600	1,875	1,558	1,875	1,679
15,600	15,650	1,883	1,563	1,883	1,686
15,650	15,700	1,890	1,568	1,890	1,694
15,700	15,750	1,898	1,573	1,898	1,701
15,750	15,800	1,905	1,578	1,905	1,709
15,800	15,850	1,913	1,583	1,913	1,716
15,850	15,900	1,920	1,588	1,920	1,724
15,900	15,950	1,928	1,593	1,928	1,731
15,950	16,000	1,935	1,598	1,935	1,739

16,000

At least	But less than	Single	Married filing jointly *	Married filing separately	Head of a household
16,000	16,050	1,943	1,603	1,943	1,746
16,050	16,100	1,950	1,608	1,950	1,754
16,100	16,150	1,958	1,613	1,958	1,761
16,150	16,200	1,965	1,618	1,965	1,769
16,200	16,250	1,973	1,623	1,973	1,776
16,250	16,300	1,980	1,628	1,980	1,784
16,300	16,350	1,988	1,633	1,988	1,791
16,350	16,400	1,995	1,638	1,995	1,799
16,400	16,450	2,003	1,643	2,003	1,806
16,450	16,500	2,010	1,648	2,010	1,814
16,500	16,550	2,018	1,653	2,018	1,821
16,550	16,600	2,025	1,658	2,025	1,829
16,600	16,650	2,033	1,663	2,033	1,836
16,650	16,700	2,040	1,668	2,040	1,844
16,700	16,750	2,048	1,673	2,048	1,851
16,750	16,800	2,055	1,678	2,055	1,859
16,800	16,850	2,063	1,683	2,063	1,866
16,850	16,900	2,070	1,688	2,070	1,874
16,900	16,950	2,078	1,693	2,078	1,881
16,950	17,000	2,085	1,698	2,085	1,889

17,000

At least	But less than	Single	Married filing jointly *	Married filing separately	Head of a household
17,000	17,050	2,093	1,703	2,093	1,896
17,050	17,100	2,100	1,708	2,100	1,904
17,100	17,150	2,108	1,713	2,108	1,911
17,150	17,200	2,115	1,718	2,115	1,919
17,200	17,250	2,123	1,723	2,123	1,926
17,250	17,300	2,130	1,728	2,130	1,934
17,300	17,350	2,138	1,733	2,138	1,941
17,350	17,400	2,145	1,738	2,145	1,949
17,400	17,450	2,153	1,743	2,153	1,956
17,450	17,500	2,160	1,748	2,160	1,964
17,500	17,550	2,168	1,753	2,168	1,971
17,550	17,600	2,175	1,758	2,175	1,979
17,600	17,650	2,183	1,763	2,183	1,986
17,650	17,700	2,190	1,768	2,190	1,994
17,700	17,750	2,198	1,773	2,198	2,001
17,750	17,800	2,205	1,778	2,205	2,009
17,800	17,850	2,213	1,783	2,213	2,016
17,850	17,900	2,220	1,788	2,220	2,024
17,900	17,950	2,228	1,793	2,228	2,031
17,950	18,000	2,235	1,798	2,235	2,039

18,000

At least	But less than	Single	Married filing jointly *	Married filing separately	Head of a household
18,000	18,050	2,243	1,803	2,243	2,046
18,050	18,100	2,250	1,808	2,250	2,054
18,100	18,150	2,258	1,813	2,258	2,061
18,150	18,200	2,265	1,818	2,265	2,069
18,200	18,250	2,273	1,823	2,273	2,076
18,250	18,300	2,280	1,828	2,280	2,084
18,300	18,350	2,288	1,833	2,288	2,091
18,350	18,400	2,295	1,838	2,295	2,099
18,400	18,450	2,303	1,843	2,303	2,106
18,450	18,500	2,310	1,849	2,310	2,114
18,500	18,550	2,318	1,856	2,318	2,121
18,550	18,600	2,325	1,864	2,325	2,129
18,600	18,650	2,333	1,871	2,333	2,136
18,650	18,700	2,340	1,879	2,340	2,144
18,700	18,750	2,348	1,886	2,348	2,151
18,750	18,800	2,355	1,894	2,355	2,159
18,800	18,850	2,363	1,901	2,363	2,166
18,850	18,900	2,370	1,909	2,370	2,174
18,900	18,950	2,378	1,916	2,378	2,181
18,950	19,000	2,385	1,924	2,385	2,189

19,000

At least	But less than	Single	Married filing jointly *	Married filing separately	Head of a household
19,000	19,050	2,393	1,931	2,393	2,196
19,050	19,100	2,400	1,939	2,400	2,204
19,100	19,150	2,408	1,946	2,408	2,211
19,150	19,200	2,415	1,954	2,415	2,219
19,200	19,250	2,423	1,961	2,423	2,226
19,250	19,300	2,430	1,969	2,430	2,234
19,300	19,350	2,438	1,976	2,438	2,241
19,350	19,400	2,445	1,984	2,445	2,249
19,400	19,450	2,453	1,991	2,453	2,256
19,450	19,500	2,460	1,999	2,460	2,264
19,500	19,550	2,468	2,006	2,468	2,271
19,550	19,600	2,475	2,014	2,475	2,279
19,600	19,650	2,483	2,021	2,483	2,286
19,650	19,700	2,490	2,029	2,490	2,294
19,700	19,750	2,498	2,036	2,498	2,301
19,750	19,800	2,505	2,044	2,505	2,309
19,800	19,850	2,513	2,051	2,513	2,316
19,850	19,900	2,520	2,059	2,520	2,324
19,900	19,950	2,528	2,066	2,528	2,331
19,950	20,000	2,535	2,074	2,535	2,339

20,000

At least	But less than	Single	Married filing jointly *	Married filing separately	Head of a household
20,000	20,050	2,543	2,081	2,543	2,346
20,050	20,100	2,550	2,089	2,550	2,354
20,100	20,150	2,558	2,096	2,558	2,361
20,150	20,200	2,565	2,104	2,565	2,369
20,200	20,250	2,573	2,111	2,573	2,376
20,250	20,300	2,580	2,119	2,580	2,384
20,300	20,350	2,588	2,126	2,588	2,391
20,350	20,400	2,595	2,134	2,595	2,399
20,400	20,450	2,603	2,141	2,603	2,406
20,450	20,500	2,610	2,149	2,610	2,414
20,500	20,550	2,618	2,156	2,618	2,421
20,550	20,600	2,625	2,164	2,625	2,429
20,600	20,650	2,633	2,171	2,633	2,436
20,650	20,700	2,640	2,179	2,640	2,444
20,700	20,750	2,648	2,186	2,648	2,451
20,750	20,800	2,655	2,194	2,655	2,459
20,800	20,850	2,663	2,201	2,663	2,466
20,850	20,900	2,670	2,209	2,670	2,474
20,900	20,950	2,678	2,216	2,678	2,481
20,950	21,000	2,685	2,224	2,685	2,489

(Continued)

* This column must also be used by a qualifying widow(er).

Need more information or forms? Visit IRS.gov.

21,000

At least	But less than	Single	Married filing jointly *	Married filing separately	Head of a household
21,000	21,050	2,693	2,231	2,693	2,496
21,050	21,100	2,700	2,239	2,700	2,504
21,100	21,150	2,708	2,246	2,708	2,511
21,150	21,200	2,715	2,254	2,715	2,519
21,200	21,250	2,723	2,261	2,723	2,526
21,250	21,300	2,730	2,269	2,730	2,534
21,300	21,350	2,738	2,276	2,738	2,541
21,350	21,400	2,745	2,284	2,745	2,549
21,400	21,450	2,753	2,291	2,753	2,556
21,450	21,500	2,760	2,299	2,760	2,564
21,500	21,550	2,768	2,306	2,768	2,571
21,550	21,600	2,775	2,314	2,775	2,579
21,600	21,650	2,783	2,321	2,783	2,586
21,650	21,700	2,790	2,329	2,790	2,594
21,700	21,750	2,798	2,336	2,798	2,601
21,750	21,800	2,805	2,344	2,805	2,609
21,800	21,850	2,813	2,351	2,813	2,616
21,850	21,900	2,820	2,359	2,820	2,624
21,900	21,950	2,828	2,366	2,828	2,631
21,950	22,000	2,835	2,374	2,835	2,639

22,000

At least	But less than	Single	Married filing jointly *	Married filing separately	Head of a household
22,000	22,050	2,843	2,381	2,843	2,646
22,050	22,100	2,850	2,389	2,850	2,654
22,100	22,150	2,858	2,396	2,858	2,661
22,150	22,200	2,865	2,404	2,865	2,669
22,200	22,250	2,873	2,411	2,873	2,676
22,250	22,300	2,880	2,419	2,880	2,684
22,300	22,350	2,888	2,426	2,888	2,691
22,350	22,400	2,895	2,434	2,895	2,699
22,400	22,450	2,903	2,441	2,903	2,706
22,450	22,500	2,910	2,449	2,910	2,714
22,500	22,550	2,918	2,456	2,918	2,721
22,550	22,600	2,925	2,464	2,925	2,729
22,600	22,650	2,933	2,471	2,933	2,736
22,650	22,700	2,940	2,479	2,940	2,744
22,700	22,750	2,948	2,486	2,948	2,751
22,750	22,800	2,955	2,494	2,955	2,759
22,800	22,850	2,963	2,501	2,963	2,766
22,850	22,900	2,970	2,509	2,970	2,774
22,900	22,950	2,978	2,516	2,978	2,781
22,950	23,000	2,985	2,524	2,985	2,789

23,000

At least	But less than	Single	Married filing jointly *	Married filing separately	Head of a household
23,000	23,050	2,993	2,531	2,993	2,796
23,050	23,100	3,000	2,539	3,000	2,804
23,100	23,150	3,008	2,546	3,008	2,811
23,150	23,200	3,015	2,554	3,015	2,819
23,200	23,250	3,023	2,561	3,023	2,826
23,250	23,300	3,030	2,569	3,030	2,834
23,300	23,350	3,038	2,576	3,038	2,841
23,350	23,400	3,045	2,584	3,045	2,849
23,400	23,450	3,053	2,591	3,053	2,856
23,450	23,500	3,060	2,599	3,060	2,864
23,500	23,550	3,068	2,606	3,068	2,871
23,550	23,600	3,075	2,614	3,075	2,879
23,600	23,650	3,083	2,621	3,083	2,886
23,650	23,700	3,090	2,629	3,090	2,894
23,700	23,750	3,098	2,636	3,098	2,901
23,750	23,800	3,105	2,644	3,105	2,909
23,800	23,850	3,113	2,651	3,113	2,916
23,850	23,900	3,120	2,659	3,120	2,924
23,900	23,950	3,128	2,666	3,128	2,931
23,950	24,000	3,135	2,674	3,135	2,939

24,000

At least	But less than	Single	Married filing jointly *	Married filing separately	Head of a household
24,000	24,050	3,143	2,681	3,143	2,946
24,050	24,100	3,150	2,689	3,150	2,954
24,100	24,150	3,158	2,696	3,158	2,961
24,150	24,200	3,165	2,704	3,165	2,969
24,200	24,250	3,173	2,711	3,173	2,976
24,250	24,300	3,180	2,719	3,180	2,984
24,300	24,350	3,188	2,726	3,188	2,991
24,350	24,400	3,195	2,734	3,195	2,999
24,400	24,450	3,203	2,741	3,203	3,006
24,450	24,500	3,210	2,749	3,210	3,014
24,500	24,550	3,218	2,756	3,218	3,021
24,550	24,600	3,225	2,764	3,225	3,029
24,600	24,650	3,233	2,771	3,233	3,036
24,650	24,700	3,240	2,779	3,240	3,044
24,700	24,750	3,248	2,786	3,248	3,051
24,750	24,800	3,255	2,794	3,255	3,059
24,800	24,850	3,263	2,801	3,263	3,066
24,850	24,900	3,270	2,809	3,270	3,074
24,900	24,950	3,278	2,816	3,278	3,081
24,950	25,000	3,285	2,824	3,285	3,089

25,000

At least	But less than	Single	Married filing jointly *	Married filing separately	Head of a household
25,000	25,050	3,293	2,831	3,293	3,096
25,050	25,100	3,300	2,839	3,300	3,104
25,100	25,150	3,308	2,846	3,308	3,111
25,150	25,200	3,315	2,854	3,315	3,119
25,200	25,250	3,323	2,861	3,323	3,126
25,250	25,300	3,330	2,869	3,330	3,134
25,300	25,350	3,338	2,876	3,338	3,141
25,350	25,400	3,345	2,884	3,345	3,149
25,400	25,450	3,353	2,891	3,353	3,156
25,450	25,500	3,360	2,899	3,360	3,164
25,500	25,550	3,368	2,906	3,368	3,171
25,550	25,600	3,375	2,914	3,375	3,179
25,600	25,650	3,383	2,921	3,383	3,186
25,650	25,700	3,390	2,929	3,390	3,194
25,700	25,750	3,398	2,936	3,398	3,201
25,750	25,800	3,405	2,944	3,405	3,209
25,800	25,850	3,413	2,951	3,413	3,216
25,850	25,900	3,420	2,959	3,420	3,224
25,900	25,950	3,428	2,966	3,428	3,231
25,950	26,000	3,435	2,974	3,435	3,239

26,000

At least	But less than	Single	Married filing jointly *	Married filing separately	Head of a household
26,000	26,050	3,443	2,981	3,443	3,246
26,050	26,100	3,450	2,989	3,450	3,254
26,100	26,150	3,458	2,996	3,458	3,261
26,150	26,200	3,465	3,004	3,465	3,269
26,200	26,250	3,473	3,011	3,473	3,276
26,250	26,300	3,480	3,019	3,480	3,284
26,300	26,350	3,488	3,026	3,488	3,291
26,350	26,400	3,495	3,034	3,495	3,299
26,400	26,450	3,503	3,041	3,503	3,306
26,450	26,500	3,510	3,049	3,510	3,314
26,500	26,550	3,518	3,056	3,518	3,321
26,550	26,600	3,525	3,064	3,525	3,329
26,600	26,650	3,533	3,071	3,533	3,336
26,650	26,700	3,540	3,079	3,540	3,344
26,700	26,750	3,548	3,086	3,548	3,351
26,750	26,800	3,555	3,094	3,555	3,359
26,800	26,850	3,563	3,101	3,563	3,366
26,850	26,900	3,570	3,109	3,570	3,374
26,900	26,950	3,578	3,116	3,578	3,381
26,950	27,000	3,585	3,124	3,585	3,389

27,000

At least	But less than	Single	Married filing jointly *	Married filing separately	Head of a household
27,000	27,050	3,593	3,131	3,593	3,396
27,050	27,100	3,600	3,139	3,600	3,404
27,100	27,150	3,608	3,146	3,608	3,411
27,150	27,200	3,615	3,154	3,615	3,419
27,200	27,250	3,623	3,161	3,623	3,426
27,250	27,300	3,630	3,169	3,630	3,434
27,300	27,350	3,638	3,176	3,638	3,441
27,350	27,400	3,645	3,184	3,645	3,449
27,400	27,450	3,653	3,191	3,653	3,456
27,450	27,500	3,660	3,199	3,660	3,464
27,500	27,550	3,668	3,206	3,668	3,471
27,550	27,600	3,675	3,214	3,675	3,479
27,600	27,650	3,683	3,221	3,683	3,486
27,650	27,700	3,690	3,229	3,690	3,494
27,700	27,750	3,698	3,236	3,698	3,501
27,750	27,800	3,705	3,244	3,705	3,509
27,800	27,850	3,713	3,251	3,713	3,516
27,850	27,900	3,720	3,259	3,720	3,524
27,900	27,950	3,728	3,266	3,728	3,531
27,950	28,000	3,735	3,274	3,735	3,539

28,000

At least	But less than	Single	Married filing jointly *	Married filing separately	Head of a household
28,000	28,050	3,743	3,281	3,743	3,546
28,050	28,100	3,750	3,289	3,750	3,554
28,100	28,150	3,758	3,296	3,758	3,561
28,150	28,200	3,765	3,304	3,765	3,569
28,200	28,250	3,773	3,311	3,773	3,576
28,250	28,300	3,780	3,319	3,780	3,584
28,300	28,350	3,788	3,326	3,788	3,591
28,350	28,400	3,795	3,334	3,795	3,599
28,400	28,450	3,803	3,341	3,803	3,606
28,450	28,500	3,810	3,349	3,810	3,614
28,500	28,550	3,818	3,356	3,818	3,621
28,550	28,600	3,825	3,364	3,825	3,629
28,600	28,650	3,833	3,371	3,833	3,636
28,650	28,700	3,840	3,379	3,840	3,644
28,700	28,750	3,848	3,386	3,848	3,651
28,750	28,800	3,855	3,394	3,855	3,659
28,800	28,850	3,863	3,401	3,863	3,666
28,850	28,900	3,870	3,409	3,870	3,674
28,900	28,950	3,878	3,416	3,878	3,681
28,950	29,000	3,885	3,424	3,885	3,689

29,000

At least	But less than	Single	Married filing jointly *	Married filing separately	Head of a household
29,000	29,050	3,893	3,431	3,893	3,696
29,050	29,100	3,900	3,439	3,900	3,704
29,100	29,150	3,908	3,446	3,908	3,711
29,150	29,200	3,915	3,454	3,915	3,719
29,200	29,250	3,923	3,461	3,923	3,726
29,250	29,300	3,930	3,469	3,930	3,734
29,300	29,350	3,938	3,476	3,938	3,741
29,350	29,400	3,945	3,484	3,945	3,749
29,400	29,450	3,953	3,491	3,953	3,756
29,450	29,500	3,960	3,499	3,960	3,764
29,500	29,550	3,968	3,506	3,968	3,771
29,550	29,600	3,975	3,514	3,975	3,779
29,600	29,650	3,983	3,521	3,983	3,786
29,650	29,700	3,990	3,529	3,990	3,794
29,700	29,750	3,998	3,536	3,998	3,801
29,750	29,800	4,005	3,544	4,005	3,809
29,800	29,850	4,013	3,551	4,013	3,816
29,850	29,900	4,020	3,559	4,020	3,824
29,900	29,950	4,028	3,566	4,028	3,831
29,950	30,000	4,035	3,574	4,035	3,839

* This column must also be used by a qualifying widow(er).

(Continued)

If line 43 (taxable income) is—		And you are—			
At least	But less than	Single	Married filing jointly *	Married filing separately	Head of a household
		Your tax is—			

30,000

At least	But less than	Single	Married filing jointly *	Married filing separately	Head of a household
30,000	30,050	4,043	3,581	4,043	3,846
30,050	30,100	4,050	3,589	4,050	3,854
30,100	30,150	4,058	3,596	4,058	3,861
30,150	30,200	4,065	3,604	4,065	3,869
30,200	30,250	4,073	3,611	4,073	3,876
30,250	30,300	4,080	3,619	4,080	3,884
30,300	30,350	4,088	3,626	4,088	3,891
30,350	30,400	4,095	3,634	4,095	3,899
30,400	30,450	4,103	3,641	4,103	3,906
30,450	30,500	4,110	3,649	4,110	3,914
30,500	30,550	4,118	3,656	4,118	3,921
30,550	30,600	4,125	3,664	4,125	3,929
30,600	30,650	4,133	3,671	4,133	3,936
30,650	30,700	4,140	3,679	4,140	3,944
30,700	30,750	4,148	3,686	4,148	3,951
30,750	30,800	4,155	3,694	4,155	3,959
30,800	30,850	4,163	3,701	4,163	3,966
30,850	30,900	4,170	3,709	4,170	3,974
30,900	30,950	4,178	3,716	4,178	3,981
30,950	31,000	4,185	3,724	4,185	3,989

31,000

At least	But less than	Single	Married filing jointly *	Married filing separately	Head of a household
31,000	31,050	4,193	3,731	4,193	3,996
31,050	31,100	4,200	3,739	4,200	4,004
31,100	31,150	4,208	3,746	4,208	4,011
31,150	31,200	4,215	3,754	4,215	4,019
31,200	31,250	4,223	3,761	4,223	4,026
31,250	31,300	4,230	3,769	4,230	4,034
31,300	31,350	4,238	3,776	4,238	4,041
31,350	31,400	4,245	3,784	4,245	4,049
31,400	31,450	4,253	3,791	4,253	4,056
31,450	31,500	4,260	3,799	4,260	4,064
31,500	31,550	4,268	3,806	4,268	4,071
31,550	31,600	4,275	3,814	4,275	4,079
31,600	31,650	4,283	3,821	4,283	4,086
31,650	31,700	4,290	3,829	4,290	4,094
31,700	31,750	4,298	3,836	4,298	4,101
31,750	31,800	4,305	3,844	4,305	4,109
31,800	31,850	4,313	3,851	4,313	4,116
31,850	31,900	4,320	3,859	4,320	4,124
31,900	31,950	4,328	3,866	4,328	4,131
31,950	32,000	4,335	3,874	4,335	4,139

32,000

At least	But less than	Single	Married filing jointly *	Married filing separately	Head of a household
32,000	32,050	4,343	3,881	4,343	4,146
32,050	32,100	4,350	3,889	4,350	4,154
32,100	32,150	4,358	3,896	4,358	4,161
32,150	32,200	4,365	3,904	4,365	4,169
32,200	32,250	4,373	3,911	4,373	4,176
32,250	32,300	4,380	3,919	4,380	4,184
32,300	32,350	4,388	3,926	4,388	4,191
32,350	32,400	4,395	3,934	4,395	4,199
32,400	32,450	4,403	3,941	4,403	4,206
32,450	32,500	4,410	3,949	4,410	4,214
32,500	32,550	4,418	3,956	4,418	4,221
32,550	32,600	4,425	3,964	4,425	4,229
32,600	32,650	4,433	3,971	4,433	4,236
32,650	32,700	4,440	3,979	4,440	4,244
32,700	32,750	4,448	3,986	4,448	4,251
32,750	32,800	4,455	3,994	4,455	4,259
32,800	32,850	4,463	4,001	4,463	4,266
32,850	32,900	4,470	4,009	4,470	4,274
32,900	32,950	4,478	4,016	4,478	4,281
32,950	33,000	4,485	4,024	4,485	4,289

33,000

At least	But less than	Single	Married filing jointly *	Married filing separately	Head of a household
33,000	33,050	4,493	4,031	4,493	4,296
33,050	33,100	4,500	4,039	4,500	4,304
33,100	33,150	4,508	4,046	4,508	4,311
33,150	33,200	4,515	4,054	4,515	4,319
33,200	33,250	4,523	4,061	4,523	4,326
33,250	33,300	4,530	4,069	4,530	4,334
33,300	33,350	4,538	4,076	4,538	4,341
33,350	33,400	4,545	4,084	4,545	4,349
33,400	33,450	4,553	4,091	4,553	4,356
33,450	33,500	4,560	4,099	4,560	4,364
33,500	33,550	4,568	4,106	4,568	4,371
33,550	33,600	4,575	4,114	4,575	4,379
33,600	33,650	4,583	4,121	4,583	4,386
33,650	33,700	4,590	4,129	4,590	4,394
33,700	33,750	4,598	4,136	4,598	4,401
33,750	33,800	4,605	4,144	4,605	4,409
33,800	33,850	4,613	4,151	4,613	4,416
33,850	33,900	4,620	4,159	4,620	4,424
33,900	33,950	4,628	4,166	4,628	4,431
33,950	34,000	4,635	4,174	4,635	4,439

34,000

At least	But less than	Single	Married filing jointly *	Married filing separately	Head of a household
34,000	34,050	4,643	4,181	4,643	4,446
34,050	34,100	4,650	4,189	4,650	4,454
34,100	34,150	4,658	4,196	4,658	4,461
34,150	34,200	4,665	4,204	4,665	4,469
34,200	34,250	4,673	4,211	4,673	4,476
34,250	34,300	4,680	4,219	4,680	4,484
34,300	34,350	4,688	4,226	4,688	4,491
34,350	34,400	4,695	4,234	4,695	4,499
34,400	34,450	4,703	4,241	4,703	4,506
34,450	34,500	4,710	4,249	4,710	4,514
34,500	34,550	4,718	4,256	4,718	4,521
34,550	34,600	4,725	4,264	4,725	4,529
34,600	34,650	4,733	4,271	4,733	4,536
34,650	34,700	4,740	4,279	4,740	4,544
34,700	34,750	4,748	4,286	4,748	4,551
34,750	34,800	4,755	4,294	4,755	4,559
34,800	34,850	4,763	4,301	4,763	4,566
34,850	34,900	4,770	4,309	4,770	4,574
34,900	34,950	4,778	4,316	4,778	4,581
34,950	35,000	4,785	4,324	4,785	4,589

35,000

At least	But less than	Single	Married filing jointly *	Married filing separately	Head of a household
35,000	35,050	4,793	4,331	4,793	4,596
35,050	35,100	4,800	4,339	4,800	4,604
35,100	35,150	4,808	4,346	4,808	4,611
35,150	35,200	4,815	4,354	4,815	4,619
35,200	35,250	4,823	4,361	4,823	4,626
35,250	35,300	4,830	4,369	4,830	4,634
35,300	35,350	4,838	4,376	4,838	4,641
35,350	35,400	4,845	4,384	4,845	4,649
35,400	35,450	4,853	4,391	4,853	4,656
35,450	35,500	4,860	4,399	4,860	4,664
35,500	35,550	4,868	4,406	4,868	4,671
35,550	35,600	4,875	4,414	4,875	4,679
35,600	35,650	4,883	4,421	4,883	4,686
35,650	35,700	4,890	4,429	4,890	4,694
35,700	35,750	4,898	4,436	4,898	4,701
35,750	35,800	4,905	4,444	4,905	4,709
35,800	35,850	4,913	4,451	4,913	4,716
35,850	35,900	4,920	4,459	4,920	4,724
35,900	35,950	4,928	4,466	4,928	4,731
35,950	36,000	4,935	4,474	4,935	4,739

36,000

At least	But less than	Single	Married filing jointly *	Married filing separately	Head of a household
36,000	36,050	4,943	4,481	4,943	4,746
36,050	36,100	4,950	4,489	4,950	4,754
36,100	36,150	4,958	4,496	4,958	4,761
36,150	36,200	4,965	4,504	4,965	4,769
36,200	36,250	4,973	4,511	4,973	4,776
36,250	36,300	4,980	4,519	4,980	4,784
36,300	36,350	4,988	4,526	4,988	4,791
36,350	36,400	4,995	4,534	4,995	4,799
36,400	36,450	5,003	4,541	5,003	4,806
36,450	36,500	5,010	4,549	5,010	4,814
36,500	36,550	5,018	4,556	5,018	4,821
36,550	36,600	5,025	4,564	5,025	4,829
36,600	36,650	5,033	4,571	5,033	4,836
36,650	36,700	5,040	4,579	5,040	4,844
36,700	36,750	5,048	4,586	5,048	4,851
36,750	36,800	5,055	4,594	5,055	4,859
36,800	36,850	5,063	4,601	5,063	4,866
36,850	36,900	5,070	4,609	5,070	4,874
36,900	36,950	5,078	4,616	5,078	4,881
36,950	37,000	5,085	4,624	5,085	4,889

37,000

At least	But less than	Single	Married filing jointly *	Married filing separately	Head of a household
37,000	37,050	5,093	4,631	5,093	4,896
37,050	37,100	5,100	4,639	5,100	4,904
37,100	37,150	5,108	4,646	5,108	4,911
37,150	37,200	5,115	4,654	5,115	4,919
37,200	37,250	5,123	4,661	5,123	4,926
37,250	37,300	5,130	4,669	5,130	4,934
37,300	37,350	5,138	4,676	5,138	4,941
37,350	37,400	5,145	4,684	5,145	4,949
37,400	37,450	5,153	4,691	5,153	4,956
37,450	37,500	5,163	4,699	5,163	4,964
37,500	37,550	5,175	4,706	5,175	4,971
37,550	37,600	5,188	4,714	5,188	4,979
37,600	37,650	5,200	4,721	5,200	4,986
37,650	37,700	5,213	4,729	5,213	4,994
37,700	37,750	5,225	4,736	5,225	5,001
37,750	37,800	5,238	4,744	5,238	5,009
37,800	37,850	5,250	4,751	5,250	5,016
37,850	37,900	5,263	4,759	5,263	5,024
37,900	37,950	5,275	4,766	5,275	5,031
37,950	38,000	5,288	4,774	5,288	5,039

38,000

At least	But less than	Single	Married filing jointly *	Married filing separately	Head of a household
38,000	38,050	5,300	4,781	5,300	5,046
38,050	38,100	5,313	4,789	5,313	5,054
38,100	38,150	5,325	4,796	5,325	5,061
38,150	38,200	5,338	4,804	5,338	5,069
38,200	38,250	5,350	4,811	5,350	5,076
38,250	38,300	5,363	4,819	5,363	5,084
38,300	38,350	5,375	4,826	5,375	5,091
38,350	38,400	5,388	4,834	5,388	5,099
38,400	38,450	5,400	4,841	5,400	5,106
38,450	38,500	5,413	4,849	5,413	5,114
38,500	38,550	5,425	4,856	5,425	5,121
38,550	38,600	5,438	4,864	5,438	5,129
38,600	38,650	5,450	4,871	5,450	5,136
38,650	38,700	5,463	4,879	5,463	5,144
38,700	38,750	5,475	4,886	5,475	5,151
38,750	38,800	5,488	4,894	5,488	5,159
38,800	38,850	5,500	4,901	5,500	5,166
38,850	38,900	5,513	4,909	5,513	5,174
38,900	38,950	5,525	4,916	5,525	5,181
38,950	39,000	5,538	4,924	5,538	5,189

* This column must also be used by a qualifying widow(er).

(Continued)

Need more information or forms? Visit IRS.gov.

If line 43 (taxable income) is—		And you are—			
At least	But less than	Single	Married filing jointly *	Married filing separately	Head of a household
		Your tax is—			

39,000

At least	But less than	Single	MFJ *	MFS	HoH
39,000	39,050	5,550	4,931	5,550	5,196
39,050	39,100	5,563	4,939	5,563	5,204
39,100	39,150	5,575	4,946	5,575	5,211
39,150	39,200	5,588	4,954	5,588	5,219
39,200	39,250	5,600	4,961	5,600	5,226
39,250	39,300	5,613	4,969	5,613	5,234
39,300	39,350	5,625	4,976	5,625	5,241
39,350	39,400	5,638	4,984	5,638	5,249
39,400	39,450	5,650	4,991	5,650	5,256
39,450	39,500	5,663	4,999	5,663	5,264
39,500	39,550	5,675	5,006	5,675	5,271
39,550	39,600	5,688	5,014	5,688	5,279
39,600	39,650	5,700	5,021	5,700	5,286
39,650	39,700	5,713	5,029	5,713	5,294
39,700	39,750	5,725	5,036	5,725	5,301
39,750	39,800	5,738	5,044	5,738	5,309
39,800	39,850	5,750	5,051	5,750	5,316
39,850	39,900	5,763	5,059	5,763	5,324
39,900	39,950	5,775	5,066	5,775	5,331
39,950	40,000	5,788	5,074	5,788	5,339

40,000

At least	But less than	Single	MFJ *	MFS	HoH
40,000	40,050	5,800	5,081	5,800	5,346
40,050	40,100	5,813	5,089	5,813	5,354
40,100	40,150	5,825	5,096	5,825	5,361
40,150	40,200	5,838	5,104	5,838	5,369
40,200	40,250	5,850	5,111	5,850	5,376
40,250	40,300	5,863	5,119	5,863	5,384
40,300	40,350	5,875	5,126	5,875	5,391
40,350	40,400	5,888	5,134	5,888	5,399
40,400	40,450	5,900	5,141	5,900	5,406
40,450	40,500	5,913	5,149	5,913	5,414
40,500	40,550	5,925	5,156	5,925	5,421
40,550	40,600	5,938	5,164	5,938	5,429
40,600	40,650	5,950	5,171	5,950	5,436
40,650	40,700	5,963	5,179	5,963	5,444
40,700	40,750	5,975	5,186	5,975	5,451
40,750	40,800	5,988	5,194	5,988	5,459
40,800	40,850	6,000	5,201	6,000	5,466
40,850	40,900	6,013	5,209	6,013	5,474
40,900	40,950	6,025	5,216	6,025	5,481
40,950	41,000	6,038	5,224	6,038	5,489

41,000

At least	But less than	Single	MFJ *	MFS	HoH
41,000	41,050	6,050	5,231	6,050	5,496
41,050	41,100	6,063	5,239	6,063	5,504
41,100	41,150	6,075	5,246	6,075	5,511
41,150	41,200	6,088	5,254	6,088	5,519
41,200	41,250	6,100	5,261	6,100	5,526
41,250	41,300	6,113	5,269	6,113	5,534
41,300	41,350	6,125	5,276	6,125	5,541
41,350	41,400	6,138	5,284	6,138	5,549
41,400	41,450	6,150	5,291	6,150	5,556
41,450	41,500	6,163	5,299	6,163	5,564
41,500	41,550	6,175	5,306	6,175	5,571
41,550	41,600	6,188	5,314	6,188	5,579
41,600	41,650	6,200	5,321	6,200	5,586
41,650	41,700	6,213	5,329	6,213	5,594
41,700	41,750	6,225	5,336	6,225	5,601
41,750	41,800	6,238	5,344	6,238	5,609
41,800	41,850	6,250	5,351	6,250	5,616
41,850	41,900	6,263	5,359	6,263	5,624
41,900	41,950	6,275	5,366	6,275	5,631
41,950	42,000	6,288	5,374	6,288	5,639

42,000

At least	But less than	Single	MFJ *	MFS	HoH
42,000	42,050	6,300	5,381	6,300	5,646
42,050	42,100	6,313	5,389	6,313	5,654
42,100	42,150	6,325	5,396	6,325	5,661
42,150	42,200	6,338	5,404	6,338	5,669
42,200	42,250	6,350	5,411	6,350	5,676
42,250	42,300	6,363	5,419	6,363	5,684
42,300	42,350	6,375	5,426	6,375	5,691
42,350	42,400	6,388	5,434	6,388	5,699
42,400	42,450	6,400	5,441	6,400	5,706
42,450	42,500	6,413	5,449	6,413	5,714
42,500	42,550	6,425	5,456	6,425	5,721
42,550	42,600	6,438	5,464	6,438	5,729
42,600	42,650	6,450	5,471	6,450	5,736
42,650	42,700	6,463	5,479	6,463	5,744
42,700	42,750	6,475	5,486	6,475	5,751
42,750	42,800	6,488	5,494	6,488	5,759
42,800	42,850	6,500	5,501	6,500	5,766
42,850	42,900	6,513	5,509	6,513	5,774
42,900	42,950	6,525	5,516	6,525	5,781
42,950	43,000	6,538	5,524	6,538	5,789

43,000

At least	But less than	Single	MFJ *	MFS	HoH
43,000	43,050	6,550	5,531	6,550	5,796
43,050	43,100	6,563	5,539	6,563	5,804
43,100	43,150	6,575	5,546	6,575	5,811
43,150	43,200	6,588	5,554	6,588	5,819
43,200	43,250	6,600	5,561	6,600	5,826
43,250	43,300	6,613	5,569	6,613	5,834
43,300	43,350	6,625	5,576	6,625	5,841
43,350	43,400	6,638	5,584	6,638	5,849
43,400	43,450	6,650	5,591	6,650	5,856
43,450	43,500	6,663	5,599	6,663	5,864
43,500	43,550	6,675	5,606	6,675	5,871
43,550	43,600	6,688	5,614	6,688	5,879
43,600	43,650	6,700	5,621	6,700	5,886
43,650	43,700	6,713	5,629	6,713	5,894
43,700	43,750	6,725	5,636	6,725	5,901
43,750	43,800	6,738	5,644	6,738	5,909
43,800	43,850	6,750	5,651	6,750	5,916
43,850	43,900	6,763	5,659	6,763	5,924
43,900	43,950	6,775	5,666	6,775	5,931
43,950	44,000	6,788	5,674	6,788	5,939

44,000

At least	But less than	Single	MFJ *	MFS	HoH
44,000	44,050	6,800	5,681	6,800	5,946
44,050	44,100	6,813	5,689	6,813	5,954
44,100	44,150	6,825	5,696	6,825	5,961
44,150	44,200	6,838	5,704	6,838	5,969
44,200	44,250	6,850	5,711	6,850	5,976
44,250	44,300	6,863	5,719	6,863	5,984
44,300	44,350	6,875	5,726	6,875	5,991
44,350	44,400	6,888	5,734	6,888	5,999
44,400	44,450	6,900	5,741	6,900	6,006
44,450	44,500	6,913	5,749	6,913	6,014
44,500	44,550	6,925	5,756	6,925	6,021
44,550	44,600	6,938	5,764	6,938	6,029
44,600	44,650	6,950	5,771	6,950	6,036
44,650	44,700	6,963	5,779	6,963	6,044
44,700	44,750	6,975	5,786	6,975	6,051
44,750	44,800	6,988	5,794	6,988	6,059
44,800	44,850	7,000	5,801	7,000	6,066
44,850	44,900	7,013	5,809	7,013	6,074
44,900	44,950	7,025	5,816	7,025	6,081
44,950	45,000	7,038	5,824	7,038	6,089

45,000

At least	But less than	Single	MFJ *	MFS	HoH
45,000	45,050	7,050	5,831	7,050	6,096
45,050	45,100	7,063	5,839	7,063	6,104
45,100	45,150	7,075	5,846	7,075	6,111
45,150	45,200	7,088	5,854	7,088	6,119
45,200	45,250	7,100	5,861	7,100	6,126
45,250	45,300	7,113	5,869	7,113	6,134
45,300	45,350	7,125	5,876	7,125	6,141
45,350	45,400	7,138	5,884	7,138	6,149
45,400	45,450	7,150	5,891	7,150	6,156
45,450	45,500	7,163	5,899	7,163	6,164
45,500	45,550	7,175	5,906	7,175	6,171
45,550	45,600	7,188	5,914	7,188	6,179
45,600	45,650	7,200	5,921	7,200	6,186
45,650	45,700	7,213	5,929	7,213	6,194
45,700	45,750	7,225	5,936	7,225	6,201
45,750	45,800	7,238	5,944	7,238	6,209
45,800	45,850	7,250	5,951	7,250	6,216
45,850	45,900	7,263	5,959	7,263	6,224
45,900	45,950	7,275	5,966	7,275	6,231
45,950	46,000	7,288	5,974	7,288	6,239

46,000

At least	But less than	Single	MFJ *	MFS	HoH
46,000	46,050	7,300	5,981	7,300	6,246
46,050	46,100	7,313	5,989	7,313	6,254
46,100	46,150	7,325	5,996	7,325	6,261
46,150	46,200	7,338	6,004	7,338	6,269
46,200	46,250	7,350	6,011	7,350	6,276
46,250	46,300	7,363	6,019	7,363	6,284
46,300	46,350	7,375	6,026	7,375	6,291
46,350	46,400	7,388	6,034	7,388	6,299
46,400	46,450	7,400	6,041	7,400	6,306
46,450	46,500	7,413	6,049	7,413	6,314
46,500	46,550	7,425	6,056	7,425	6,321
46,550	46,600	7,438	6,064	7,438	6,329
46,600	46,650	7,450	6,071	7,450	6,336
46,650	46,700	7,463	6,079	7,463	6,344
46,700	46,750	7,475	6,086	7,475	6,351
46,750	46,800	7,488	6,094	7,488	6,359
46,800	46,850	7,500	6,101	7,500	6,366
46,850	46,900	7,513	6,109	7,513	6,374
46,900	46,950	7,525	6,116	7,525	6,381
46,950	47,000	7,538	6,124	7,538	6,389

47,000

At least	But less than	Single	MFJ *	MFS	HoH
47,000	47,050	7,550	6,131	7,550	6,396
47,050	47,100	7,563	6,139	7,563	6,404
47,100	47,150	7,575	6,146	7,575	6,411
47,150	47,200	7,588	6,154	7,588	6,419
47,200	47,250	7,600	6,161	7,600	6,426
47,250	47,300	7,613	6,169	7,613	6,434
47,300	47,350	7,625	6,176	7,625	6,441
47,350	47,400	7,638	6,184	7,638	6,449
47,400	47,450	7,650	6,191	7,650	6,456
47,450	47,500	7,663	6,199	7,663	6,464
47,500	47,550	7,675	6,206	7,675	6,471
47,550	47,600	7,688	6,214	7,688	6,479
47,600	47,650	7,700	6,221	7,700	6,486
47,650	47,700	7,713	6,229	7,713	6,494
47,700	47,750	7,725	6,236	7,725	6,501
47,750	47,800	7,738	6,244	7,738	6,509
47,800	47,850	7,750	6,251	7,750	6,516
47,850	47,900	7,763	6,259	7,763	6,524
47,900	47,950	7,775	6,266	7,775	6,531
47,950	48,000	7,788	6,274	7,788	6,539

(Continued)

* This column must also be used by a qualifying widow(er).

Need more information or forms? Visit IRS.gov.

48,000

If line 43 (taxable income) is— At least	But less than	Single	Married filing jointly *	Married filing separately	Head of a household
				Your tax is—	
48,000	48,050	7,800	6,281	7,800	6,546
48,050	48,100	7,813	6,289	7,813	6,554
48,100	48,150	7,825	6,296	7,825	6,561
48,150	48,200	7,838	6,304	7,838	6,569
48,200	48,250	7,850	6,311	7,850	6,576
48,250	48,300	7,863	6,319	7,863	6,584
48,300	48,350	7,875	6,326	7,875	6,591
48,350	48,400	7,888	6,334	7,888	6,599
48,400	48,450	7,900	6,341	7,900	6,606
48,450	48,500	7,913	6,349	7,913	6,614
48,500	48,550	7,925	6,356	7,925	6,621
48,550	48,600	7,938	6,364	7,938	6,629
48,600	48,650	7,950	6,371	7,950	6,636
48,650	48,700	7,963	6,379	7,963	6,644
48,700	48,750	7,975	6,386	7,975	6,651
48,750	48,800	7,988	6,394	7,988	6,659
48,800	48,850	8,000	6,401	8,000	6,666
48,850	48,900	8,013	6,409	8,013	6,674
48,900	48,950	8,025	6,416	8,025	6,681
48,950	49,000	8,038	6,424	8,038	6,689

49,000

At least	But less than	Single	Married filing jointly *	Married filing separately	Head of a household
49,000	49,050	8,050	6,431	8,050	6,696
49,050	49,100	8,063	6,439	8,063	6,704
49,100	49,150	8,075	6,446	8,075	6,711
49,150	49,200	8,088	6,454	8,088	6,719
49,200	49,250	8,100	6,461	8,100	6,726
49,250	49,300	8,113	6,469	8,113	6,734
49,300	49,350	8,125	6,476	8,125	6,741
49,350	49,400	8,138	6,484	8,138	6,749
49,400	49,450	8,150	6,491	8,150	6,756
49,450	49,500	8,163	6,499	8,163	6,764
49,500	49,550	8,175	6,506	8,175	6,771
49,550	49,600	8,188	6,514	8,188	6,779
49,600	49,650	8,200	6,521	8,200	6,786
49,650	49,700	8,213	6,529	8,213	6,794
49,700	49,750	8,225	6,536	8,225	6,801
49,750	49,800	8,238	6,544	8,238	6,809
49,800	49,850	8,250	6,551	8,250	6,816
49,850	49,900	8,263	6,559	8,263	6,824
49,900	49,950	8,275	6,566	8,275	6,831
49,950	50,000	8,288	6,574	8,288	6,839

50,000

At least	But less than	Single	Married filing jointly *	Married filing separately	Head of a household
50,000	50,050	8,300	6,581	8,300	6,846
50,050	50,100	8,313	6,589	8,313	6,854
50,100	50,150	8,325	6,596	8,325	6,861
50,150	50,200	8,338	6,604	8,338	6,869
50,200	50,250	8,350	6,611	8,350	6,879
50,250	50,300	8,363	6,619	8,363	6,891
50,300	50,350	8,375	6,626	8,375	6,904
50,350	50,400	8,388	6,634	8,388	6,916
50,400	50,450	8,400	6,641	8,400	6,929
50,450	50,500	8,413	6,649	8,413	6,941
50,500	50,550	8,425	6,656	8,425	6,954
50,550	50,600	8,438	6,664	8,438	6,966
50,600	50,650	8,450	6,671	8,450	6,979
50,650	50,700	8,463	6,679	8,463	6,991
50,700	50,750	8,475	6,686	8,475	7,004
50,750	50,800	8,488	6,694	8,488	7,016
50,800	50,850	8,500	6,701	8,500	7,029
50,850	50,900	8,513	6,709	8,513	7,041
50,900	50,950	8,525	6,716	8,525	7,054
50,950	51,000	8,538	6,724	8,538	7,066

51,000

At least	But less than	Single	Married filing jointly *	Married filing separately	Head of a household
51,000	51,050	8,550	6,731	8,550	7,079
51,050	51,100	8,563	6,739	8,563	7,091
51,100	51,150	8,575	6,746	8,575	7,104
51,150	51,200	8,588	6,754	8,588	7,116
51,200	51,250	8,600	6,761	8,600	7,129
51,250	51,300	8,613	6,769	8,613	7,141
51,300	51,350	8,625	6,776	8,625	7,154
51,350	51,400	8,638	6,784	8,638	7,166
51,400	51,450	8,650	6,791	8,650	7,179
51,450	51,500	8,663	6,799	8,663	7,191
51,500	51,550	8,675	6,806	8,675	7,204
51,550	51,600	8,688	6,814	8,688	7,216
51,600	51,650	8,700	6,821	8,700	7,229
51,650	51,700	8,713	6,829	8,713	7,241
51,700	51,750	8,725	6,836	8,725	7,254
51,750	51,800	8,738	6,844	8,738	7,266
51,800	51,850	8,750	6,851	8,750	7,279
51,850	51,900	8,763	6,859	8,763	7,291
51,900	51,950	8,775	6,866	8,775	7,304
51,950	52,000	8,788	6,874	8,788	7,316

52,000

At least	But less than	Single	Married filing jointly *	Married filing separately	Head of a household
52,000	52,050	8,800	6,881	8,800	7,329
52,050	52,100	8,813	6,889	8,813	7,341
52,100	52,150	8,825	6,896	8,825	7,354
52,150	52,200	8,838	6,904	8,838	7,366
52,200	52,250	8,850	6,911	8,850	7,379
52,250	52,300	8,863	6,919	8,863	7,391
52,300	52,350	8,875	6,926	8,875	7,404
52,350	52,400	8,888	6,934	8,888	7,416
52,400	52,450	8,900	6,941	8,900	7,429
52,450	52,500	8,913	6,949	8,913	7,441
52,500	52,550	8,925	6,956	8,925	7,454
52,550	52,600	8,938	6,964	8,938	7,466
52,600	52,650	8,950	6,971	8,950	7,479
52,650	52,700	8,963	6,979	8,963	7,491
52,700	52,750	8,975	6,986	8,975	7,504
52,750	52,800	8,988	6,994	8,988	7,516
52,800	52,850	9,000	7,001	9,000	7,529
52,850	52,900	9,013	7,009	9,013	7,541
52,900	52,950	9,025	7,016	9,025	7,554
52,950	53,000	9,038	7,024	9,038	7,566

53,000

At least	But less than	Single	Married filing jointly *	Married filing separately	Head of a household
53,000	53,050	9,050	7,031	9,050	7,579
53,050	53,100	9,063	7,039	9,063	7,591
53,100	53,150	9,075	7,046	9,075	7,604
53,150	53,200	9,088	7,054	9,088	7,616
53,200	53,250	9,100	7,061	9,100	7,629
53,250	53,300	9,113	7,069	9,113	7,641
53,300	53,350	9,125	7,076	9,125	7,654
53,350	53,400	9,138	7,084	9,138	7,666
53,400	53,450	9,150	7,091	9,150	7,679
53,450	53,500	9,163	7,099	9,163	7,691
53,500	53,550	9,175	7,106	9,175	7,704
53,550	53,600	9,188	7,114	9,188	7,716
53,600	53,650	9,200	7,121	9,200	7,729
53,650	53,700	9,213	7,129	9,213	7,741
53,700	53,750	9,225	7,136	9,225	7,754
53,750	53,800	9,238	7,144	9,238	7,766
53,800	53,850	9,250	7,151	9,250	7,779
53,850	53,900	9,263	7,159	9,263	7,791
53,900	53,950	9,275	7,166	9,275	7,804
53,950	54,000	9,288	7,174	9,288	7,816

54,000

At least	But less than	Single	Married filing jointly *	Married filing separately	Head of a household
54,000	54,050	9,300	7,181	9,300	7,829
54,050	54,100	9,313	7,189	9,313	7,841
54,100	54,150	9,325	7,196	9,325	7,854
54,150	54,200	9,338	7,204	9,338	7,866
54,200	54,250	9,350	7,211	9,350	7,879
54,250	54,300	9,363	7,219	9,363	7,891
54,300	54,350	9,375	7,226	9,375	7,904
54,350	54,400	9,388	7,234	9,388	7,916
54,400	54,450	9,400	7,241	9,400	7,929
54,450	54,500	9,413	7,249	9,413	7,941
54,500	54,550	9,425	7,256	9,425	7,954
54,550	54,600	9,438	7,264	9,438	7,966
54,600	54,650	9,450	7,271	9,450	7,979
54,650	54,700	9,463	7,279	9,463	7,991
54,700	54,750	9,475	7,286	9,475	8,004
54,750	54,800	9,488	7,294	9,488	8,016
54,800	54,850	9,500	7,301	9,500	8,029
54,850	54,900	9,513	7,309	9,513	8,041
54,900	54,950	9,525	7,316	9,525	8,054
54,950	55,000	9,538	7,324	9,538	8,066

55,000

At least	But less than	Single	Married filing jointly *	Married filing separately	Head of a household
55,000	55,050	9,550	7,331	9,550	8,079
55,050	55,100	9,563	7,339	9,563	8,091
55,100	55,150	9,575	7,346	9,575	8,104
55,150	55,200	9,588	7,354	9,588	8,116
55,200	55,250	9,600	7,361	9,600	8,129
55,250	55,300	9,613	7,369	9,613	8,141
55,300	55,350	9,625	7,376	9,625	8,154
55,350	55,400	9,638	7,384	9,638	8,166
55,400	55,450	9,650	7,391	9,650	8,179
55,450	55,500	9,663	7,399	9,663	8,191
55,500	55,550	9,675	7,406	9,675	8,204
55,550	55,600	9,688	7,414	9,688	8,216
55,600	55,650	9,700	7,421	9,700	8,229
55,650	55,700	9,713	7,429	9,713	8,241
55,700	55,750	9,725	7,436	9,725	8,254
55,750	55,800	9,738	7,444	9,738	8,266
55,800	55,850	9,750	7,451	9,750	8,279
55,850	55,900	9,763	7,459	9,763	8,291
55,900	55,950	9,775	7,466	9,775	8,304
55,950	56,000	9,788	7,474	9,788	8,316

56,000

At least	But less than	Single	Married filing jointly *	Married filing separately	Head of a household
56,000	56,050	9,800	7,481	9,800	8,329
56,050	56,100	9,813	7,489	9,813	8,341
56,100	56,150	9,825	7,496	9,825	8,354
56,150	56,200	9,838	7,504	9,838	8,366
56,200	56,250	9,850	7,511	9,850	8,379
56,250	56,300	9,863	7,519	9,863	8,391
56,300	56,350	9,875	7,526	9,875	8,404
56,350	56,400	9,888	7,534	9,888	8,416
56,400	56,450	9,900	7,541	9,900	8,429
56,450	56,500	9,913	7,549	9,913	8,441
56,500	56,550	9,925	7,556	9,925	8,454
56,550	56,600	9,938	7,564	9,938	8,466
56,600	56,650	9,950	7,571	9,950	8,479
56,650	56,700	9,963	7,579	9,963	8,491
56,700	56,750	9,975	7,586	9,975	8,504
56,750	56,800	9,988	7,594	9,988	8,516
56,800	56,850	10,000	7,601	10,000	8,529
56,850	56,900	10,013	7,609	10,013	8,541
56,900	56,950	10,025	7,616	10,025	8,554
56,950	57,000	10,038	7,624	10,038	8,566

(Continued)

* This column must also be used by a qualifying widow(er).

Need more information or forms? Visit IRS.gov.

If line 43 (taxable income) is—		And you are—				If line 43 (taxable income) is—		And you are—				If line 43 (taxable income) is—		And you are—			
At least	But less than	Single	Married filing jointly *	Married filing separately	Head of a household	At least	But less than	Single	Married filing jointly *	Married filing separately	Head of a household	At least	But less than	Single	Married filing jointly *	Married filing separately	Head of a household
		Your tax is—						Your tax is—						Your tax is—			

57,000 / 60,000 / 63,000

At least	But less than	Single	MFJ	MFS	HoH	At least	But less than	Single	MFJ	MFS	HoH	At least	But less than	Single	MFJ	MFS	HoH
57,000	57,050	10,050	7,631	10,050	8,579	60,000	60,050	10,800	8,081	10,800	9,329	63,000	63,050	11,550	8,531	11,550	10,079
57,050	57,100	10,063	7,639	10,063	8,591	60,050	60,100	10,813	8,089	10,813	9,341	63,050	63,100	11,563	8,539	11,563	10,091
57,100	57,150	10,075	7,646	10,075	8,604	60,100	60,150	10,825	8,096	10,825	9,354	63,100	63,150	11,575	8,546	11,575	10,104
57,150	57,200	10,088	7,654	10,088	8,616	60,150	60,200	10,838	8,104	10,838	9,366	63,150	63,200	11,588	8,554	11,588	10,116
57,200	57,250	10,100	7,661	10,100	8,629	60,200	60,250	10,850	8,111	10,850	9,379	63,200	63,250	11,600	8,561	11,600	10,129
57,250	57,300	10,113	7,669	10,113	8,641	60,250	60,300	10,863	8,119	10,863	9,391	63,250	63,300	11,613	8,569	11,613	10,141
57,300	57,350	10,125	7,676	10,125	8,654	60,300	60,350	10,875	8,126	10,875	9,404	63,300	63,350	11,625	8,576	11,625	10,154
57,350	57,400	10,138	7,684	10,138	8,666	60,350	60,400	10,888	8,134	10,888	9,416	63,350	63,400	11,638	8,584	11,638	10,166
57,400	57,450	10,150	7,691	10,150	8,679	60,400	60,450	10,900	8,141	10,900	9,429	63,400	63,450	11,650	8,591	11,650	10,179
57,450	57,500	10,163	7,699	10,163	8,691	60,450	60,500	10,913	8,149	10,913	9,441	63,450	63,500	11,663	8,599	11,663	10,191
57,500	57,550	10,175	7,706	10,175	8,704	60,500	60,550	10,925	8,156	10,925	9,454	63,500	63,550	11,675	8,606	11,675	10,204
57,550	57,600	10,188	7,714	10,188	8,716	60,550	60,600	10,938	8,164	10,938	9,466	63,550	63,600	11,688	8,614	11,688	10,216
57,600	57,650	10,200	7,721	10,200	8,729	60,600	60,650	10,950	8,171	10,950	9,479	63,600	63,650	11,700	8,621	11,700	10,229
57,650	57,700	10,213	7,729	10,213	8,741	60,650	60,700	10,963	8,179	10,963	9,491	63,650	63,700	11,713	8,629	11,713	10,241
57,700	57,750	10,225	7,736	10,225	8,754	60,700	60,750	10,975	8,186	10,975	9,504	63,700	63,750	11,725	8,636	11,725	10,254
57,750	57,800	10,238	7,744	10,238	8,766	60,750	60,800	10,988	8,194	10,988	9,516	63,750	63,800	11,738	8,644	11,738	10,266
57,800	57,850	10,250	7,751	10,250	8,779	60,800	60,850	11,000	8,201	11,000	9,529	63,800	63,850	11,750	8,651	11,750	10,279
57,850	57,900	10,263	7,759	10,263	8,791	60,850	60,900	11,013	8,209	11,013	9,541	63,850	63,900	11,763	8,659	11,763	10,291
57,900	57,950	10,275	7,766	10,275	8,804	60,900	60,950	11,025	8,216	11,025	9,554	63,900	63,950	11,775	8,666	11,775	10,304
57,950	58,000	10,288	7,774	10,288	8,816	60,950	61,000	11,038	8,224	11,038	9,566	63,950	64,000	11,788	8,674	11,788	10,316

58,000 / 61,000 / 64,000

At least	But less than	Single	MFJ	MFS	HoH	At least	But less than	Single	MFJ	MFS	HoH	At least	But less than	Single	MFJ	MFS	HoH
58,000	58,050	10,300	7,781	10,300	8,829	61,000	61,050	11,050	8,231	11,050	9,579	64,000	64,050	11,800	8,681	11,800	10,329
58,050	58,100	10,313	7,789	10,313	8,841	61,050	61,100	11,063	8,239	11,063	9,591	64,050	64,100	11,813	8,689	11,813	10,341
58,100	58,150	10,325	7,796	10,325	8,854	61,100	61,150	11,075	8,246	11,075	9,604	64,100	64,150	11,825	8,696	11,825	10,366
58,150	58,200	10,338	7,804	10,338	8,866	61,150	61,200	11,088	8,254	11,088	9,616	64,150	64,200	11,838	8,704	11,838	10,366
58,200	58,250	10,350	7,811	10,350	8,879	61,200	61,250	11,100	8,261	11,100	9,629	64,200	64,250	11,850	8,711	11,850	10,379
58,250	58,300	10,363	7,819	10,363	8,891	61,250	61,300	11,113	8,269	11,113	9,641	64,250	64,300	11,863	8,719	11,863	10,391
58,300	58,350	10,375	7,826	10,375	8,904	61,300	61,350	11,125	8,276	11,125	9,654	64,300	64,350	11,875	8,726	11,875	10,404
58,350	58,400	10,388	7,834	10,388	8,916	61,350	61,400	11,138	8,284	11,138	9,666	64,350	64,400	11,888	8,734	11,888	10,416
58,400	58,450	10,400	7,841	10,400	8,929	61,400	61,450	11,150	8,291	11,150	9,679	64,400	64,450	11,900	8,741	11,900	10,429
58,450	58,500	10,413	7,849	10,413	8,941	61,450	61,500	11,163	8,299	11,163	9,691	64,450	64,500	11,913	8,749	11,913	10,441
58,500	58,550	10,425	7,856	10,425	8,954	61,500	61,550	11,175	8,306	11,175	9,704	64,500	64,550	11,925	8,756	11,925	10,454
58,550	58,600	10,438	7,864	10,438	8,966	61,550	61,600	11,188	8,314	11,188	9,716	64,550	64,600	11,938	8,764	11,938	10,466
58,600	58,650	10,450	7,871	10,450	8,979	61,600	61,650	11,200	8,321	11,200	9,729	64,600	64,650	11,950	8,771	11,950	10,479
58,650	58,700	10,463	7,879	10,463	8,991	61,650	61,700	11,213	8,329	11,213	9,741	64,650	64,700	11,963	8,779	11,963	10,491
58,700	58,750	10,475	7,886	10,475	9,004	61,700	61,750	11,225	8,336	11,225	9,754	64,700	64,750	11,975	8,786	11,975	10,504
58,750	58,800	10,488	7,894	10,488	9,016	61,750	61,800	11,238	8,344	11,238	9,766	64,750	64,800	11,988	8,794	11,988	10,516
58,800	58,850	10,500	7,901	10,500	9,029	61,800	61,850	11,250	8,351	11,250	9,779	64,800	64,850	12,000	8,801	12,000	10,529
58,850	58,900	10,513	7,909	10,513	9,041	61,850	61,900	11,263	8,359	11,263	9,791	64,850	64,900	12,013	8,809	12,013	10,541
58,900	58,950	10,525	7,916	10,525	9,054	61,900	61,950	11,275	8,366	11,275	9,804	64,900	64,950	12,025	8,816	12,025	10,554
58,950	59,000	10,538	7,924	10,538	9,066	61,950	62,000	11,288	8,374	11,288	9,816	64,950	65,000	12,038	8,824	12,038	10,566

59,000 / 62,000 / 65,000

At least	But less than	Single	MFJ	MFS	HoH	At least	But less than	Single	MFJ	MFS	HoH	At least	But less than	Single	MFJ	MFS	HoH
59,000	59,050	10,550	7,931	10,550	9,079	62,000	62,050	11,300	8,381	11,300	9,829	65,000	65,050	12,050	8,831	12,050	10,579
59,050	59,100	10,563	7,939	10,563	9,091	62,050	62,100	11,313	8,389	11,313	9,841	65,050	65,100	12,063	8,839	12,063	10,591
59,100	59,150	10,575	7,946	10,575	9,104	62,100	62,150	11,325	8,396	11,325	9,854	65,100	65,150	12,075	8,846	12,075	10,604
59,150	59,200	10,588	7,954	10,588	9,116	62,150	62,200	11,338	8,404	11,338	9,866	65,150	65,200	12,088	8,854	12,088	10,616
59,200	59,250	10,600	7,961	10,600	9,129	62,200	62,250	11,350	8,411	11,350	9,879	65,200	65,250	12,100	8,861	12,100	10,629
59,250	59,300	10,613	7,969	10,613	9,141	62,250	62,300	11,363	8,419	11,363	9,891	65,250	65,300	12,113	8,869	12,113	10,641
59,300	59,350	10,625	7,976	10,625	9,154	62,300	62,350	11,375	8,426	11,375	9,904	65,300	65,350	12,125	8,876	12,125	10,654
59,350	59,400	10,638	7,984	10,638	9,166	62,350	62,400	11,388	8,434	11,388	9,916	65,350	65,400	12,138	8,884	12,138	10,666
59,400	59,450	10,650	7,991	10,650	9,179	62,400	62,450	11,400	8,441	11,400	9,929	65,400	65,450	12,150	8,891	12,150	10,679
59,450	59,500	10,663	7,999	10,663	9,191	62,450	62,500	11,413	8,449	11,413	9,941	65,450	65,500	12,163	8,899	12,163	10,691
59,500	59,550	10,675	8,006	10,675	9,204	62,500	62,550	11,425	8,456	11,425	9,954	65,500	65,550	12,175	8,906	12,175	10,704
59,550	59,600	10,688	8,014	10,688	9,216	62,550	62,600	11,438	8,464	11,438	9,966	65,550	65,600	12,188	8,914	12,188	10,716
59,600	59,650	10,700	8,021	10,700	9,229	62,600	62,650	11,450	8,471	11,450	9,979	65,600	65,650	12,200	8,921	12,200	10,729
59,650	59,700	10,713	8,029	10,713	9,241	62,650	62,700	11,463	8,479	11,463	9,991	65,650	65,700	12,213	8,929	12,213	10,741
59,700	59,750	10,725	8,036	10,725	9,254	62,700	62,750	11,475	8,486	11,475	10,004	65,700	65,750	12,225	8,936	12,225	10,754
59,750	59,800	10,738	8,044	10,738	9,266	62,750	62,800	11,488	8,494	11,488	10,016	65,750	65,800	12,238	8,944	12,238	10,766
59,800	59,850	10,750	8,051	10,750	9,279	62,800	62,850	11,500	8,501	11,500	10,029	65,800	65,850	12,250	8,951	12,250	10,779
59,850	59,900	10,763	8,059	10,763	9,291	62,850	62,900	11,513	8,509	11,513	10,041	65,850	65,900	12,263	8,959	12,263	10,791
59,900	59,950	10,775	8,066	10,775	9,304	62,900	62,950	11,525	8,516	11,525	10,054	65,900	65,950	12,275	8,966	12,275	10,804
59,950	60,000	10,788	8,074	10,788	9,316	62,950	63,000	11,538	8,524	11,538	10,066	65,950	66,000	12,288	8,974	12,288	10,816

(Continued)

* This column must also be used by a qualifying widow(er).

| If line 43 (taxable income) is— | | And you are— | | | |
At least	But less than	Single	Married filing jointly *	Married filing separately	Head of a household
		Your tax is—			

66,000

At least	But less than	Single	MFJ *	MFS	HoH
66,000	66,050	12,300	8,981	12,300	10,829
66,050	66,100	12,313	8,989	12,313	10,841
66,100	66,150	12,325	8,996	12,325	10,854
66,150	66,200	12,338	9,004	12,338	10,866
66,200	66,250	12,350	9,011	12,350	10,879
66,250	66,300	12,363	9,019	12,363	10,891
66,300	66,350	12,375	9,026	12,375	10,904
66,350	66,400	12,388	9,034	12,388	10,916
66,400	66,450	12,400	9,041	12,400	10,929
66,450	66,500	12,413	9,049	12,413	10,941
66,500	66,550	12,425	9,056	12,425	10,954
66,550	66,600	12,438	9,064	12,438	10,966
66,600	66,650	12,450	9,071	12,450	10,979
66,650	66,700	12,463	9,079	12,463	10,991
66,700	66,750	12,475	9,086	12,475	11,004
66,750	66,800	12,488	9,094	12,488	11,016
66,800	66,850	12,500	9,101	12,500	11,029
66,850	66,900	12,513	9,109	12,513	11,041
66,900	66,950	12,525	9,116	12,525	11,054
66,950	67,000	12,538	9,124	12,538	11,066

67,000

At least	But less than	Single	MFJ *	MFS	HoH
67,000	67,050	12,550	9,131	12,550	11,079
67,050	67,100	12,563	9,139	12,563	11,091
67,100	67,150	12,575	9,146	12,575	11,104
67,150	67,200	12,588	9,154	12,588	11,116
67,200	67,250	12,600	9,161	12,600	11,129
67,250	67,300	12,613	9,169	12,613	11,141
67,300	67,350	12,625	9,176	12,625	11,154
67,350	67,400	12,638	9,184	12,638	11,166
67,400	67,450	12,650	9,191	12,650	11,179
67,450	67,500	12,663	9,199	12,663	11,191
67,500	67,550	12,675	9,206	12,675	11,204
67,550	67,600	12,688	9,214	12,688	11,216
67,600	67,650	12,700	9,221	12,700	11,229
67,650	67,700	12,713	9,229	12,713	11,241
67,700	67,750	12,725	9,236	12,725	11,254
67,750	67,800	12,738	9,244	12,738	11,266
67,800	67,850	12,750	9,251	12,750	11,279
67,850	67,900	12,763	9,259	12,763	11,291
67,900	67,950	12,775	9,266	12,775	11,304
67,950	68,000	12,788	9,274	12,788	11,316

68,000

At least	But less than	Single	MFJ *	MFS	HoH
68,000	68,050	12,800	9,281	12,800	11,329
68,050	68,100	12,813	9,289	12,813	11,341
68,100	68,150	12,825	9,296	12,825	11,354
68,150	68,200	12,838	9,304	12,838	11,366
68,200	68,250	12,850	9,311	12,850	11,379
68,250	68,300	12,863	9,319	12,863	11,391
68,300	68,350	12,875	9,326	12,875	11,404
68,350	68,400	12,888	9,334	12,888	11,416
68,400	68,450	12,900	9,341	12,900	11,429
68,450	68,500	12,913	9,349	12,913	11,441
68,500	68,550	12,925	9,356	12,925	11,454
68,550	68,600	12,938	9,364	12,938	11,466
68,600	68,650	12,950	9,371	12,950	11,479
68,650	68,700	12,963	9,379	12,963	11,491
68,700	68,750	12,975	9,386	12,975	11,504
68,750	68,800	12,988	9,394	12,988	11,516
68,800	68,850	13,000	9,401	13,000	11,529
68,850	68,900	13,013	9,409	13,013	11,541
68,900	68,950	13,025	9,416	13,025	11,554
68,950	69,000	13,038	9,424	13,038	11,566

69,000

At least	But less than	Single	MFJ *	MFS	HoH
69,000	69,050	13,050	9,431	13,050	11,579
69,050	69,100	13,063	9,439	13,063	11,591
69,100	69,150	13,075	9,446	13,075	11,604
69,150	69,200	13,088	9,454	13,088	11,616
69,200	69,250	13,100	9,461	13,100	11,629
69,250	69,300	13,113	9,469	13,113	11,641
69,300	69,350	13,125	9,476	13,125	11,654
69,350	69,400	13,138	9,484	13,138	11,666
69,400	69,450	13,150	9,491	13,150	11,679
69,450	69,500	13,163	9,499	13,163	11,691
69,500	69,550	13,175	9,506	13,175	11,704
69,550	69,600	13,188	9,514	13,188	11,716
69,600	69,650	13,200	9,521	13,200	11,729
69,650	69,700	13,213	9,529	13,213	11,741
69,700	69,750	13,225	9,536	13,225	11,754
69,750	69,800	13,238	9,544	13,238	11,766
69,800	69,850	13,250	9,551	13,250	11,779
69,850	69,900	13,263	9,559	13,263	11,791
69,900	69,950	13,275	9,566	13,275	11,804
69,950	70,000	13,288	9,574	13,288	11,816

70,000

At least	But less than	Single	MFJ *	MFS	HoH
70,000	70,050	13,300	9,581	13,300	11,829
70,050	70,100	13,313	9,589	13,313	11,841
70,100	70,150	13,325	9,596	13,325	11,854
70,150	70,200	13,338	9,604	13,338	11,866
70,200	70,250	13,350	9,611	13,350	11,879
70,250	70,300	13,363	9,619	13,363	11,891
70,300	70,350	13,375	9,626	13,375	11,904
70,350	70,400	13,388	9,634	13,388	11,916
70,400	70,450	13,400	9,641	13,400	11,929
70,450	70,500	13,413	9,649	13,413	11,941
70,500	70,550	13,425	9,656	13,425	11,954
70,550	70,600	13,438	9,664	13,438	11,966
70,600	70,650	13,450	9,671	13,450	11,979
70,650	70,700	13,463	9,679	13,463	11,991
70,700	70,750	13,475	9,686	13,475	12,004
70,750	70,800	13,488	9,694	13,488	12,016
70,800	70,850	13,500	9,701	13,500	12,029
70,850	70,900	13,513	9,709	13,513	12,041
70,900	70,950	13,525	9,716	13,525	12,054
70,950	71,000	13,538	9,724	13,538	12,066

71,000

At least	But less than	Single	MFJ *	MFS	HoH
71,000	71,050	13,550	9,731	13,550	12,079
71,050	71,100	13,563	9,739	13,563	12,091
71,100	71,150	13,575	9,746	13,575	12,104
71,150	71,200	13,588	9,754	13,588	12,116
71,200	71,250	13,600	9,761	13,600	12,129
71,250	71,300	13,613	9,769	13,613	12,141
71,300	71,350	13,625	9,776	13,625	12,154
71,350	71,400	13,638	9,784	13,638	12,166
71,400	71,450	13,650	9,791	13,650	12,179
71,450	71,500	13,663	9,799	13,663	12,191
71,500	71,550	13,675	9,806	13,675	12,204
71,550	71,600	13,688	9,814	13,688	12,216
71,600	71,650	13,700	9,821	13,700	12,229
71,650	71,700	13,713	9,829	13,713	12,241
71,700	71,750	13,725	9,836	13,725	12,254
71,750	71,800	13,738	9,844	13,738	12,266
71,800	71,850	13,750	9,851	13,750	12,279
71,850	71,900	13,763	9,859	13,763	12,291
71,900	71,950	13,775	9,866	13,775	12,304
71,950	72,000	13,788	9,874	13,788	12,316

72,000

At least	But less than	Single	MFJ *	MFS	HoH
72,000	72,050	13,800	9,881	13,800	12,329
72,050	72,100	13,813	9,889	13,813	12,341
72,100	72,150	13,825	9,896	13,825	12,354
72,150	72,200	13,838	9,904	13,838	12,366
72,200	72,250	13,850	9,911	13,850	12,379
72,250	72,300	13,863	9,919	13,863	12,391
72,300	72,350	13,875	9,926	13,875	12,404
72,350	72,400	13,888	9,934	13,888	12,416
72,400	72,450	13,900	9,941	13,900	12,429
72,450	72,500	13,913	9,949	13,913	12,441
72,500	72,550	13,925	9,956	13,925	12,454
72,550	72,600	13,938	9,964	13,938	12,466
72,600	72,650	13,950	9,971	13,950	12,479
72,650	72,700	13,963	9,979	13,963	12,491
72,700	72,750	13,975	9,986	13,975	12,504
72,750	72,800	13,988	9,994	13,988	12,516
72,800	72,850	14,000	10,001	14,000	12,529
72,850	72,900	14,013	10,009	14,013	12,541
72,900	72,950	14,025	10,016	14,025	12,554
72,950	73,000	14,038	10,024	14,038	12,566

73,000

At least	But less than	Single	MFJ *	MFS	HoH
73,000	73,050	14,050	10,031	14,050	12,579
73,050	73,100	14,063	10,039	14,063	12,591
73,100	73,150	14,075	10,046	14,075	12,604
73,150	73,200	14,088	10,054	14,088	12,616
73,200	73,250	14,100	10,061	14,100	12,629
73,250	73,300	14,113	10,069	14,113	12,641
73,300	73,350	14,125	10,076	14,125	12,654
73,350	73,400	14,138	10,084	14,138	12,666
73,400	73,450	14,150	10,091	14,150	12,679
73,450	73,500	14,163	10,099	14,163	12,691
73,500	73,550	14,175	10,106	14,175	12,704
73,550	73,600	14,188	10,114	14,188	12,716
73,600	73,650	14,200	10,121	14,200	12,729
73,650	73,700	14,213	10,129	14,213	12,741
73,700	73,750	14,225	10,136	14,225	12,754
73,750	73,800	14,238	10,144	14,238	12,766
73,800	73,850	14,250	10,151	14,250	12,779
73,850	73,900	14,263	10,159	14,263	12,791
73,900	73,950	14,275	10,166	14,275	12,804
73,950	74,000	14,288	10,174	14,288	12,816

74,000

At least	But less than	Single	MFJ *	MFS	HoH
74,000	74,050	14,300	10,181	14,300	12,829
74,050	74,100	14,313	10,189	14,313	12,841
74,100	74,150	14,325	10,196	14,325	12,854
74,150	74,200	14,338	10,204	14,338	12,866
74,200	74,250	14,350	10,211	14,350	12,879
74,250	74,300	14,363	10,219	14,363	12,891
74,300	74,350	14,375	10,226	14,375	12,904
74,350	74,400	14,388	10,234	14,388	12,916
74,400	74,450	14,400	10,241	14,400	12,929
74,450	74,500	14,413	10,249	14,413	12,941
74,500	74,550	14,425	10,256	14,425	12,954
74,550	74,600	14,438	10,264	14,438	12,966
74,600	74,650	14,450	10,271	14,450	12,979
74,650	74,700	14,463	10,279	14,463	12,991
74,700	74,750	14,475	10,286	14,475	13,004
74,750	74,800	14,488	10,294	14,488	13,016
74,800	74,850	14,500	10,301	14,500	13,029
74,850	74,900	14,513	10,309	14,513	13,041
74,900	74,950	14,525	10,319	14,525	13,054
74,950	75,000	14,538	10,331	14,538	13,066

* This column must also be used by a qualifying widow(er).

(Continued)

Need more information or forms? Visit IRS.gov.

If line 43 (taxable income) is—		And you are—			
At least	But less than	Single	Married filing jointly *	Married filing separately	Head of a household
		Your tax is—			

75,000

At least	But less than	Single	Married filing jointly *	Married filing separately	Head of a household
75,000	75,050	14,550	10,344	14,550	13,079
75,050	75,100	14,563	10,356	14,563	13,091
75,100	75,150	14,575	10,369	14,575	13,104
75,150	75,200	14,588	10,381	14,588	13,116
75,200	75,250	14,600	10,394	14,600	13,129
75,250	75,300	14,613	10,406	14,613	13,141
75,300	75,350	14,625	10,419	14,625	13,154
75,350	75,400	14,638	10,431	14,638	13,166
75,400	75,450	14,650	10,444	14,650	13,179
75,450	75,500	14,663	10,456	14,663	13,191
75,500	75,550	14,675	10,469	14,675	13,204
75,550	75,600	14,688	10,481	14,688	13,216
75,600	75,650	14,700	10,494	14,701	13,229
75,650	75,700	14,713	10,506	14,715	13,241
75,700	75,750	14,725	10,519	14,729	13,254
75,750	75,800	14,738	10,531	14,743	13,266
75,800	75,850	14,750	10,544	14,757	13,279
75,850	75,900	14,763	10,556	14,771	13,291
75,900	75,950	14,775	10,569	14,785	13,304
75,950	76,000	14,788	10,581	14,799	13,316

76,000

At least	But less than	Single	Married filing jointly *	Married filing separately	Head of a household
76,000	76,050	14,800	10,594	14,813	13,329
76,050	76,100	14,813	10,606	14,827	13,341
76,100	76,150	14,825	10,619	14,841	13,354
76,150	76,200	14,838	10,631	14,855	13,366
76,200	76,250	14,850	10,644	14,869	13,379
76,250	76,300	14,863	10,656	14,883	13,391
76,300	76,350	14,875	10,669	14,897	13,404
76,350	76,400	14,888	10,681	14,911	13,416
76,400	76,450	14,900	10,694	14,925	13,429
76,450	76,500	14,913	10,706	14,939	13,441
76,500	76,550	14,925	10,719	14,953	13,454
76,550	76,600	14,938	10,731	14,967	13,466
76,600	76,650	14,950	10,744	14,981	13,479
76,650	76,700	14,963	10,756	14,995	13,491
76,700	76,750	14,975	10,769	15,009	13,504
76,750	76,800	14,988	10,781	15,023	13,516
76,800	76,850	15,000	10,794	15,037	13,529
76,850	76,900	15,013	10,806	15,051	13,541
76,900	76,950	15,025	10,819	15,065	13,554
76,950	77,000	15,038	10,831	15,079	13,566

77,000

At least	But less than	Single	Married filing jointly *	Married filing separately	Head of a household
77,000	77,050	15,050	10,844	15,093	13,579
77,050	77,100	15,063	10,856	15,107	13,591
77,100	77,150	15,075	10,869	15,121	13,604
77,150	77,200	15,088	10,881	15,135	13,616
77,200	77,250	15,100	10,894	15,149	13,629
77,250	77,300	15,113	10,906	15,163	13,641
77,300	77,350	15,125	10,919	15,177	13,654
77,350	77,400	15,138	10,931	15,191	13,666
77,400	77,450	15,150	10,944	15,205	13,679
77,450	77,500	15,163	10,956	15,219	13,691
77,500	77,550	15,175	10,969	15,233	13,704
77,550	77,600	15,188	10,981	15,247	13,716
77,600	77,650	15,200	10,994	15,261	13,729
77,650	77,700	15,213	11,006	15,275	13,741
77,700	77,750	15,225	11,019	15,289	13,754
77,750	77,800	15,238	11,031	15,303	13,766
77,800	77,850	15,250	11,044	15,317	13,779
77,850	77,900	15,263	11,056	15,331	13,791
77,900	77,950	15,275	11,069	15,345	13,804
77,950	78,000	15,288	11,081	15,359	13,816

78,000

At least	But less than	Single	Married filing jointly *	Married filing separately	Head of a household
78,000	78,050	15,300	11,094	15,373	13,829
78,050	78,100	15,313	11,106	15,387	13,841
78,100	78,150	15,325	11,119	15,401	13,854
78,150	78,200	15,338	11,131	15,415	13,866
78,200	78,250	15,350	11,144	15,429	13,879
78,250	78,300	15,363	11,156	15,443	13,891
78,300	78,350	15,375	11,169	15,457	13,904
78,350	78,400	15,388	11,181	15,471	13,916
78,400	78,450	15,400	11,194	15,485	13,929
78,450	78,500	15,413	11,206	15,499	13,941
78,500	78,550	15,425	11,219	15,513	13,954
78,550	78,600	15,438	11,231	15,527	13,966
78,600	78,650	15,450	11,244	15,541	13,979
78,650	78,700	15,463	11,256	15,555	13,991
78,700	78,750	15,475	11,269	15,569	14,004
78,750	78,800	15,488	11,281	15,583	14,016
78,800	78,850	15,500	11,294	15,597	14,029
78,850	78,900	15,513	11,306	15,611	14,041
78,900	78,950	15,525	11,319	15,625	14,054
78,950	79,000	15,538	11,331	15,639	14,066

79,000

At least	But less than	Single	Married filing jointly *	Married filing separately	Head of a household
79,000	79,050	15,550	11,344	15,653	14,079
79,050	79,100	15,563	11,356	15,667	14,091
79,100	79,150	15,575	11,369	15,681	14,104
79,150	79,200	15,588	11,381	15,695	14,116
79,200	79,250	15,600	11,394	15,709	14,129
79,250	79,300	15,613	11,406	15,723	14,141
79,300	79,350	15,625	11,419	15,737	14,154
79,350	79,400	15,638	11,431	15,751	14,166
79,400	79,450	15,650	11,444	15,765	14,179
79,450	79,500	15,663	11,456	15,779	14,191
79,500	79,550	15,675	11,469	15,793	14,204
79,550	79,600	15,688	11,481	15,807	14,216
79,600	79,650	15,700	11,494	15,821	14,229
79,650	79,700	15,713	11,506	15,835	14,241
79,700	79,750	15,725	11,519	15,849	14,254
79,750	79,800	15,738	11,531	15,863	14,266
79,800	79,850	15,750	11,544	15,877	14,279
79,850	79,900	15,763	11,556	15,891	14,291
79,900	79,950	15,775	11,569	15,905	14,304
79,950	80,000	15,788	11,581	15,919	14,316

80,000

At least	But less than	Single	Married filing jointly *	Married filing separately	Head of a household
80,000	80,050	15,800	11,594	15,933	14,329
80,050	80,100	15,813	11,606	15,947	14,341
80,100	80,150	15,825	11,619	15,961	14,354
80,150	80,200	15,838	11,631	15,975	14,366
80,200	80,250	15,850	11,644	15,989	14,379
80,250	80,300	15,863	11,656	16,003	14,391
80,300	80,350	15,875	11,669	16,017	14,404
80,350	80,400	15,888	11,681	16,031	14,416
80,400	80,450	15,900	11,694	16,045	14,429
80,450	80,500	15,913	11,706	16,059	14,441
80,500	80,550	15,925	11,719	16,073	14,454
80,550	80,600	15,938	11,731	16,087	14,466
80,600	80,650	15,950	11,744	16,101	14,479
80,650	80,700	15,963	11,756	16,115	14,491
80,700	80,750	15,975	11,769	16,129	14,504
80,750	80,800	15,988	11,781	16,143	14,516
80,800	80,850	16,000	11,794	16,157	14,529
80,850	80,900	16,013	11,806	16,171	14,541
80,900	80,950	16,025	11,819	16,185	14,554
80,950	81,000	16,038	11,831	16,199	14,566

81,000

At least	But less than	Single	Married filing jointly *	Married filing separately	Head of a household
81,000	81,050	16,050	11,844	16,213	14,579
81,050	81,100	16,063	11,856	16,227	14,591
81,100	81,150	16,075	11,869	16,241	14,604
81,150	81,200	16,088	11,881	16,255	14,616
81,200	81,250	16,100	11,894	16,269	14,629
81,250	81,300	16,113	11,906	16,283	14,641
81,300	81,350	16,125	11,919	16,297	14,654
81,350	81,400	16,138	11,931	16,311	14,666
81,400	81,450	16,150	11,944	16,325	14,679
81,450	81,500	16,163	11,956	16,339	14,691
81,500	81,550	16,175	11,969	16,353	14,704
81,550	81,600	16,188	11,981	16,367	14,716
81,600	81,650	16,200	11,994	16,381	14,729
81,650	81,700	16,213	12,006	16,395	14,741
81,700	81,750	16,225	12,019	16,409	14,754
81,750	81,800	16,238	12,031	16,423	14,766
81,800	81,850	16,250	12,044	16,437	14,779
81,850	81,900	16,263	12,056	16,451	14,791
81,900	81,950	16,275	12,069	16,465	14,804
81,950	82,000	16,288	12,081	16,479	14,816

82,000

At least	But less than	Single	Married filing jointly *	Married filing separately	Head of a household
82,000	82,050	16,300	12,094	16,493	14,829
82,050	82,100	16,313	12,106	16,507	14,841
82,100	82,150	16,325	12,119	16,521	14,854
82,150	82,200	16,338	12,131	16,535	14,866
82,200	82,250	16,350	12,144	16,549	14,879
82,250	82,300	16,363	12,156	16,563	14,891
82,300	82,350	16,375	12,169	16,577	14,904
82,350	82,400	16,388	12,181	16,591	14,916
82,400	82,450	16,400	12,194	16,605	14,929
82,450	82,500	16,413	12,206	16,619	14,941
82,500	82,550	16,425	12,219	16,633	14,954
82,550	82,600	16,438	12,231	16,647	14,966
82,600	82,650	16,450	12,244	16,661	14,979
82,650	82,700	16,463	12,256	16,675	14,991
82,700	82,750	16,475	12,269	16,689	15,004
82,750	82,800	16,488	12,281	16,703	15,016
82,800	82,850	16,500	12,294	16,717	15,029
82,850	82,900	16,513	12,306	16,731	15,041
82,900	82,950	16,525	12,319	16,745	15,054
82,950	83,000	16,538	12,331	16,759	15,066

83,000

At least	But less than	Single	Married filing jointly *	Married filing separately	Head of a household
83,000	83,050	16,550	12,344	16,773	15,079
83,050	83,100	16,563	12,356	16,787	15,091
83,100	83,150	16,575	12,369	16,801	15,104
83,150	83,200	16,588	12,381	16,815	15,116
83,200	83,250	16,600	12,394	16,829	15,129
83,250	83,300	16,613	12,406	16,843	15,141
83,300	83,350	16,625	12,419	16,857	15,154
83,350	83,400	16,638	12,431	16,871	15,166
83,400	83,450	16,650	12,444	16,885	15,179
83,450	83,500	16,663	12,456	16,899	15,191
83,500	83,550	16,675	12,469	16,913	15,204
83,550	83,600	16,688	12,481	16,927	15,216
83,600	83,650	16,700	12,494	16,941	15,229
83,650	83,700	16,713	12,506	16,955	15,241
83,700	83,750	16,725	12,519	16,969	15,254
83,750	83,800	16,738	12,531	16,983	15,266
83,800	83,850	16,750	12,544	16,997	15,279
83,850	83,900	16,763	12,556	17,011	15,291
83,900	83,950	16,775	12,569	17,025	15,304
83,950	84,000	16,788	12,581	17,039	15,316

(Continued)

* This column must also be used by a qualifying widow(er).

Need more information or forms? Visit IRS.gov.

If line 43 (taxable income) is—		And you are—			
At least	But less than	Single	Married filing jointly *	Married filing separately	Head of a household
		Your tax is—			

84,000

At least	But less than	Single	Married filing jointly *	Married filing separately	Head of a household
84,000	84,050	16,800	12,594	17,053	15,329
84,050	84,100	16,813	12,606	17,067	15,341
84,100	84,150	16,825	12,619	17,081	15,354
84,150	84,200	16,838	12,631	17,095	15,366
84,200	84,250	16,850	12,644	17,109	15,379
84,250	84,300	16,863	12,656	17,123	15,391
84,300	84,350	16,875	12,669	17,137	15,404
84,350	84,400	16,888	12,681	17,151	15,416
84,400	84,450	16,900	12,694	17,165	15,429
84,450	84,500	16,913	12,706	17,179	15,441
84,500	84,550	16,925	12,719	17,193	15,454
84,550	84,600	16,938	12,731	17,207	15,466
84,600	84,650	16,950	12,744	17,221	15,479
84,650	84,700	16,963	12,756	17,235	15,491
84,700	84,750	16,975	12,769	17,249	15,504
84,750	84,800	16,988	12,781	17,263	15,516
84,800	84,850	17,000	12,794	17,277	15,529
84,850	84,900	17,013	12,806	17,291	15,541
84,900	84,950	17,025	12,819	17,305	15,554
84,950	85,000	17,038	12,831	17,319	15,566

85,000

At least	But less than	Single	Married filing jointly *	Married filing separately	Head of a household
85,000	85,050	17,050	12,844	17,333	15,579
85,050	85,100	17,063	12,856	17,347	15,591
85,100	85,150	17,075	12,869	17,361	15,604
85,150	85,200	17,088	12,881	17,375	15,616
85,200	85,250	17,100	12,894	17,389	15,629
85,250	85,300	17,113	12,906	17,403	15,641
85,300	85,350	17,125	12,919	17,417	15,654
85,350	85,400	17,138	12,931	17,431	15,666
85,400	85,450	17,150	12,944	17,445	15,679
85,450	85,500	17,163	12,956	17,459	15,691
85,500	85,550	17,175	12,969	17,473	15,704
85,550	85,600	17,188	12,981	17,487	15,716
85,600	85,650	17,200	12,994	17,501	15,729
85,650	85,700	17,213	13,006	17,515	15,741
85,700	85,750	17,225	13,019	17,529	15,754
85,750	85,800	17,238	13,031	17,543	15,766
85,800	85,850	17,250	13,044	17,557	15,779
85,850	85,900	17,263	13,056	17,571	15,791
85,900	85,950	17,275	13,069	17,585	15,804
85,950	86,000	17,288	13,081	17,599	15,816

86,000

At least	But less than	Single	Married filing jointly *	Married filing separately	Head of a household
86,000	86,050	17,300	13,094	17,613	15,829
86,050	86,100	17,313	13,106	17,627	15,841
86,100	86,150	17,325	13,119	17,641	15,854
86,150	86,200	17,338	13,131	17,655	15,866
86,200	86,250	17,350	13,144	17,669	15,879
86,250	86,300	17,363	13,156	17,683	15,891
86,300	86,350	17,375	13,169	17,697	15,904
86,350	86,400	17,388	13,181	17,711	15,916
86,400	86,450	17,400	13,194	17,725	15,929
86,450	86,500	17,413	13,206	17,739	15,941
86,500	86,550	17,425	13,219	17,753	15,954
86,550	86,600	17,438	13,231	17,767	15,966
86,600	86,650	17,450	13,244	17,781	15,979
86,650	86,700	17,463	13,256	17,795	15,991
86,700	86,750	17,475	13,269	17,809	16,004
86,750	86,800	17,488	13,281	17,823	16,016
86,800	86,850	17,500	13,294	17,837	16,029
86,850	86,900	17,513	13,306	17,851	16,041
86,900	86,950	17,525	13,319	17,865	16,054
86,950	87,000	17,538	13,331	17,879	16,066

87,000

At least	But less than	Single	Married filing jointly *	Married filing separately	Head of a household
87,000	87,050	17,550	13,344	17,893	16,079
87,050	87,100	17,563	13,356	17,907	16,091
87,100	87,150	17,575	13,369	17,921	16,104
87,150	87,200	17,588	13,381	17,935	16,116
87,200	87,250	17,600	13,394	17,949	16,129
87,250	87,300	17,613	13,406	17,963	16,141
87,300	87,350	17,625	13,419	17,977	16,154
87,350	87,400	17,638	13,431	17,991	16,166
87,400	87,450	17,650	13,444	18,005	16,179
87,450	87,500	17,663	13,456	18,019	16,191
87,500	87,550	17,675	13,469	18,033	16,204
87,550	87,600	17,688	13,481	18,047	16,216
87,600	87,650	17,700	13,494	18,061	16,229
87,650	87,700	17,713	13,506	18,075	16,241
87,700	87,750	17,725	13,519	18,089	16,254
87,750	87,800	17,738	13,531	18,103	16,266
87,800	87,850	17,750	13,544	18,117	16,279
87,850	87,900	17,763	13,556	18,131	16,291
87,900	87,950	17,775	13,569	18,145	16,304
87,950	88,000	17,788	13,581	18,159	16,316

88,000

At least	But less than	Single	Married filing jointly *	Married filing separately	Head of a household
88,000	88,050	17,800	13,594	18,173	16,329
88,050	88,100	17,813	13,606	18,187	16,341
88,100	88,150	17,825	13,619	18,201	16,354
88,150	88,200	17,838	13,631	18,215	16,366
88,200	88,250	17,850	13,644	18,229	16,379
88,250	88,300	17,863	13,656	18,243	16,391
88,300	88,350	17,875	13,669	18,257	16,404
88,350	88,400	17,888	13,681	18,271	16,416
88,400	88,450	17,900	13,694	18,285	16,429
88,450	88,500	17,913	13,706	18,299	16,441
88,500	88,550	17,925	13,719	18,313	16,454
88,550	88,600	17,938	13,731	18,327	16,466
88,600	88,650	17,950	13,744	18,341	16,479
88,650	88,700	17,963	13,756	18,355	16,491
88,700	88,750	17,975	13,769	18,369	16,504
88,750	88,800	17,988	13,781	18,383	16,516
88,800	88,850	18,000	13,794	18,397	16,529
88,850	88,900	18,013	13,806	18,411	16,541
88,900	88,950	18,025	13,819	18,425	16,554
88,950	89,000	18,038	13,831	18,439	16,566

89,000

At least	But less than	Single	Married filing jointly *	Married filing separately	Head of a household
89,000	89,050	18,050	13,844	18,453	16,579
89,050	89,100	18,063	13,856	18,467	16,591
89,100	89,150	18,075	13,869	18,481	16,604
89,150	89,200	18,088	13,881	18,495	16,616
89,200	89,250	18,100	13,894	18,509	16,629
89,250	89,300	18,113	13,906	18,523	16,641
89,300	89,350	18,125	13,919	18,537	16,654
89,350	89,400	18,138	13,931	18,551	16,666
89,400	89,450	18,150	13,944	18,565	16,679
89,450	89,500	18,163	13,956	18,579	16,691
89,500	89,550	18,175	13,969	18,593	16,704
89,550	89,600	18,188	13,981	18,607	16,716
89,600	89,650	18,200	13,994	18,621	16,729
89,650	89,700	18,213	14,006	18,635	16,741
89,700	89,750	18,225	14,019	18,649	16,754
89,750	89,800	18,238	14,031	18,663	16,766
89,800	89,850	18,250	14,044	18,677	16,779
89,850	89,900	18,263	14,056	18,691	16,791
89,900	89,950	18,275	14,069	18,705	16,804
89,950	90,000	18,288	14,081	18,719	16,816

90,000

At least	But less than	Single	Married filing jointly *	Married filing separately	Head of a household
90,000	90,050	18,300	14,094	18,733	16,829
90,050	90,100	18,313	14,106	18,747	16,841
90,100	90,150	18,325	14,119	18,761	16,854
90,150	90,200	18,338	14,131	18,775	16,866
90,200	90,250	18,350	14,144	18,789	16,879
90,250	90,300	18,363	14,156	18,803	16,891
90,300	90,350	18,375	14,169	18,817	16,904
90,350	90,400	18,388	14,181	18,831	16,916
90,400	90,450	18,400	14,194	18,845	16,929
90,450	90,500	18,413	14,206	18,859	16,941
90,500	90,550	18,425	14,219	18,873	16,954
90,550	90,600	18,438	14,231	18,887	16,966
90,600	90,650	18,450	14,244	18,901	16,979
90,650	90,700	18,463	14,256	18,915	16,991
90,700	90,750	18,475	14,269	18,929	17,004
90,750	90,800	18,488	14,281	18,943	17,016
90,800	90,850	18,502	14,294	18,957	17,029
90,850	90,900	18,516	14,306	18,971	17,041
90,900	90,950	18,530	14,319	18,985	17,054
90,950	91,000	18,544	14,331	18,999	17,066

91,000

At least	But less than	Single	Married filing jointly *	Married filing separately	Head of a household
91,000	91,050	18,558	14,344	19,013	17,079
91,050	91,100	18,572	14,356	19,027	17,091
91,100	91,150	18,586	14,369	19,041	17,104
91,150	91,200	18,600	14,381	19,055	17,116
91,200	91,250	18,614	14,394	19,069	17,129
91,250	91,300	18,628	14,406	19,083	17,141
91,300	91,350	18,642	14,419	19,097	17,154
91,350	91,400	18,656	14,431	19,111	17,166
91,400	91,450	18,670	14,444	19,125	17,179
91,450	91,500	18,684	14,456	19,139	17,191
91,500	91,550	18,698	14,469	19,153	17,204
91,550	91,600	18,712	14,481	19,167	17,216
91,600	91,650	18,726	14,494	19,181	17,229
91,650	91,700	18,740	14,506	19,195	17,241
91,700	91,750	18,754	14,519	19,209	17,254
91,750	91,800	18,768	14,531	19,223	17,266
91,800	91,850	18,782	14,544	19,237	17,279
91,850	91,900	18,796	14,556	19,251	17,291
91,900	91,950	18,810	14,569	19,265	17,304
91,950	92,000	18,824	14,581	19,279	17,316

92,000

At least	But less than	Single	Married filing jointly *	Married filing separately	Head of a household
92,000	92,050	18,838	14,594	19,293	17,329
92,050	92,100	18,852	14,606	19,307	17,341
92,100	92,150	18,866	14,619	19,321	17,354
92,150	92,200	18,880	14,631	19,335	17,366
92,200	92,250	18,894	14,644	19,349	17,379
92,250	92,300	18,908	14,656	19,363	17,391
92,300	92,350	18,922	14,669	19,377	17,404
92,350	92,400	18,936	14,681	19,391	17,416
92,400	92,450	18,950	14,694	19,405	17,429
92,450	92,500	18,964	14,706	19,419	17,441
92,500	92,550	18,978	14,719	19,433	17,454
92,550	92,600	18,992	14,731	19,447	17,466
92,600	92,650	19,006	14,744	19,461	17,479
92,650	92,700	19,020	14,756	19,475	17,491
92,700	92,750	19,034	14,769	19,489	17,504
92,750	92,800	19,048	14,781	19,503	17,516
92,800	92,850	19,062	14,794	19,517	17,529
92,850	92,900	19,076	14,806	19,531	17,541
92,900	92,950	19,090	14,819	19,545	17,554
92,950	93,000	19,104	14,831	19,559	17,566

(Continued)

* This column must also be used by a qualifying widow(er).

Need more information or forms? Visit IRS.gov.

If line 43 (taxable income) is—		And you are—			
At least	But less than	Single	Married filing jointly *	Married filing separately	Head of a household
		Your tax is—			

93,000

At least	But less than	Single	Married filing jointly *	Married filing separately	Head of a household
93,000	93,050	19,118	14,844	19,573	17,579
93,050	93,100	19,132	14,856	19,587	17,591
93,100	93,150	19,146	14,869	19,601	17,604
93,150	93,200	19,160	14,881	19,615	17,616
93,200	93,250	19,174	14,894	19,629	17,629
93,250	93,300	19,188	14,906	19,643	17,641
93,300	93,350	19,202	14,919	19,657	17,654
93,350	93,400	19,216	14,931	19,671	17,666
93,400	93,450	19,230	14,944	19,685	17,679
93,450	93,500	19,244	14,956	19,699	17,691
93,500	93,550	19,258	14,969	19,713	17,704
93,550	93,600	19,272	14,981	19,727	17,716
93,600	93,650	19,286	14,994	19,741	17,729
93,650	93,700	19,300	15,006	19,755	17,741
93,700	93,750	19,314	15,019	19,769	17,754
93,750	93,800	19,328	15,031	19,783	17,766
93,800	93,850	19,342	15,044	19,797	17,779
93,850	93,900	19,356	15,056	19,811	17,791
93,900	93,950	19,370	15,069	19,825	17,804
93,950	94,000	19,384	15,081	19,839	17,816

94,000

At least	But less than	Single	Married filing jointly *	Married filing separately	Head of a household
94,000	94,050	19,398	15,094	19,853	17,829
94,050	94,100	19,412	15,106	19,867	17,841
94,100	94,150	19,426	15,119	19,881	17,854
94,150	94,200	19,440	15,131	19,895	17,866
94,200	94,250	19,454	15,144	19,909	17,879
94,250	94,300	19,468	15,156	19,923	17,891
94,300	94,350	19,482	15,169	19,937	17,904
94,350	94,400	19,496	15,181	19,951	17,916
94,400	94,450	19,510	15,194	19,965	17,929
94,450	94,500	19,524	15,206	19,979	17,941
94,500	94,550	19,538	15,219	19,993	17,954
94,550	94,600	19,552	15,231	20,007	17,966
94,600	94,650	19,566	15,244	20,021	17,979
94,650	94,700	19,580	15,256	20,035	17,991
94,700	94,750	19,594	15,269	20,049	18,004
94,750	94,800	19,608	15,281	20,063	18,016
94,800	94,850	19,622	15,294	20,077	18,029
94,850	94,900	19,636	15,306	20,091	18,041
94,900	94,950	19,650	15,319	20,105	18,054
94,950	95,000	19,664	15,331	20,119	18,066

95,000

At least	But less than	Single	Married filing jointly *	Married filing separately	Head of a household
95,000	95,050	19,678	15,344	20,133	18,079
95,050	95,100	19,692	15,356	20,147	18,091
95,100	95,150	19,706	15,369	20,161	18,104
95,150	95,200	19,720	15,381	20,175	18,116
95,200	95,250	19,734	15,394	20,189	18,129
95,250	95,300	19,748	15,406	20,203	18,141
95,300	95,350	19,762	15,419	20,217	18,154
95,350	95,400	19,776	15,431	20,231	18,166
95,400	95,450	19,790	15,444	20,245	18,179
95,450	95,500	19,804	15,456	20,259	18,191
95,500	95,550	19,818	15,469	20,273	18,204
95,550	95,600	19,832	15,481	20,287	18,216
95,600	95,650	19,846	15,494	20,301	18,229
95,650	95,700	19,860	15,506	20,315	18,241
95,700	95,750	19,874	15,519	20,329	18,254
95,750	95,800	19,888	15,531	20,343	18,266
95,800	95,850	19,902	15,544	20,357	18,279
95,850	95,900	19,916	15,556	20,371	18,291
95,900	95,950	19,930	15,569	20,385	18,304
95,950	96,000	19,944	15,581	20,399	18,316

96,000

At least	But less than	Single	Married filing jointly *	Married filing separately	Head of a household
96,000	96,050	19,958	15,594	20,413	18,329
96,050	96,100	19,972	15,606	20,427	18,341
96,100	96,150	19,986	15,619	20,441	18,354
96,150	96,200	20,000	15,631	20,455	18,366
96,200	96,250	20,014	15,644	20,469	18,379
96,250	96,300	20,028	15,656	20,483	18,391
96,300	96,350	20,042	15,669	20,497	18,404
96,350	96,400	20,056	15,681	20,511	18,416
96,400	96,450	20,070	15,694	20,525	18,429
96,450	96,500	20,084	15,706	20,539	18,441
96,500	96,550	20,098	15,719	20,553	18,454
96,550	96,600	20,112	15,731	20,567	18,466
96,600	96,650	20,126	15,744	20,581	18,479
96,650	96,700	20,140	15,756	20,595	18,491
96,700	96,750	20,154	15,769	20,609	18,504
96,750	96,800	20,168	15,781	20,623	18,516
96,800	96,850	20,182	15,794	20,637	18,529
96,850	96,900	20,196	15,806	20,651	18,541
96,900	96,950	20,210	15,819	20,665	18,554
96,950	97,000	20,224	15,831	20,679	18,566

97,000

At least	But less than	Single	Married filing jointly *	Married filing separately	Head of a household
97,000	97,050	20,238	15,844	20,693	18,579
97,050	97,100	20,252	15,856	20,707	18,591
97,100	97,150	20,266	15,869	20,721	18,604
97,150	97,200	20,280	15,881	20,735	18,616
97,200	97,250	20,294	15,894	20,749	18,629
97,250	97,300	20,308	15,906	20,763	18,641
97,300	97,350	20,322	15,919	20,777	18,654
97,350	97,400	20,336	15,931	20,791	18,666
97,400	97,450	20,350	15,944	20,805	18,679
97,450	97,500	20,364	15,956	20,819	18,691
97,500	97,550	20,378	15,969	20,833	18,704
97,550	97,600	20,392	15,981	20,847	18,716
97,600	97,650	20,406	15,994	20,861	18,729
97,650	97,700	20,420	16,006	20,875	18,741
97,700	97,750	20,434	16,019	20,889	18,754
97,750	97,800	20,448	16,031	20,903	18,766
97,800	97,850	20,462	16,044	20,917	18,779
97,850	97,900	20,476	16,056	20,931	18,791
97,900	97,950	20,490	16,069	20,945	18,804
97,950	98,000	20,504	16,081	20,959	18,816

98,000

At least	But less than	Single	Married filing jointly *	Married filing separately	Head of a household
98,000	98,050	20,518	16,094	20,973	18,829
98,050	98,100	20,532	16,106	20,987	18,841
98,100	98,150	20,546	16,119	21,001	18,854
98,150	98,200	20,560	16,131	21,015	18,866
98,200	98,250	20,574	16,144	21,029	18,879
98,250	98,300	20,588	16,156	21,043	18,891
98,300	98,350	20,602	16,169	21,057	18,904
98,350	98,400	20,616	16,181	21,071	18,916
98,400	98,450	20,630	16,194	21,085	18,929
98,450	98,500	20,644	16,206	21,099	18,941
98,500	98,550	20,658	16,219	21,113	18,954
98,550	98,600	20,672	16,231	21,127	18,966
98,600	98,650	20,686	16,244	21,141	18,979
98,650	98,700	20,700	16,256	21,155	18,991
98,700	98,750	20,714	16,269	21,169	19,004
98,750	98,800	20,728	16,281	21,183	19,016
98,800	98,850	20,742	16,294	21,197	19,029
98,850	98,900	20,756	16,306	21,211	19,041
98,900	98,950	20,770	16,319	21,225	19,054
98,950	99,000	20,784	16,331	21,239	19,066

99,000

At least	But less than	Single	Married filing jointly *	Married filing separately	Head of a household
99,000	99,050	20,798	16,344	21,253	19,079
99,050	99,100	20,812	16,356	21,267	19,091
99,100	99,150	20,826	16,369	21,281	19,104
99,150	99,200	20,840	16,381	21,295	19,116
99,200	99,250	20,854	16,394	21,309	19,129
99,250	99,300	20,868	16,406	21,323	19,141
99,300	99,350	20,882	16,419	21,337	19,154
99,350	99,400	20,896	16,431	21,351	19,166
99,400	99,450	20,910	16,444	21,365	19,179
99,450	99,500	20,924	16,456	21,379	19,191
99,500	99,550	20,938	16,469	21,393	19,204
99,550	99,600	20,952	16,481	21,407	19,216
99,600	99,650	20,966	16,494	21,421	19,229
99,650	99,700	20,980	16,506	21,435	19,241
99,700	99,750	20,994	16,519	21,449	19,254
99,750	99,800	21,008	16,531	21,463	19,266
99,800	99,850	21,022	16,544	21,477	19,279
99,850	99,900	21,036	16,556	21,491	19,291
99,900	99,950	21,050	16,569	21,505	19,304
99,950	100,000	21,064	16,581	21,519	19,316

$100,000 or over
use the Tax Computation Worksheet

* This column must also be used by a qualifying widow(er).

2015 Tax Computation Worksheet—Line 44

 See the instructions for line 44 to see if you must use the worksheet below to figure your tax.

Note. If you are required to use this worksheet to figure the tax on an amount from another form or worksheet, such as the Qualified Dividends and Capital Gain Tax Worksheet, the Schedule D Tax Worksheet, Schedule J, Form 8615, or the Foreign Earned Income Tax Worksheet, enter the amount from that form or worksheet in column (a) of the row that applies to the amount you are looking up. Enter the result on the appropriate line of the form or worksheet that you are completing.

Section A—Use if your filing status is **Single.** Complete the row below that applies to you.

Taxable income. If line 43 is—	(a) Enter the amount from line 43	(b) Multiplication amount	(c) Multiply (a) by (b)	(d) Subtraction amount	Tax. Subtract (d) from (c). Enter the result here and on Form 1040, line 44
At least $100,000 but not over $189,300	$	× 28% (0.28)	$	$ 6,928.75	$
Over $189,300 but not over $411,500	$	× 33% (0.33)	$	$ 16,393.75	$
Over $411,500 but not over $413,200	$	× 35% (0.35)	$	$ 24,623.75	$
Over $413,200	$	× 39.6% (0.396)	$	$ 43,630.95	$

Section B—Use if your filing status is **Married filing jointly** or **Qualifying widow(er).** Complete the row below that applies to you.

Taxable income. If line 43 is—	(a) Enter the amount from line 43	(b) Multiplication amount	(c) Multiply (a) by (b)	(d) Subtraction amount	Tax. Subtract (d) from (c). Enter the result here and on Form 1040, line 44
At least $100,000 but not over $151,200	$	× 25% (0.25)	$	$ 8,412.50	$
Over $151,200 but not over $230,450	$	× 28% (0.28)	$	$ 12,948.50	$
Over $230,450 but not over $411,500	$	× 33% (0.33)	$	$ 24,471.00	$
Over $411,500 but not over $464,850	$	× 35% (0.35)	$	$ 32,701.00	$
Over $464,850	$	× 39.6% (0.396)	$	$ 54,084.10	$

Section C—Use if your filing status is **Married filing separately.** Complete the row below that applies to you.

Taxable income. If line 43 is—	(a) Enter the amount from line 43	(b) Multiplication amount	(c) Multiply (a) by (b)	(d) Subtraction amount	Tax. Subtract (d) from (c). Enter the result here and on Form 1040, line 44
At least $100,000 but not over $115,225	$	× 28% (0.28)	$	$ 6,474.25	$
Over $115,225 but not over $205,750	$	× 33% (0.33)	$	$ 12,235.50	$
Over $205,750 but not over $232,425	$	× 35% (0.35)	$	$ 16,350.50	$
Over $232,425	$	× 39.6% (0.396)	$	$ 27,042.05	$

Section D—Use if your filing status is **Head of household.** Complete the row below that applies to you.

Taxable income. If line 43 is—	(a) Enter the amount from line 43	(b) Multiplication amount	(c) Multiply (a) by (b)	(d) Subtraction amount	Tax. Subtract (d) from (c). Enter the result here and on Form 1040, line 44
At least $100,000 but not over $129,600	$	× 25% (0.25)	$	$ 5,677.50	$
Over $129,600 but not over $209,850	$	× 28% (0.28)	$	$ 9,565.50	$
Over $209,850 but not over $411,500	$	× 33% (0.33)	$	$ 20,058.00	$
Over $411,500 but not over $439,000	$	× 35% (0.35)	$	$ 28,288.00	$
Over $439,000	$	× 39.6% (0.396)	$	$ 48,482.00	$

Need more information or forms? Visit IRS.gov.

General Information

The IRS Mission. Provide America's taxpayers top-quality service by helping them understand and meet their tax responsibilities and enforce the law with integrity and fairness to all.

How To Avoid Common Mistakes

Mistakes can delay your refund or result in notices being sent to you. One of the best ways to file an accurate return is to file electronically. Tax software does the math for you and will help you avoid mistakes. You may be eligible to use free tax software that will take the guesswork out of preparing your return. Free File makes available free brand-name software and free *e-file*. Visit *www.irs.gov/freefile* for details. Join the eight in 10 taxpayers who get their refunds faster by using direct deposit and *e-file*.

• Make sure you entered the correct name and social security number (SSN) for each dependent you claim on line 6c. Check that each dependent's name and SSN agrees with his or her social security card. For each child under age 17 who is a qualifying child for the child tax credit, make sure you checked the box in line 6c, column (4).

• Check your math, especially for the child tax credit, earned income credit (EIC), taxable social security benefits, total income, itemized deductions or standard deduction, deduction for exemptions, taxable income, total tax, federal income tax withheld, and refund or amount you owe.

• Be sure you used the correct method to figure your tax. See the instructions for line 44.

• Be sure to enter your SSN in the space provided on page 1 of Form 1040. If you are married filing a joint or separate return, also enter your spouse's SSN. Be sure to enter your SSN in the space next to your name. Check that your name and SSN agree with your social security card.

• Make sure your name and address are correct. Enter your (and your spouse's) name in the same order as shown on your last return.

• If you live in an apartment, be sure to include your apartment number in your address.

• If you are taking the standard deduction, see the instructions for line 40 to be sure you entered the correct amount.

• If you received capital gain distributions but weren't required to file Schedule D, make sure you checked the box on line 13.

• If you are taking the EIC, be sure you used the correct column of the EIC Table for your filing status and the number of children you have.

• Remember to sign and date Form 1040 and enter your occupation(s).

• Attach your Form(s) W-2 and other required forms and schedules. Put all forms and schedules in the proper order. See *Assemble Your Return,* earlier.

• If you owe tax and are paying by check or money order, be sure to include all the required information on your payment. See the instructions for line 78 for details.

• Do not file more than one original return for the same year, even if you haven't gotten your refund or haven't heard from the IRS since you filed. Filing more than one original return for the same year, or sending in more than one copy of the same return (unless we ask you to do so), could delay your refund.

Innocent Spouse Relief

Generally, both you and your spouse are each responsible for paying the full amount of tax, interest, and penalties on your joint return. However, you may qualify for relief from liability for tax on a joint return if (a) there is an understatement of tax because your spouse omitted income or claimed false deductions or credits, (b) you are divorced, separated, or no longer living with your spouse, or (c) given all the facts and circumstances, it wouldn't be fair to hold you liable for the tax. You may also qualify for relief if you were a married resident of a community property state but didn't file a joint return and are now liable for an unpaid or understated tax. File Form 8857 to request relief. In some cases, Form 8857 may need to be filed within 2 years of the date on which the IRS first attempted to collect the tax from you. Do not file Form 8857 with your Form 1040. For more information, see Pub. 971 and Form 8857 or you can call the Innocent Spouse office toll-free at 1-855-851-2009.

Income Tax Withholding and Estimated Tax Payments for 2016

If the amount you owe or the amount you overpaid is large, you may want to file a new Form W-4 with your employer to change the amount of income tax withheld from your 2016 pay. For details on how to complete Form W-4, see Pub. 505. If you have pension or annuity income, use Form W-4P. If you receive certain government payments (such as unemployment compensation or social security benefits), you can have tax withheld from those payments by giving the payer Form W-4V.

 You can use the IRS Withholding Calculator instead of Pub. 505 or the worksheets included with Form W-4 or W-4P, to determine whether you need to have your withholding increased or decreased.

In general, you do not have to make estimated tax payments if you expect that your 2016 Form 1040 will show a tax refund or a tax balance due of less than $1,000. If your total estimated tax for 2016 is $1,000 or more, see Form 1040-ES and Pub. 505 for a worksheet you can use to see if you have to make estimated tax payments. For more details, see Pub. 505.

Secure Your Tax Records from Identity Theft

Identity theft occurs when someone uses your personal information, such as your name, social security number (SSN), or other identifying information, without your permission, to commit fraud or other crimes. An identity thief may use your SSN to get a job or may file a tax return using your SSN to receive a refund.

To reduce your risk:
- Protect your SSN,
- Ensure your employer is protecting your SSN, and
- Be careful when choosing a tax preparer.

If your tax records are affected by identity theft and you receive a notice from the IRS, respond right away to the name and phone number printed on the IRS notice or letter. For more information, see Pub. 4535.

If your SSN has been lost or stolen or you suspect you are a victim of tax-related identity theft, visit *www.irs.gov/identitytheft* to learn what steps you should take.

Victims of identity theft who are experiencing economic harm or a systemic problem, or are seeking help in resolving tax problems that haven't been resolved through normal channels, may be eligible for Taxpayer Advocate Service (TAS) assistance. You can reach TAS by calling the National Taxpayer Advocate helpline at 1-877-777-4778. People who are deaf, hard of hearing, or have a speech disability and who have access to TTY/TDD equipment can call 1-800-829-4059. Deaf or hard-of-hearing individuals can also contact the IRS through relay services such as the Federal Relay Service available at *www.gsa.gov/fedrelay*.

Protect yourself from suspicious emails or phishing schemes. Phishing is the creation and use of email and websites designed to mimic legitimate business emails and websites. The most common form is sending an email to a user falsely claiming to be an established legitimate enterprise in an attempt to scam the user into surrendering private information that will be used for identity theft.

The IRS doesn't initiate contacts with taxpayers via emails. Also, the IRS doesn't request detailed personal information through email or ask taxpayers for the PIN numbers, passwords, or similar secret access information for their credit card, bank, or other financial accounts.

If you receive an unsolicited email claiming to be from the IRS, forward the message to *phishing@irs.gov*. You may also report misuse of the IRS name, logo, forms, or other IRS property to the Treasury Inspector General for Tax Administration toll-free at 1-800-366-4484. People who are deaf, hard of hearing, or have a speech disability and who have access to TTY/TDD equipment can call 1-800-877-8339. You can forward suspicious emails to the Federal Trade Commission at *spam@uce.gov* or contact them at *www.ftc.gov/idtheft* or 1-877-IDTHEFT (1-877-438-4338). People who are deaf, hard of hearing, or have a speech disability and who have access to TTY/TDD equipment can call 1-866-653-4261.

Visit IRS.gov and enter "identity theft" in the search box to learn more about identity theft and how to reduce your risk.

How Do You Make a Gift To Reduce Debt Held By the Public?

If you wish to do so, make a check payable to "Bureau of the Fiscal Service." You can send it to: Bureau of the Fiscal Service, Attn: Dept G, P.O. Box 2188, Parkersburg, WV 26106-2188. Or you can enclose the check with your income tax return when you file. In the memo section of the check, make a note that it is a gift to reduce the debt held by the public. Do not add your gift to any tax you may owe. See the instructions for line 78 for details on how to pay any tax you owe. For information on how to make this type of gift online, go to *www.treasurydirect.gov* and click on "How To Make a Contribution to Reduce the Debt."

 You may be able to deduct this gift on your 2016 tax return.

How Long Should Records Be Kept?

Keep a copy of your tax return, worksheets you used, and records of all items appearing on it (such as Forms W-2 and 1099) until the statute of limitations runs out for that return. Usually, this is 3 years from the date the return was due or filed or 2 years from the date the tax was paid, whichever is later. You should keep some records longer. For example, keep property records (including those on your home) as long as they are needed to figure the basis of the original or replacement property. For more details, see chapter 1 of Pub. 17.

Amended Return

File Form 1040X to change a return you already filed. Generally, Form 1040X must be filed within 3 years after the date the original return was filed or within 2 years after the date the tax was paid, whichever is later. But you may have more time to file Form 1040X if you live in a federally declared disaster area or you are physically or mentally unable to manage your financial affairs. See Pub. 556 for details.

Use the *Where's My Amended Return* application on IRS.gov to track the status of your amended return. It can take up to 3 weeks from the date you mailed it to show up in our system.

Need a Copy of Your Tax Return Information?

Tax return transcripts are free and generally are used to validate income and tax filing status for mortgage applications, student and small business loan applications, and during tax preparation. To get a free transcript:
- Visit *www.irs.gov/Individuals/Get-Transcript,*
- Use Form 4506-T or 4506T-EZ, or
- Call us at 1-800-908-9946.

If you need a copy of your actual tax return, use Form 4506. There is a fee for each return requested. See Form 4506 for the current fee. If your main home, principal place of business, or tax records are located in a federally declared disaster area, this fee will be waived.

Death of a Taxpayer

If a taxpayer died before filing a return for 2015, the taxpayer's spouse or personal representative may have to file and sign a return for that taxpayer. A personal representative can be an executor, administrator, or anyone who is in charge of the deceased taxpayer's property. If the deceased taxpayer didn't have to file a return but had tax withheld, a return must be filed to get a refund. The person who files the return must enter "Deceased," the deceased taxpayer's name, and the date of death across the top of the return. If this information isn't provided, it may delay the processing of the return.

If your spouse died in 2015 and you didn't remarry in 2015, or if your spouse died in 2016 before filing a return for 2015, you can file a joint return. A joint return should show your spouse's 2015 income before death and your income for all of 2015. Enter "Filing as surviving spouse" in the area where you sign the return. If someone else is the personal representative, he or she must also sign.

The surviving spouse or personal representative should promptly notify all payers of income, including financial institutions, of the taxpayer's death. This will ensure the proper reporting of income earned by the taxpayer's estate or heirs. A deceased taxpayer's social security number shouldn't be used for tax years after the year of death, except for estate tax return purposes.

Claiming a Refund for a Deceased Taxpayer

If you are filing a joint return as a surviving spouse, you only need to file the tax return to claim the refund. If you are a court-appointed representative, file the return and include a copy of the certificate that shows your appointment. All other filers requesting the deceased taxpayer's refund must file the return and attach Form 1310.

For more details, use *Tax Topic 356* or see Pub. 559.

Past Due Returns

If you or someone you know needs to file past due tax returns, use *Tax Topic 153* or go to *www.irs.gov/individuals* for help in filing those returns. Send the return to the address that applies to you in the latest Form 1040 instructions. For example, if you are filing a 2012 return in 2016, use the address at the end of these instructions. However, if you got an IRS notice, mail the return to the address in the notice.

How To Get Tax Help

If you have questions about a tax issue, need help preparing your tax return, or want to download free publications, forms, or instructions, go to IRS.gov and find resources that can help you right away.

Preparing and filing your tax return. Find free options to prepare and file your return on IRS.gov or in your local community if you qualify.
- Go to IRS.gov and click on the Filing tab to see your options.
- Enter "Free File" in the search box to see whether you can use brand-name software to prepare and *e-file* your federal tax return for free.
- Enter "VITA" in the search box, download the free IRS2Go app, or call 1-800-906-9887 to find the nearest Volunteer Income Tax Assistance or Tax Counseling for the Elderly (TCE) location for free tax preparation.
- Enter "TCE" in the search box, download the free IRS2Go app, or call 1-888-227-7669 to find the nearest Tax Counseling for the Elderly location for free tax preparation.

In general, the Volunteer Income Tax Assistance (VITA) program offers free tax help to people who make $54,000 or less, persons with disabilities, the elderly, and limited-English-speaking taxpayers who need help preparing their own tax returns. The Tax Counseling for the Elderly (TCE) program offers free tax help for all taxpayers, particularly those who are 60 years of age and older. TCE volunteers specialize in answering questions about pensions and retirement-related issues unique to seniors.

 Getting answers to your tax law questions. On IRS.gov get answers to your tax questions anytime, anywhere.
- Go to *www.irs.gov/Help-&-Resources* for a variety of tools that will help you with your taxes.
- Enter "ITA" in the search box on IRS.gov for the Interactive Tax Assistant, a tool that will ask you questions on a number of tax law topics and provide answers. You can print the entire interview and the final response.
- Enter "Pub 17" in the search box on IRS.gov to get Pub. 17, Your Federal Income Tax for Individuals, which features details on tax-saving opportunities, 2015 tax changes, and thousands of interactive links to help you find answers to your questions.
- Additionally, you may be able to access tax law information in your electronic filing software.

Tax forms and publications. You can download or print all of the forms and publications you may need on *www.irs.gov/formspubs*. Otherwise, you can go to *www.irs.gov/orderforms* to place an order and have forms mailed to you. You should receive your order within 10 business days.

Direct deposit. The fastest way to receive a tax refund is by combining direct deposit and IRS *e-file*. Direct deposit securely and electronically transfers your refund directly into your financial account. Eight in 10 taxpayers use direct deposit to receive their refund. The majority of refunds are received within 21 days or less.

Getting a transcript or copy of a return.
- Go to *www.irs.gov/Individuals/Get-Transcript*.
- Call the transcript toll-free line at 1-800-908-9946.
- Mail Form 4506-T or Form 4506T-EZ (both available on IRS.gov).

Using online tools to help prepare your return. Go to IRS.gov and click on the Tools bar to use these and other self-service options.
- The *Earned Income Tax Credit Assistant* determines if you are eligible for the EIC.

- The *Online EIN Application* helps you get an employer identification number.
- The *IRS Withholding Calculator* estimates the amount you should have withheld from your paycheck for federal income tax purposes.
- The *Electronic Filing PIN Request* helps to verify your identity when you do not have your prior year AGI or prior year self-selected PIN available.
- The *First Time Homebuyer Credit Account Look-up* tool provides information on your repayments and account balance.

For help with the alternative minimum tax, go to *IRS.gov/AMT*.

Understanding identity theft issues.
- Go to *www.irs.gov/uac/Identity-Protection* for information and videos.
- See *Secure Your Tax Records from Identity Theft* under *General Information*, earlier.

Checking on the status of a refund.
- Go to *www.irs.gov/refunds*.
- Download the free IRS2Go app to your smart phone and use it to check your refund status.
- Call the automated refund hotline at 1-800-829-1954. See *Refund Information*, later.

Making a tax payment. The IRS uses the latest encryption technology so electronic payments are safe and secure. You can make electronic payments online, by phone, or from a mobile device. Paying electronically is quick, easy, and faster than mailing in a check or money order. Go to *www.irs.gov/payments* to make a payment using any of the following options.
- *IRS Direct Pay* (for individual taxpayers who have a checking or savings account).
- **Debit or credit card** (approved payment processors online or by phone).
- **Electronic Funds Withdrawal** (available during *e-file*).
- **Electronic Federal Tax Payment System** (best option for businesses; enrollment required).
- **Check or money order.**

IRS2Go provides access to mobile-friendly payment options like IRS Direct Pay, offering you a free, secure way to pay directly from your bank account. You can also make debit or credit card payments through an approved payment processor. Simply download IRS2Go from Google Play, the Apple App Store, or the Amazon Appstore, and make your payments anytime, anywhere.

What if I can't pay now? Click on the "Pay Your Tax Bill" icon on IRS.gov for more information about these additional options.
- Apply for an *online payment agreement* to meet your tax obligation in monthly installments if you can't pay your taxes in full today. Once you complete the online process, you will receive immediate notification of whether your agreement has been approved.
- An offer in compromise allows you to settle your tax debt for less than the full amount you owe. Use the *Offer in Compromise Pre-Qualifier* to confirm your eligibility.

Checking the status of an amended return. Go to IRS.gov and click on the Tools tab and then *Where's My Amended Return?*

Understanding an IRS notice or letter. Enter "Understanding your notice" in the search box on IRS.gov to find additional information about your IRS notice or letter.

Visiting the IRS. Locate the nearest Taxpayer Assistance Center using the Office Locator tool on IRS.gov. Enter "office locator" in the search box. Or choose the "Contact Us" option on the IRS2Go app and search Local Offices. Before you visit, use the Locator tool to check hours and services available.

Watching IRS videos. The IRS Video portal *www.irsvideos.gov* contains video and audio presentations for individuals, small businesses, and tax professionals. You'll find video clips of tax topics, archived versions of panel discussions and Webinars, and audio archives of tax practitioner phone forums.

Getting tax information in other languages. For taxpayers whose native language isn't English, we have the following resources available.

1. Taxpayers can find information on IRS.gov in the following languages.
   a. *Spanish*.
   b. *Chinese*.
   c. *Vietnamese*.
   d. *Korean*.
   e. *Russian*.

2. The IRS Taxpayer Assistance Centers provide over-the-phone interpreter service in over 170 languages, and the service is available free to taxpayers.

Interest and Penalties

You do not have to figure the amount of any interest or penalties you may owe. Because figuring these amounts can be complicated, we will do it for you if you want. We will send you a bill for any amount due.

If you include interest or penalties (other than the estimated tax penalty) with your payment, identify and enter the amount in the bottom margin of Form 1040, page 2. Do not include interest or penalties (other than the estimated tax penalty) in the amount you owe on line 78.

Interest

We will charge you interest on taxes not paid by their due date, even if an extension of time to file is granted. We will also charge you interest on penalties imposed for failure to file, negligence, fraud, substantial valuation misstatements, substantial understatements of tax, and reportable transaction understatements. Interest is charged on the penalty from the due date of the return (including extensions).

Penalties

Late filing. If you do not file your return by the due date (including extensions), the penalty is usually 5% of the amount due for each month or part of a month your return is late, unless you have a reasonable explanation. If you do, include it with your return. The penalty can be as much as 25% of the tax due. The penalty is 15% per month, up to a maximum of 75%, if the failure to file is fraudulent. If your return is more than 60 days late, the minimum penalty will be $135 or the amount of any tax you owe, whichever is smaller.

Late payment of tax. If you pay your taxes late, the penalty is usually $\frac{1}{2}$ of 1% of the unpaid amount for each month or part of a month the tax isn't paid. The penalty can be as much as 25% of the unpaid amount. It applies to any unpaid tax on the return. This penalty is in addition to interest charges on late payments.

Frivolous return. In addition to any other penalties, the law imposes a penalty of $5,000 for filing a frivolous return. A frivolous return is one that doesn't contain information needed to figure the correct tax or shows a substantially incorrect tax because you take a frivolous position or desire to delay or interfere with the tax laws. This includes altering or striking out the preprinted language above the space where you sign. For a list of positions identified as frivolous, see Notice 2010-33, 2010-17 I.R.B. 609, available at *www.irs.gov/irb/2010-17_IRB/ar13.html*.

Other. Other penalties can be imposed for negligence, substantial understatement of tax, reportable transaction understatements, filing an erroneous refund claim, and fraud. Criminal penalties may be imposed for willful failure to file, tax evasion, making a false statement, or identity theft. See Pub. 17 for details on some of these penalties.

Taxpayer Bill of Rights

All taxpayers have fundamental rights they should be aware of when dealing with the IRS. The Taxpayer Bill of Rights, which the IRS adopted in June of 2014, takes existing rights in the tax code and groups them into the following 10 broad categories, making them easier to understand. Explore your rights and our obligations to protect them.

The right to be informed. Taxpayers have the right to know what they need to do to comply with the tax laws. They are entitled to clear explanations of the laws and IRS procedures in all tax forms, instructions, publications, notices, and correspondence. They have the right to be informed of IRS decisions about their tax accounts and to receive clear explanations of the outcomes.

The right to quality service. Taxpayers have the right to receive prompt, courteous, and professional assistance in their dealings with the IRS, to be spoken to in a way they can easily understand, to receive clear and easily understandable communications from the IRS, and to speak to a supervisor about inadequate service.

The right to pay no more than the correct amount of tax. Taxpayers have the right to pay only the amount of tax legally due, including interest and penalties, and to have the IRS apply all tax payments properly.

The right to challenge the IRS's position and be heard. Taxpayers have the right to raise objections and provide additional documentation in response to formal IRS actions or proposed actions, to expect that the IRS will consider their timely objections and documentation promptly and fairly, and to receive a response if the IRS does not agree with their position.

The right to appeal an IRS decision in an independent forum. Taxpayers are entitled to a fair and impartial administrative appeal of most IRS decisions, including many penalties, and have the right to receive a written response regarding the Office of Appeals' decision. Taxpayers generally have the right to take their cases to court.

The right to finality. Taxpayers have the right to know the maximum amount of time they have to challenge the IRS's position as well as the maximum amount of time the IRS has to audit a particular tax year or collect a tax debt. Taxpayers have the right to know when the IRS has finished an audit.

The right to privacy. Taxpayers have the right to expect that any IRS inquiry, examination, or enforcement action will comply with the law and be no more intrusive than necessary, and will respect all due process rights, including search and seizure protections and will provide, where applicable, a collection due process hearing.

The right to confidentiality. Taxpayers have the right to expect that any information they provide to the IRS will not be disclosed unless authorized by the taxpayer or by law. Taxpayers have the right to expect appropriate action will be taken against employees, return preparers, and others who wrongfully use or disclose taxpayer return information.

The right to retain representation. Taxpayers have the right to retain an authorized representative of their choice to represent them in their dealings with the IRS. Taxpayers have the right to seek assistance from a *Low Income Taxpayer Clinic* if they can't afford representation.

The right to a fair and just tax system. Taxpayers have the right to expect the tax system to consider facts and circumstances that might affect their underlying liabilities, ability to pay, or ability to provide information timely. Taxpayers have the right to receive assistance from the *Taxpayer Advocate Service* if they are experiencing financial difficulty or if the IRS has not resolved their tax issues properly and timely through its normal channels.

Learn more at *www.irs.gov/taxpayerrights*.

Refund Information

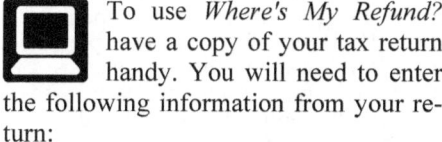 Visit IRS.gov and click on *Where's My Refund*, or use the free IRS2Go app, 24 hours a day, 7 days a week. Information about your return will generally be available within 24 hours after the IRS receives your e-filed return, or 4 weeks after you mail a paper return. But if you filed Form 8379 with your return, allow 14 weeks (11 weeks if you filed electronically) before checking your refund status.

 To use *Where's My Refund?* have a copy of your tax return handy. You will need to enter the following information from your return:

• Your social security number (or individual taxpayer identification number),

• Your filing status, and

• The exact whole dollar amount of your refund.

Where's My Refund? will provide an actual personalized refund date as soon as the IRS processes your tax return and approves your refund.

 Updates to refund status are made once a day - usually at night.

If you do not have Internet access, you can call 1-800-829-1954 24 hours a day, 7 days a week, for automated refund information. Our phone and walk-in assistors can research the status of your refund only if it's been 21 days or more since you filed electronically or more than 6 weeks since you mailed your paper return.

Do not send in a copy of your return unless asked to do so.

To get a refund, you generally must file your return within 3 years from the date the return was due (including extensions).

Where's My Refund? doesn't track refunds that are claimed on an amended tax return.

Refund information also is available in Spanish at *www.irs.gov/Spanish* and 1-800-829-1954.

Tax Topics

You can read these Tax Topics at *www.irs.gov/taxtopics*.

List of Tax Topics

All topics are available in Spanish.

List of Tax Topics

(Continued)

Tax Topic numbers are effective January 1, 2016.

Disclosure, Privacy Act, and Paperwork Reduction Act Notice

The IRS Restructuring and Reform Act of 1998, the Privacy Act of 1974, and the Paperwork Reduction Act of 1980 require that when we ask you for information we must first tell you our legal right to ask for the information, why we are asking for it, and how it will be used. We must also tell you what could happen if we do not receive it and whether your response is voluntary, required to obtain a benefit, or mandatory under the law.

This notice applies to all papers you file with us, including this tax return. It also applies to any questions we need to ask you so we can complete, correct, or process your return; figure your tax; and collect tax, interest, or penalties.

Our legal right to ask for information is Internal Revenue Code sections 6001, 6011, and 6012(a), and their regulations. They say that you must file a return or statement with us for any tax you are liable for. Your response is mandatory under these sections. Code section 6109 requires you to provide your identifying number on the return. This is so we know who you are, and can process your return and other papers. You must fill in all parts of the tax form that apply to you. But you do not have to check the boxes for the Presidential Election Campaign Fund or for the third-party designee. You also do not have to provide your daytime phone number.

You are not required to provide the information requested on a form that is subject to the Paperwork Reduction Act unless the form displays a valid OMB control number. Books or records relating to a form or its instructions must be retained as long as their contents may become material in the administration of any Internal Revenue law.

We ask for tax return information to carry out the tax laws of the United States. We need it to figure and collect the right amount of tax.

If you do not file a return, do not provide the information we ask for, or provide fraudulent information, you may be charged penalties and be subject to criminal prosecution. We may also have to disallow the exemptions, exclusions, credits, deductions, or adjustments shown on the tax return. This could make the tax higher or delay any refund. Interest may also be charged.

Generally, tax returns and return information are confidential, as stated in Code section 6103. However, Code section 6103 allows or requires the Internal Revenue Service to disclose or give the information shown on your tax return to others as described in the Code. For example, we may disclose your tax information to the Department of Justice to enforce the tax laws, both civil and criminal, and to cities, states, the District of Columbia, and U.S. commonwealths or possessions to carry out their tax laws. We may disclose your tax information to the Department of Treasury and contractors for tax administration purposes; and to other persons as necessary to obtain information needed to determine the amount of or to collect the tax you owe. We may disclose your tax information to the Comptroller General of the United States to permit the Comptroller General to review the Internal Revenue Service. We may disclose your tax information to committees of Congress; federal, state, and local child support agencies; and to other federal agencies for the purposes of determining entitlement for benefits or the eligibility for and the repayment of loans. We may also disclose this information to other countries under a tax treaty, to federal and state agencies to enforce federal nontax criminal laws, or to federal law enforcement and intelligence agencies to combat terrorism.

Please keep this notice with your records. It may help you if we ask you for other information. If you have questions about the rules for filing and giving information, please call or visit any Internal Revenue Service office.

We Welcome Comments on Forms

We try to create forms and instructions that can be easily understood. Often this is difficult to do because our tax laws are very complex. For some people with income mostly from wages, filling in the forms is easy. For others who have businesses, pensions, stocks, rental income, or other investments, it is more difficult.

If you have suggestions for making these forms simpler, we would be happy to hear from you. You can send us comments from www.irs.gov/formspubs/. Click on "More Information" and then on "Give us feedback." Or you can send your comments to Internal Revenue Service, Tax Forms and Publications Division, 1111 Constitution Ave. NW, IR-6526, Washington, DC 20224. Do not send your return to this address. Instead, see the addresses at the end of these instructions.

Although we can't respond individually to each comment received, we do appreciate your feedback and will consider your comments as we revise our tax forms and instructions.

Estimates of Taxpayer Burden

The following table shows burden estimates based on current statutory requirements as of November 2015, for taxpayers filing a 2015 Form 1040, 1040A, or 1040EZ tax return. Time spent and out-of-pocket costs are presented separately. Time burden is broken out by taxpayer activity, with recordkeeping representing the largest component. Out-of-pocket costs include any expenses incurred by taxpayers to prepare and submit their tax returns. Examples include tax return preparation and submission fees, postage and photocopying costs, and tax preparation software costs. While these estimates do not include burden associated with post-filing activities, IRS operational data indicate that electronically prepared and filed returns have fewer arithmetic errors, implying lower post-filing burden.

Reported time and cost burdens are national averages and do not necessarily reflect a "typical" case. Most taxpayers experience lower than average burden, with taxpayer burden varying considerably by taxpayer type. For instance, the estimated average time burden for all taxpayers filing a Form 1040, 1040A, or 1040EZ is 13 hours, with an average cost of $200 per return. This average includes all associated forms and schedules, across all preparation methods and taxpayer activities. The average burden for taxpayers filing Form 1040 is about 16 hours and $270; the average burden for taxpayers filing Form 1040A is about 7 hours and $90;

and the average for Form 1040EZ filers is about 5 hours and $40.

Within each of these estimates there is significant variation in taxpayer activity. For example, nonbusiness taxpayers are expected to have an average burden of about 8 hours and $110, while business taxpayers are expected to have an average burden of about 22 hours and $410. Similarly, tax preparation fees and other out-of-pocket costs vary extensively depending on the tax situation of the taxpayer, the type of software or professional preparer used, and the geographic location.

If you have comments concerning the time and cost estimates below, you can contact us at either one of the addresses shown under *We Welcome Comments on Forms*.

Estimated Average Taxpayer Burden for Individuals by Activity

Primary Form Filed or Type of Taxpayer	Percentage of Returns	Average Burden					Average Cost (Dollars)*
		Average Time (Hours)					
		Total Time	Record Keeping	Tax Planning	Form Completion and Submission	All Other	
All taxpayers	100	13	6	2	4	1	$200
Primary forms filed							
1040	69	16	8	2	4	1	270
1040A	19	7	2	1	3	1	90
1040EZ	12	5	1	1	2	1	40
Type of taxpayer							
Nonbusiness**	70	8	3	1	3	1	110
Business**	30	22	12	4	5	2	410

*Dollars rounded to the nearest $10.

**You are considered a "business" filer if you file one or more of the following with Form 1040: Schedule C, C-EZ, E, or F or Form 2106 or 2106-EZ. You are considered a "nonbusiness" filer if you do not file any of those schedules or forms with Form 1040 or if you file Form 1040A or 1040EZ.

Order Form for Forms and Publications

 You can view and download the tax forms and publications you need at www.irs.gov/formspubs. You can also place an order for forms at www.irs.gov/orderforms to avoid having to complete and mail the order form.

The most frequently ordered forms and publications are listed on the order form. You will receive two copies of each form, one copy of the instructions, and one copy of each publication you order. To help reduce waste, please order only the items you need to prepare your return.

How To Use the Order Form

Circle the items you need on the order form. Use the blank spaces to order items not listed. If you need more space, attach a separate sheet of paper.

Print or type your name and address accurately in the space provided on the order form to ensure delivery of your order. Enclose the order form in an envelope and mail it to the IRS address shown next. You should receive your order within 10 business days after we receive your request.

Do not send your tax return to the address shown here. Instead, see the addresses at the end of these instructions.

Mail Your Order Form To:

Internal Revenue Service
1201 N. Mitsubishi Motorway
Bloomington, IL 61705-6613

▲ *Cut here* ▲

Save Money and Time by Going Online!
Download or order these and other forms and publications at www.irs.gov/formspubs

Order Form

Please print.

Name
_____

Postal mailing address _____ Apt./Suite/Room _____

City _____ State _____ ZIP code _____

Foreign country _____ International postal code _____

Daytime phone number
(_____) _____

Circle the forms and publications you need. The instructions for any form you order will be included.

Use the **blank spaces** to order items not listed.

Use your QR Reader app on your smartphone to scan this code and get connected to the IRS Forms and Publications homepage.

1040	Schedule F (1040)	1040-V	4868	8959	Pub. 505	Pub. 551	Pub. 946
Schedule A (1040)	Schedule H (1040)	1040X	5405	8960	Pub. 523	Pub. 554	Pub. 970
Schedule B (1040A or 1040)	Schedule J (1040)	2106	6251	8962	Pub. 525	Pub. 575	Pub. 972
Schedule C (1040)	Schedule R (1040A or 1040)	2441	8283	8965	Pub. 526	Pub. 583	Pub. 4681
Schedule C-EZ (1040)	Schedule SE (1040)	3903	8606	Pub. 1	Pub. 527	Pub. 587	
Schedule D (1040)	Schedule 8812 (1040A or 1040)	4506	8822	Pub. 334	Pub. 529	Pub. 590-A	
Form 8949	1040A	4506-T	8829	Pub. 463	Pub. 535	Pub. 590-B	
Schedule E (1040)	1040EZ	4562	8863	Pub. 501	Pub. 547	Pub. 596	
Schedule EIC (1040A or 1040)	1040-ES (2016)	4684	8917	Pub. 502	Pub. 550	Pub. 915	

Income and Outlays. These pie charts show the relative sizes of the major categories of federal income and outlays for fiscal year 2014.

Income

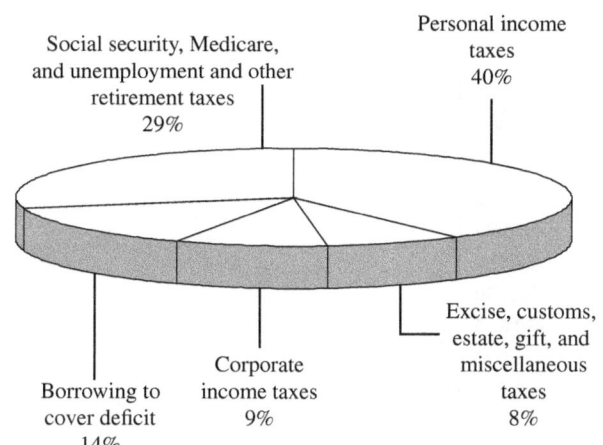

Social security, Medicare, and unemployment and other retirement taxes
29%

Personal income taxes
40%

Borrowing to cover deficit
14%

Corporate income taxes
9%

Excise, customs, estate, gift, and miscellaneous taxes
8%

Outlays*

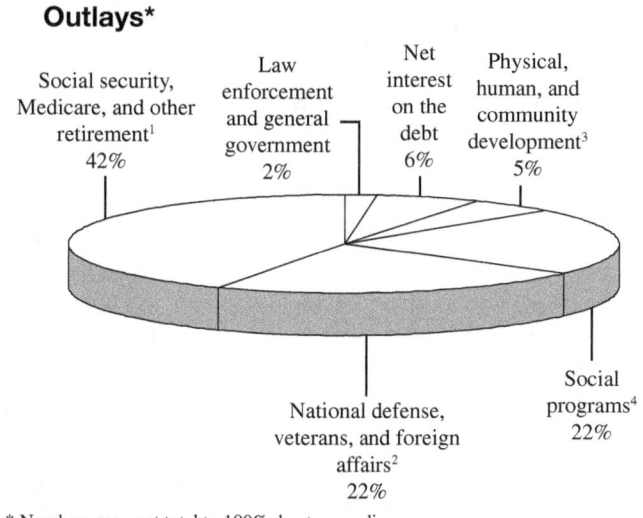

Social security, Medicare, and other retirement[1]
42%

Law enforcement and general government
2%

Net interest on the debt
6%

Physical, human, and community development[3]
5%

National defense, veterans, and foreign affairs[2]
22%

Social programs[4]
22%

* Numbers may not total to 100% due to rounding.

On or before the first Monday in February of each year the President is required by law to submit to the Congress a budget proposal for the fiscal year that begins the following October. The budget plan sets forth the President's proposed receipts, spending, and the surplus or deficit for the Federal Government. The plan includes recommendations for new legislation as well as recommendations to change, eliminate, and add programs. After receipt of the President's proposal, the Congress reviews the proposal and makes changes. It first passes a budget resolution setting its own targets for receipts, outlays, and surplus or deficit. Next, individual spending and revenue bills that are consistent with the goals of the budget resolution are enacted.

In fiscal year 2014 (which began on October 1, 2013, and ended on September 30, 2014), Federal income was $3.021 trillion and outlays were $3.506 trillion, leaving a deficit of $485 billion.

Footnotes for Certain Federal Outlays

1. **Social security, Medicare, and other retirement:** These programs provide income support for the retired and disabled and medical care for the elderly.

2. **National defense, veterans, and foreign affairs:** About 17% of outlays were to equip, modernize, and pay our armed forces and to fund national defense activities; about 4% were for veterans benefits and services; and about 1% were for international activities, including military and economic assistance to foreign countries and the maintenance of U.S. embassies abroad.

3. **Physical, human, and community development:** These outlays were for agriculture; natural resources; environment; transportation; aid for elementary and secondary education and direct assistance to college students; job training; deposit insurance, commerce and housing credit, and community development; and space, energy, and general science programs.

4. **Social programs:** About 16% of total outlays were for Medicaid, food stamps, temporary assistance for needy families, supplemental security income, and related programs; and the remaining outlays were for health research and public health programs, unemployment compensation, assisted housing, and social services.

Note. The percentages shown here exclude undistributed offsetting receipts, which were $88 billion in fiscal year 2014. In the budget, these receipts are offset against spending in figuring the outlay totals shown above. These receipts are for the U.S. Government's share of its employee retirement programs, rents and royalties on the Outer Continental Shelf, and proceeds from the sale of assets.

2015 Tax Rate Schedules

 The Tax Rate Schedules are shown so you can see the tax rate that applies to all levels of taxable income. Do not use them to figure your tax. Instead, see the instructions for line 44.

Schedule X—If your filing status is **Single**

If your taxable income is:		The tax is:	of the amount
Over—	But not over—		over—
$0	$9,225	---------- 10%	$0
9,225	37,450	$922.50 + 15%	9,225
37,450	90,750	5,156.25 + 25%	37,450
90,750	189,300	18,481.25 + 28%	90,750
189,300	411,500	46,075.25 + 33%	189,300
411,500	413,200	119,401.25 + 35%	411,500
413,200	----------	119,996.25 + 39.6%	413,200

Schedule Y-1—If your filing status is **Married filing jointly** or **Qualifying widow(er)**

If your taxable income is:		The tax is:	of the amount
Over—	But not over—		over—
$0	$18,450	---------- 10%	$0
18,450	74,900	$1,845.00 + 15%	18,450
74,900	151,200	10,312.50 + 25%	74,900
151,200	230,450	29,387.50 + 28%	151,200
230,450	411,500	51,577.50 + 33%	230,450
411,500	464,850	111,324.00 + 35%	411,500
464,850	----------	129,996.50 + 39.6%	464,850

Schedule Y-2—If your filing status is **Married filing separately**

If your taxable income is:		The tax is:	of the amount
Over—	But not over—		over—
$0	$9,225	---------- 10%	$0
9,225	37,450	$922.50 + 15%	9,225
37,450	75,600	5,156.25 + 25%	37,450
75,600	115,225	14,693.75 + 28%	75,600
115,225	205,750	25,788.75 + 33%	115,225
205,750	232,425	55,662.00 + 35%	205,750
232,425	----------	64,998.25 + 39.6%	232,425

Schedule Z—If your filing status is **Head of household**

If your taxable income is:		The tax is:	of the amount
Over—	But not over—		over—
$0	$13,150	---------- 10%	$0
13,150	50,200	$1,315.00 + 15%	13,150
50,200	129,600	6,872.50 + 25%	50,200
129,600	209,850	26,722.50 + 28%	129,600
209,850	411,500	49,192.50 + 33%	209,850
411,500	439,000	115,737.00 + 35%	411,500
439,000	----------	125,362.00 + 39.6%	439,000

Index to Instructions

Where Do You File? Mail your return to the address shown below that applies to you. If you want to use a private delivery service, see *Private Delivery Services* under *Filing Requirements,* earlier.

 Envelopes without enough postage will be returned to you by the post office. Your envelope may need additional postage if it contains more than five pages or is oversized (for example, it is over $\frac{1}{4}$" thick). Also, include your complete return address.

IF you live in...	THEN use this address if you:	
	Are requesting a refund or are not enclosing a check or money order...	**Are enclosing a check or money order...**
Florida, Louisiana, Mississippi, Texas	Department of the Treasury Internal Revenue Service Austin, TX 73301-0002	Internal Revenue Service P.O. Box 1214 Charlotte, NC 28201-1214
Alaska, Arizona, California, Colorado, Hawaii, Idaho, Nevada, New Mexico, Oregon, Utah, Washington, Wyoming	Department of the Treasury Internal Revenue Service Fresno, CA 93888-0002	Internal Revenue Service P.O. Box 7704 San Francisco, CA 94120-7704
Arkansas, Illinois, Indiana, Iowa, Kansas, Michigan, Minnesota, Montana, Nebraska, North Dakota, Ohio, Oklahoma, South Dakota, Wisconsin	Department of the Treasury Internal Revenue Service Fresno, CA 93888-0002	Internal Revenue Service P.O. Box 802501 Cincinnati, OH 45280-2501
Alabama, Georgia, Kentucky, New Jersey, North Carolina, South Carolina, Tennessee, Virginia	Department of the Treasury Internal Revenue Service Kansas City, MO 64999-0002	Internal Revenue Service P.O. Box 931000 Louisville, KY 40293-1000
Connecticut, Delaware, District of Columbia, Maine, Maryland, Massachusetts, Missouri, New Hampshire, New York, Pennsylvania, Rhode Island, Vermont, West Virginia	Department of the Treasury Internal Revenue Service Kansas City, MO 64999-0002	Internal Revenue Service P.O. Box 37008 Hartford, CT 06176-7008
A foreign country, U.S. possession or territory*, or use an APO or FPO address, or file Form 2555, 2555-EZ, or 4563, or are a dual-status alien	Department of the Treasury Internal Revenue Service Austin, TX 73301-0215	Internal Revenue Service P.O. Box 1303 Charlotte, NC 28201-1303

*If you live in American Samoa, Puerto Rico, Guam, the U.S. Virgin Islands, or the Northern Mariana Islands, see Pub. 570.